UNCHARTED WATERS

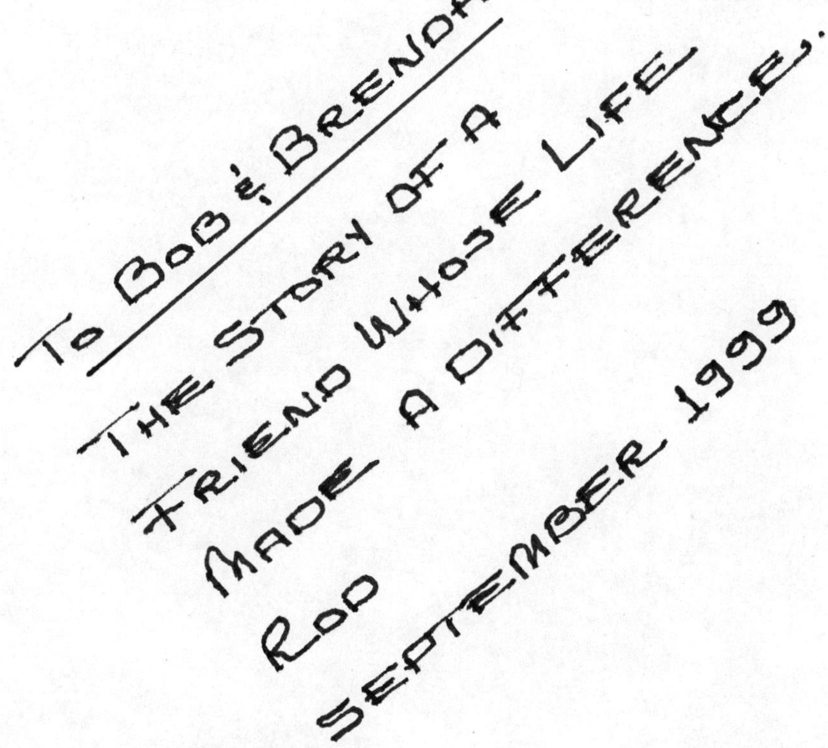

Uncharted Waters

C. Hudson Southwell

Astana Publishing • Calgary, Canada

UNCHARTED WATERS

Other Scripture quotations are from the King James Version (KJV).

Printed and bound in Canada by Friesens Corporation.

Published by Astana Publishing, Calgary, Canada.

Canadian Cataloguing in Publication Data

Southwell, C. H. (C. Hudson)
Uncharted waters

Includes bibliographical references.
ISBN 0-9685440-0-2

1. Southwell, C. H. (C. Hudson) 2. Missionaries–Malaysia–Sarawak–Biography 3. World War, 1939-1945–Prisoners and prisons, Japanese. I. Title.

BV3370.N6S68 1999 266'.0092 C99-900684-3

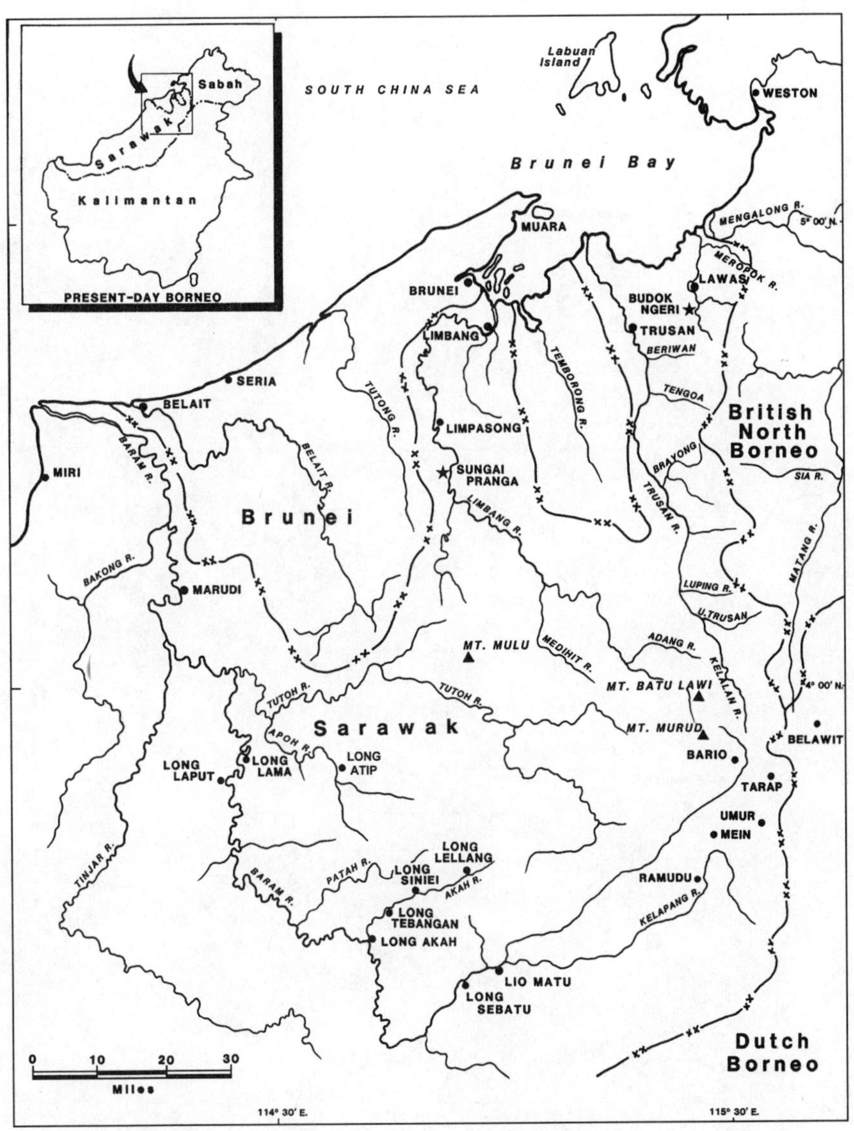

Northern Part of Island of Borneo – From Early Maps Drawn by C. H. Southwell

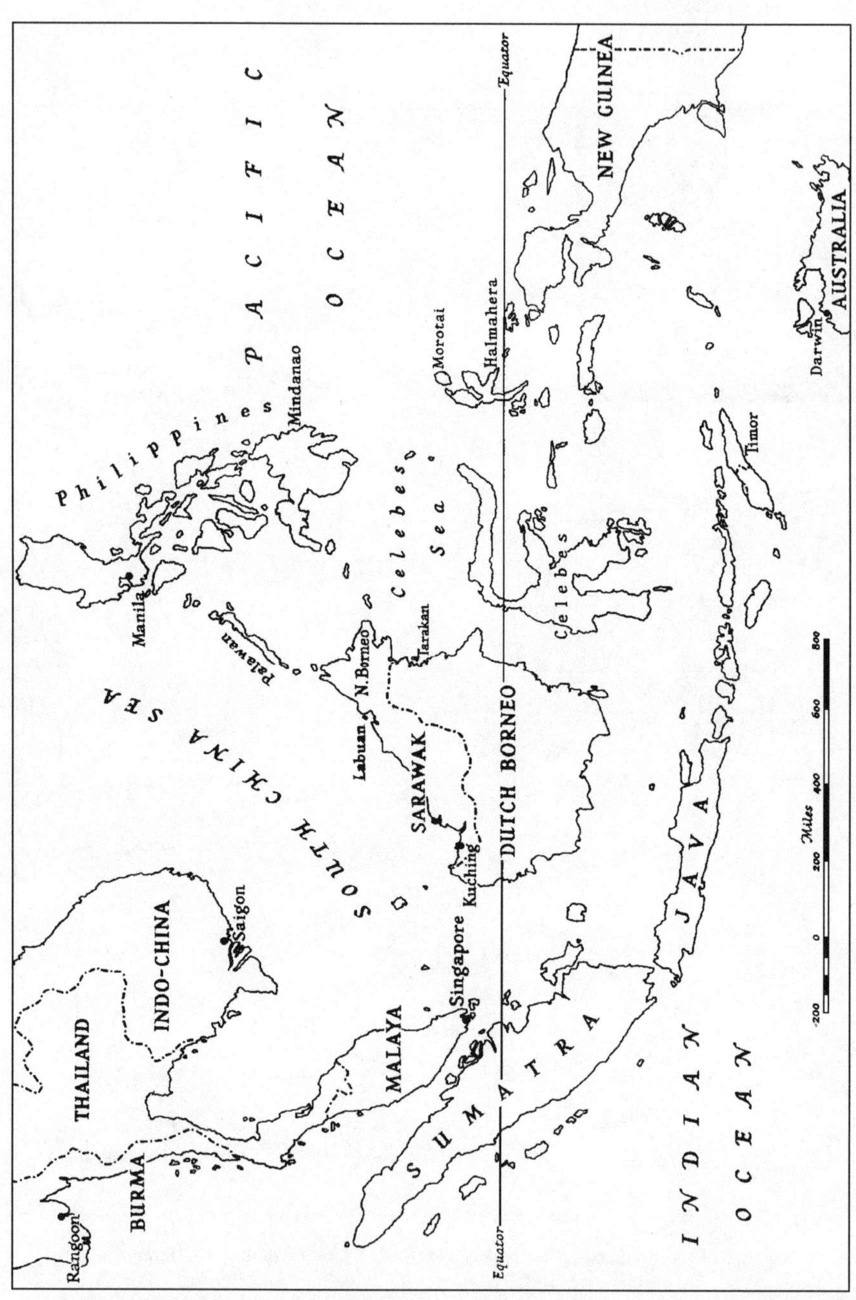

Borneo in Southeast Asia – From Early Map Drawn by Royal Geographical Society

Contents

Prologue

Fear nothing for me;
the decision is in higher Hands.
– James Brooke

As the year 2000 approaches, I share in the universal sense of anticipation and excitement leading up to a major milestone in human history. This date also gives me special cause for reflection. It marks a personal centennial. I was born in the year 1900.

Looking back, I recognize that I have lived a fascinating life filled with unusual experiences that were divinely orchestrated.

With a complex and changing world on the brink of a new millennium, I see the once-remote Pacific nations of Malaysia and Indonesia gaining prominence. It is a corner of the world where I spent most of my life, and an area that still intrigues me. Over the course of almost a full century, my life became interwoven with these places and more particularly the people of the island of Borneo with its "wild men," its headhunters and its legendary White Rajahs.

To appreciate this mysterious and romantic island, and my subsequent life and adventures there, it is helpful to understand something of its historical setting. The parts of Borneo that I know best entered the modern era under the hundred-year reign of the White Rajahs, and I have recorded my own life-story against this background.

The regime of the White Rajahs in Borneo began with the English adventurer and explorer James Brooke, who in December 1838 set sail from Devenport, England, bound for the islands of the east. Prevailing winds bore him off course as far as Rio de Janiero so he did not reach Singapore until June of the following year. From there, he set out for Borneo, and on August 15, 1839, he entered the mouth of the Sarawak River, at the western tip of the island, and ventured upstream to the town of Kuching. In the weeks that followed, he established a valuable lifelong friendship with the ruling Prince Hassim.

James quickly concluded that Sarawak was a trader's paradise, although he himself was not a trader. He was an explorer. From Kuching, he visited the islands to the east of Borneo, and then returned to Singapore, ill with malaria. He dreamed of visiting Manila and seeking adventure in China but never reached either. Instead, toward the end of August 1840, he found himself once again sailing to Sarawak.

Little had changed in the eight months since his first visit. A small uprising against Prince Hassim was still in progress, with the Sultan of Sambas in Dutch Borneo supplying the rebels with guns and ammunition. James allied himself with the prince and attacked a rebel stronghold at Balidah, a few miles upriver from Kuching, destroying the fort and securing the surrender of the rebels. Then he turned his attention to the pirates who were terrorizing the coast of Borneo.

The most feared of these pirate bands came from the islands to the south of Manila. They came in war *prahus* heavily armed with cannons and muskets. Some of these boats were over ninety feet long with as many as seventy rowers at the oars, and cut into the bulwarks were ports through which the pirates worked their guns. Their most valuable plunder — money, slaves, and costly silks — went to the ship commanders and free men, while the rest went to the slaves who manned the oars. At that time, an estimated 25,000 men on the north coast of Borneo were living off piracy. They plundered and massacred at will. They were the scourge of the East Indies, and James swore to destroy them.

While gathering support for this venture, James gained the confidence of the native Dayaks and strengthened his position with Prince Hassim. These new alliances, in turn, altered the political balance between the Prince and his powerful relative, the Sultan of Brunei. After a year filled with palace intrigue, Prince Hassim decided to abdicate and to transfer his control of Sarawak to James. The following year, the Sultan of Brunei affixed his royal seal to letters officially consenting to the transfer of power. On August 18, 1942, these letters were solemnly read out in the presence of the Malay princes, and the history of Sarawak took a new direction. James Brooke, at age thirty-nine, became Rajah with absolute rule over all the Malays and Dayaks in the country.

Upon assuming control, James issued a series of laws in the Malay language, demanding free trade, free passage of all goods, the abolition of slavery, the imposition of an equitable tax system, and a fair profit for the antimony miners. In its context, it was an astonishing program.

In 1847, after nearly nine years away from his native land, James Brooke returned to a hero's welcome. Everywhere he went he was showered with honours. Queen Victoria made him a Knight Commander of the Bath; at the age of forty-four he was officially Sir James Brooke, KCB, Rajah of Sarawak, Governor of Labuan, Commissioner and Consul-General in Borneo.

The Rajah's status was soon challenged, however. Following his return to Sarawak, he was again confronted with the increasingly serious problem of piracy. "During the first six months of 1849," wrote his secretary Spenser St. John, "almost all intercourse by sea ceased, as few who attempted to pass the mouths of the pirate rivers escaped unhurt. I calculated at the time that above 500 of the Sultan's subjects had been killed or taken captive between January and July, 1849." It was clear that something had to be done about the pirates, but it was no longer a question of sending a few small ships against them. They had grown into a vast and formidable force with many of their vessels equipped with swivel guns.

The Rajah knew that only a greater force could stop them, so he assembled a fleet of his own and launched a search and destroy operation. Within a few days of leaving Kuching, the Rajah's fleet engaged a large pirate force returning to their bases on the Kaluka and Sarebas Rivers. In four hours of intense fighting, some 400 pirates were killed, but a much greater number, perhaps 2,500, succeeded in taking refuge in the jungle. The Rajah pursued the pirates up the Sarebas River until their progress was blocked by felled trees. The Malays and Dayaks were landed, and about fifty more pirates were killed in the jungles. Another 450 were said to have died as the result of fighting against native tribes.

When news of the battle reached England, certain members of Parliament and detractors in the press railed against this mass slaughter, painting the Rajah as a reckless and bloodthirsty adventurer. It seemed they had conveniently forgotten that detailed reports on the savagery of the pirates had been accumulating for years. The Rajah's anger over their allegations turned to incredulity as calls began for a public inquiry. The requirement to repeatedly validate his actions to uncomprehending critics left him exhausted. His health deteriorated and he longed for a reprieve by the sea in Dorset.

Upon the Rajah's arrival in England, Prime Minister Gladstone spoke in his support. A public dinner was given for him, with guests including members of Parliament, governors of the Bank of England, directors of the East India Company, and a host of army and navy officers and merchants. To the end of his life, Sir James was baffled by the British Government, which seemed to regard him simultaneously as both an honourable and cherished ally and as an interloper who had the audacity to found a colony without asking permission from London. All through the history of Sarawak under the Rajahs there was that curious and unhappy ambivalence.

Near the end of 1858, Sir James suffered a stroke while delivering a speech in Manchester. He never completely recovered. He was fifty-five but looked seventy — old, tired, at odds with himself and the world. Over the next ten years he made only two more trips to Sarawak. From an obscure cottage in Devonshire, he wrote voluminous letters to his nephew Charles, who had left the navy to join his staff in Sarawak in 1852. Despite his failing health, Sir James Brooke was still Rajah of Sarawak, and he continued to give orders from a distance of twelve thousand miles which were received forty days later.

The Rajah's last message to Charles was sent on April 7, 1868. "If I die," he wrote, "you take possession of Sarawak, for you are my heir by appointment. Be just to our people."

On June 9th, Sir James suffered another stroke, and two days later he was dead.

Charles Johnson Brooke had been acting Rajah so long that when the time came for the proclamation, he was like a man receiving a deed of title for something he already possessed. People who knew him said there was no change in him. Indeed, he had acted like a Rajah almost from the moment he set foot on Sarawak.

In almost every way Charles was the opposite of James: precise, quick-tempered, and unrelenting in the demands he made on his subordinates. He could be terrifying when he fixed an inferior with the gaze of his cold grey eyes. As a natural administrator with a fine business sense, he was an efficient ruler who kept a keen eye on the profit and loss accounts in the Treasury. His most formative years in Sarawak were spent among the Sea Dayaks, so he acquired their manners and their ways of thinking. James had felt close to the Malays; Charles was happier in the company of the Dayaks and the Chinese. His mind worked in Oriental ways, whereas James had remained English to the core.

When he became Rajah, Charles inherited a territory vastly greater than that originally acquired by Sir James Brooke from Prince Hassim. Gradually over the years Charles acquired additional portions of Brunei. The largest area, Baram, was ceded to him in 1882. Trusan followed in 1884, and Limbang in 1890. By that time Charles was ruling over a country as large as England and Scotland combined, with the help of about twenty European officers. The Lawas region was added in 1904.

As Charles grew older, he became more and more preoccupied by the future of Sarawak. While he was very much a Victorian, he took exception with the way native peoples were handled by the colonizing nations. He accused the colonial officials of employing expediency as their most potent weapon. In 1907, he published a brochure in which he argued that colonies should be thrown open to the world, not maintained as private estates by the European powers. In his day, few even thought such things, let alone dared to say them. Senior officials in Whitehall dreaded his visits to London.

The year following his appointment as Rajah, Charles married Margaret Alice Lili de Windt, an enchanting young woman. Three children were born early in the marriage, a girl and twin boys. Then tragedy struck. While returning to England by ocean steamer in 1873, Charles and Margaret lost all three children within a few hours. One day they were well; the next day they were gasping for breath in the stifling heat of the Red Sea. No one knew for certain what killed them — cholera, heat stroke and a tin of poisoned milk were all mentioned later as possibilities. The children were buried at sea.

With tremendous courage Margaret returned to Sarawak and started a new family. The first of three additional children, Charles Vyner de Windt Brooke, was born in London on September 26th, 1874. He was two when he was taken to Sarawak for the first time, where he stayed only a few months; he came out again for a brief visit when he was twelve, this time accompanied by his two younger brothers, Bertram and Harry. Vyner's childhood was dominated by his iron-willed father, who regarded any sign of weakness as a crime, and by his beautiful and accomplished mother, who regarded him as inadequate because he did not share her passion for literature and the arts. As a result, he admired his parents without loving them.

At age seventeen, following a third brief visit to Sarawak, Vyner entered Magdalene College, Cambridge, where for the first time he found himself among people he genuinely liked. He had become a tall, strikingly handsome youth who distinguished himself in athletics. From childhood, he developed a strong sense of fairness which, although admirable, often drew him into fistfights. He spent his allowance prodigally, bought horses and was in debt to his father for many years afterwards.

In August 1897, after six years' absence from Sarawak, Vyner was appointed to the Sarawak Government Service, attached to the Rajah's staff in Kuching. The following February he went to work as a District Officer at Simanggang, where he came in daily contact with the notorious headhunters of Borneo.

From the beginning it had been the Rajah's intention to train his sons in the field. He had not approved of Vyner's fighting, his occasional gambling or his frivolity. The Rajah hoped that Simanggang would provide the disciplined environment his son needed and, indeed, most of the work of the outstation landed on Vyner's untried shoulders. There was no telegraph and few letters. Orders came by runner from Kuching, and the Rajah's inspection tours were infrequent. It became Vyner's responsibility to keep proper documents, check records, administer law and order, and dispense medicines. He established a good relationship with the Dayaks and quickly learned their language.

In 1903, Vyner was made Resident of the Third Division, encompassing the large area around the Rejang River. His reports on imports and exports, the state of local finances and the planting of rice were interspersed with detailed accounts of raids by headhunters. On one occasion, eighty women and children were beheaded in a longhouse on the Rejang River while their men were working in the fields.

Each tribal raid brought a punitive expedition led by the Rajah's forces: an attack on a longhouse surrounded by poisoned spikes, with the enemy lurking among the trees. At the end there was the familiar black smoke cloud hanging in the sky, antique jars confiscated as punishment, and a few bodies lying in the long grass. Amazingly, few lives were lost in those expeditions.

Vyner did his work well, and the Rajah, who once thought him the least worthy of his three sons, changed his mind completely. An official notice appeared in the *Sarawak Gazette* on June 4, 1904, confirming Vyner as Rajah Muda and successor to his father. Henceforth, whenever the Rajah was absent from Sarawak, Vyner became acting Rajah of the State, entitled not only to the honours but also to the burdens which go with absolute monarchy.

Vyner was fun-loving, social, impulsive, and at the same time sensitive, vulnerable and never completely sure of himself. Being placed in charge during his father's absence served to refine his character. He undertook his new responsibilities diligently and Sarawak became the passionate focus of his life.

With the advent of a new century, there was change in the air. By 1906, for example, Kuching had street lights for the first time, and the residents no longer suffered the taunts of Singaporeans, their neighbors across the South China Sea who had had street lighting for thirty years. Twenty-five thousand people lived in Kuching, and it was said the population of Sarawak was close to 700,000. Every year trade with the outside world was increasing.

Economic growth expanded further following the discovery of oil near Miri. Charles Hose, as a young District Officer in the Baram area, had suspected its presence in large quantities twenty-five years before, but it was not until 1909 that the Rajah negotiated an agreement with Shell for oil exploration and production. The Rajah had an aversion towards large corporations, but he maintained that he would welcome foreign investors if he could be sure that they would deal fairly with the native peoples. The following year he permitted two hundred acres of land at the mouth of the Sarawak River to be sold to an American company for manufacturing artificial rubber.

Vyner had his roots in this new developing age. Unlike his father, who refused to ride in motorcars (though he had no objection to travelling in trains and steamships), he was among the first to drive a car in England, and he was the very first to drive one in Sarawak. He enjoyed speed and liked tinkering with machines. He also delighted in plans for modernizing Sarawak, but all his plans came to nothing when in the early months of 1910 he became seriously ill. He was removed to Singapore and operated on for an abscess of the liver. In May of that year he was carried onto a ship and sent back to England for a convalescence which lasted the rest of the year. People in Kuching thought they would never see the Rajah Muda again.

In February 1911, government officials, opening the pages of the painfully official *Sarawak Gazette* with its calendar of saints days, lists of ships' arrivals and departures, and reports from outstations, were astounded by the brief announcement of Vyner's engagement to Sylvia Brett, youngest daughter of Viscount Esher.

The engagement was followed almost immediately by the wedding, which the Rajah viewed with considerable reserve. He was inclined to regard the Eshers as rich upstarts, without substance. More particularly, he wondered whether Sylvia, with her high-society friends, and Vyner, with his flashy cars and his air of a young man-about-town, would opt for the bright lights of London rather than the rigors of life in Sarawak. Despite the Rajah's concerns, however, it was arranged that Vyner would take his bride to Sarawak in the spring of the following year.

Before this could happen, the Rajah suffered an accident which profoundly altered his character. His horse stumbled into a blind ditch, he was thrown, and his eye was pierced by a branch. Thereafter he wore a glass eye. Hard and relentless before, he grew harder and more relentless, and for the first time a note of bitterness could be detected in his letters. In the hospital he had time to think about succession at great length. Brooding, he came to the conclusion that Vyner could not be expected to rule Sarawak alone, but needed to be supported by his brother Bertram and by an advisory committee, operating from London. It was an unworkable solution, but he held to it with grim determination. In April 1912, he wrote to Charles Willes Johnson, his nephew and legal adviser, outlining a plan of succession by which Vyner and Bertram would rule together. Upon his return to Sarawak, the Rajah announced his intention of granting royal honours to Bertram.

Vyner was extremely fond of his handsome brother, Bertram, who was responsible and efficient but knew almost nothing about conditions in Sarawak. His last visit had been in 1895, seventeen years earlier, and he had never even seen an outstation. In a hurried letter to his father, Vyner declared that he was not prepared to tolerate a situation in which his powers would be curtailed by someone who hardly knew the land. The Rajah replied, pointing out that he had authority to do as he pleased. In a heated exchange, the Rajah accused Vyner of insubordination and disloyalty, and suggested that he leave the country. Outraged, Vyner took the first available boat to Singapore and returned to England.

The Rajah was old and tired and not entirely certain that he had done the right thing. Still, at the age of eighty-two he was in remarkable form, full of pride in his achievements and determined not to slacken the reins of power. The Rajah had been an autocrat of autocrats. He had ruled Sarawak almost single-handedly for fifty years and had greatly increased its territory. Beyond the reach of English laws, he was a law unto himself. He was more than a man. He was a legend, and legends are irreplaceable.

The summer passed, and soon the Rajah was making preparations for returning to England for his annual hunt with the hounds. He was still distressed by Vyner's behavior, but his letters to his legal counsel, Charles Willes Johnson, gave indications that he was beginning to relent.

The following spring, the Rajah received reports of troubles in the interior and in his impetuous way returned to Sarawak, determined while there was still breath in him to see that his law was obeyed. He had the rebellion quelled, established a Chinese court to deal with the affairs of the Chinese, and then returned to England, where he made peace with Vyner — an uneasy peace, for neither had retreated from his original position. The next spring Vyner went out to Sarawak and ruled alone. He was still there when the First World War broke out.

The Rajah knew his place. With war spreading all over the world, with German colonies in the neighborhood of Sarawak, and with the economy of Sarawak dependent on the outcome of the war, he took the first available boat to the East. He was eighty-six, but he still regarded himself as the equal of men half his age. It was inevitable that he should take charge in time of war.

It was perhaps just as inevitable that Vyner should return to England, hoping to join the army. He passed his medical tests and was looking forward to army life, when suddenly the Colonial Office ruled against his enlistment on the grounds that he was the heir apparent to a strategic territory in the Pacific. As a result, Vyner joined an anti-aircraft regiment and worked as a machinist, shaping aeroplane parts. Only a few were aware that the obscure workman in overalls, standing all day at the lathe, known simply as C.V. Brooke, might at any moment receive orders to sail from England and rule over an Eastern principality.

In the second year of the war, the Rajah summoned him. Together with his wife, Vyner made the long, slow sea journey to Sarawak. All quarrels were forgotten, and to signify approval of his son, the Rajah issued an extraordinary proclamation on September 30, 1916, placing the Rejang area entirely under his control. It was almost his last official act. In a few days he was bedridden. By late spring of the following year, he was dead.

Seven days after his father's death, Vyner was rowed across the Sarawak River in the State barge. There, on the steps of the Government Office, the Malays, Dayaks, and Chinese were waiting to greet him. It was May 24, 1917, and Sarawak had a new Rajah.

Part I
Formative Years

I can persevere in any definite pursuit.
Few people know what may be done till they try
and persevere in what they undertake.
– William Carey

CHAPTER 1

We booked four passages on the *Newby Hall*, an old cargo steamer due to leave Melbourne in early October 1928, bound for Singapore. I took the train to Adelaide, where the ship was to dock for a few days, and there met up with my colleagues Carey Tolley and Frank Davidson, who had boarded in Melbourne. Travelling with us was Alexander Henderson, a pioneer of the Southeast Asian timber trade, who had offered to help us establish a base on the the little-known island of Borneo.

Frank Davidson, Carey Tolley, Hudson Southwell
Alexander Henderson – December 1928

After the swiftly moving events of the previous few months, we found the month-long voyage a valuable time of relaxation and orientation. As there were no other passengers, we used much of our time for study sessions to begin learning colloquial Malay.

On its route north to Singapore, the *Newby Hall* steamed between the islands of Bali and Java and stopped at Batavia (now known as Jakarta).

In Java, we stepped out into a new world. We were in Asia. Everything was different. And Singapore colorfully illustrated this when we arrived several days later on November 8th. We certainly were faced with all the ingredients for what today is known as culture shock, but our senses eagerly absorbed even the most unusual experiences. Each day carried with it the excitement of finally being in that part of the world for which we had rigorously prepared; and since our preparation had included extensive reading about events and places oriental, we were able to visualize in advance much of what we encountered.

In 1928, life in Singapore moved at a sedate pace and with all the charm of Somerset Maugham's novels penned from the old Raffles Hotel. Alexander Henderson, or Hendy as we then called him, introduced us to the bazaars and to the art of bargaining, and we all bought clothing for the tropics, including white linen suits with stiff stand-up collars fastened at the neck with twin studs.

People we met in Singapore knew little about the situation in Sarawak, but we learned of a weekly steamer from Singapore to Kuching and decided that Hendy and I should proceed there first to present our credentials to Rajah Vyner Brooke. We were carrying a letter from the Government of the state of Victoria certifying that we were Australian citizens and requesting the protection of the Sarawak Government. We also had a letter from the chairman of our Mission council in Melbourne.

Hendy and I left Singapore on Wednesday, November 10th. Our three-day stay had been a delightful experience and, although altogether too short, it was a good introduction to the blended Chinese, Malay and Indian cultures. Upon leaving the shelter of the many islands to the east of Singapore, we sailed a little to the north of due east, directly into a moderate swell coming from the South China Sea.

On Friday morning, I was up before daybreak to catch the first glimpse of Borneo. Even though the early monsoon had brought clouds and rain, straight ahead I could see the dark rocky cape of Tanjong Datu, the westernmost tip of the island. The cliff looked forbidding yet fascinating. Receding to the south of it stretched the long western coast of Dutch Borneo.

Our ship had been heading east northeast but now turned east southeast, and the main coastline of northern Borneo, lined with coconut palms, came into closer view. Ahead loomed Santubong Mountain, a peculiar rounded peak rimmed with casuarina trees and a soft sandy beach stretching along the low banks of the Sarawak River.

We entered the estuary of the river and by eleven o'clock drew alongside the wharf at Kuching, where a large crowd had gathered to meet the weekly steamer from Singapore. Malays, Chinese and a few Indians mingled with Sea Dayaks and other tribal people. The river was alive with various kinds of canoes. Bullock carts rumbled along the waterfront together with rickshaws and an occasional motorcar. On the opposite bank was the Rajah of Sarawak's fort, flanked by the *astana*, his official residence.

Kuching Wharf – November 1928

Hendy and I went ashore in the afternoon and sought out the government offices to present our official letters of introduction. Although we were unknown and had arrived unannounced, we were referred to the Rajah's private secretary, Gerard MacBryan, and to the Rajah's cousin and legal advisor, Charles Willes Johnson. These two men questioned us closely, especially Hendy, who told them he had been engaged in timber and diamond trading and in oil prospecting in Dutch Borneo. Always the great talker, Hendy went on to tell them how he had acquired a box of crown jewels from the Sultan of Pontianak.

Hendy's stories did not help our cause, and the two officials eyed him with suspicion as they continued to question him intensively. It took three days before they were sufficiently convinced that he was not trying to enter the country for trading purposes, and only then did they allow us to bring our belongings ashore.

They seemed comfortable enough with the representations I made, however, and shortly after putting us up in the government rest house, they advised us that the Rajah would approve our request to establish a mission in Sarawak. They recommended that we start in the Limbang area, in the northeast end of the country.

I immediately sent a telegram to Singapore informing Carey and Frank that they could proceed directly to Limbang.

Hendy and I stayed four more days in Kuching, during which time we visited the excellent museum founded by the second rajah many years before. We also called on the Anglican bishop. An Anglican mission had been established during the reign of the first rajah in the early 1840s, but they had worked mainly among the Ibans and Bedayu in the First and Second Divisions. For administrative purposes, the territory of Sarawak had been divided into five divisions. We were headed for the Fifth Division, comprised of the Limbang, Trusan and Lawas river systems, with Limbang town as its capital.

On November 19th, we left Kuching on the coastal steamer *Auby*. Our first stop was at Bintulu, about midway up the coast.

"We draw eight feet, and the depth at the bar is six feet, so we'll plough our way through," Captain Gibson told us. And we certainly did bump our way over that shallow silt bar before berthing a couple of miles up the Bintulu River.

Our next stop was at Miri, where the ship anchored about three miles offshore, and where we rolled in a heavy swell for four days. This was the heyday of the development of the Miri oilfield, and the hill behind the town was dotted with oil derricks.

After leaving Miri we spent one more night at sea, and the next morning we rounded Sapu Point and entered Brunei Bay. It was a beautiful calm morning and the sunrise unveiled an idyllic portrait of placid water, tropical islands, fishing boats, *kelongs*, tree-covered hills and the distant Mulu massif. We were entranced.

The Limbang River is the largest of several rivers flowing into Brunei Bay, but the entrance is not easily visible from the sea. The obvious course to the river appeared to be a wide channel skirting a range of low hills to the south and west. In earlier days, however, this course led to a subtle and dangerous trap. The entrance to that channel was barred by a bank of rocks that had been built up to raise the level of a long reef. Since the line of rocks rose to just below the surface at low tide, unsuspecting ships sailing into the channel would become stranded on the barrier and were easy prey for the pirates who would emerge from their hiding places among the mangroves.

Our ship turned eastward, through a narrow channel, and into the broad Limbang River, where we proceeded between banks lined with mangroves and nipa palms. The heat steamed from the jungle. Tropical birds chattered from their vantage points among the trees, and rare proboscis monkeys with huge pendulous noses watched us curiously.

About eight miles upriver we came alongside the wharf at Limbang town. As this was the administrative centre of the most northerly part of Sarawak, we went directly to introduce ourselves to the senior officer of the Rajah's Government.

Rajah Brooke had absolute power in Sarawak, but his paternal administration had won him the respect and loyalty of the indigenous people. The Rajah appointed Residents from the senior men of his civil service who had gained a wide knowledge of the people, their cultures and their social structures. At that time, the

Resident at Limbang was a Mr. Kortright, and he and his wife invited Hendy and me to stay with them for the night.

The Residency was a spacious bungalow with a large veranda opening onto a beautiful panorama of the Limbang delta and Brunei Bay. It was constructed entirely of *belian* timber, the famous ironwood which is termite resistant and which, when planed, takes on a lovely black surface that improves with age.

At the time of our arrival, Sarawak was at peace. Piracy had been suppressed and intertribal warfare in the interior had ceased. The taking of heads was banned, though the nationals were permitted to retain any skulls they had taken in former conflicts.

Our stay at the Residency provided an excellent opportunity to witness the kind of relationship existing between the nationals and the Government. It was the Rajah's policy to keep in close contact with the people of his country, and he encouraged his officers to do the same. So each evening at about five o'clock, the Resident or District Officer entertained any visiting nationals at an informal "court." The atmosphere was intimate and friendly; weather permitting, a table and chairs would be set on the mown grass in front of the bungalow along with mats of woven rattan. Headmen and chiefs would sit in front and all would be served with drinks — usually European spirits, but sometimes native rice beer. At this open court the leading men would report news from their longhouses or raise problems for discussion, and the Resident would often express his opinions. Such opinions were accepted as being essentially equal to law.

The fort and government offices were at the foot of the hill on which the Residency stood, but there were no police or guards in sight. With the coming of nightfall, the visitors quietly bid the Resident farewell and descended the hill to their boats or to the Chinese bazaar.

The first morning after our arrival, I was up early and walked the half-mile to the line of hills behind the Residency and climbed to the summit. In the clear morning sky the sun's first rays stretched far up the Limbang valley, reflecting off two white pinnacles, one much taller than the other, positioned closely together and joined by a saddle. The taller of the two formed a startling landmark — a 3,000-

foot pillar of limestone rising from the main body of the mountain. I had read about this striking feature while I was still in Australia, but no words could do justice to that view. That was my introduction to the interior of Borneo — my first unforgettable look at the magnificent mountain the Malays had named Batu Lawi, the "Needle of Stone."

Mount Batu Lawi

This was the land that would become my home. Far beyond Batu Lawi, the mountains of the central highlands rose to more than 7,000 feet above sea level, forming a spinal watershed for the entire island. Streams spawned by tropical rainstorms cascaded out of these highlands, cutting tortuous channels between mountains and through virgin rain forests; at lower elevations they joined to form major waterways, sometimes raging, sometimes tranquil, making their way relentlessly down through jungle and pockets of farmland and deltaic coastlands to the South China Sea.

After one more night in Limbang, the Resident provided us with his launch to transport us to Batu Danau, the furthest police outpost upriver. We had permission to stay in the government bungalow there for three months while we found a site to establish our headquarters.

Meanwhile, Carey and Frank caught a steamer from Singapore to Labuan Island and then made their way by launch across Brunei Bay to Limbang town and on upriver to join us on December 13th. It was good to be a united party again. Borneo had been in our thoughts and dreams for more than a year, and we were grateful to finally be in this new world.

We lost little time in preparing for a journey further upriver to search for a suitable location for our base of operations. Hendy was accustomed to river travel using a *tongkang* and advised us to buy one. These were wide-beam, shallow-draft boats about fifteen feet long, propelled by a long oar which was fixed at the stern and swung from side to side with a sculling action. Though *tongkangs* may have been useful for trading, we soon found them inadequate for our purposes as they were clumsy, slow and only suited for downriver travel where the currents were still subject to tidal influences.

Using this ponderous boat and two boatmen, we left on our first journey upriver. We had travelled only about two hours when we met several long canoes, carrying about two dozen men, coming downstream. They were probably even more surprised to see us than we were to see them. We all stopped our boats at a sandbank and got out on the sand.

They were rugged, vigorous looking men with fine facial features, sparkling dark eyes and straight black hair clipped in a bowl shape at the front and sides but left long at the back. We learned that they were Kelabits from deep in the interior of Borneo. None of us knew any of the Kelabit language, but their Headman knew Malay, so we were able to converse with them in simple terms.

The Headman was an impressive looking fellow, close to six feet tall and powerfully built. He wore a vest made from soft beaten bark reinforced with palm fibre stitching, and a traditional loin cloth which was wrapped around his thighs and between his legs, with the free ends hanging forward. Under each knee was a band of a special kind of vine, twisted and secured tightly, supposedly to strengthen the calf muscles. On his wrists he wore metal bangles and around his neck several strings of multi-colored beads, some round and some cylindrical. The only thing out of character was his hat, a rather stylish felt fedora.

We also could not help but notice the engraved wooden sheath hanging menacingly from his woven rattan belt. Inside was his *parang,* the long, slightly curved jungle knife that served a multiplicity of uses and without which no proud Bornean would venture out of his house. The blade of his knife was perhaps twenty inches long, and the handle was ornately carved from the antler of a deer and decorated with tufts of hair dyed red.

All of the men had extended earlobes which had been progressively stretched from infancy with ornamental weights, and some wore decorative ivory carvings inserted through a hole punched in the shell of the upper ear. As a sign of friendship, the Headman gave me a pair of ear ornaments carved from hornbill ivory in the form of tiger teeth. Hornbill ivory, taken from the casque of the helmeted hornbill bird, was one of the most sought-after products of the Borneo jungle; it is mentioned in early Chinese records as highly prized for use in carved jewellry.

These Kelabits told us that some of their party lived in the central highlands of Sarawak. They had left their longhouse about six months earlier to come to the coast for trading, but they had been delayed repeatedly by adverse omens and influences of the spirit world. As a result, they had actually travelled only about three weeks out of the six months.

We tried to explain who we were and that our purpose in coming to their land was to tell them about the greatest Spirit of all. They evidenced some interest, and after about an hour we went our separate ways. Later years would reveal that this had been a God-arranged encounter.

After leaving the Kelabits, we continued upriver, rowing against the current. Each of us was immersed in his own thoughts. We had just met some of the legendary "wild men of Borneo" — and from the wildest, most remote part of the country at that. Although headhunting had been banned in Sarawak for several years, they had not lost their menacing appearance.

"Did you get a good look at those *parangs*?" Hendy asked of no one in particular. "And the chief's hat. Very European looking . . ."

I looked over at Carey and Frank. "Nah. Couldn't be," I said. "He must have traded for it."

We all laughed. But it was not completely relaxed laughter.

We progressed slowly upriver through territory inhabited by the Bisayas, one of the smallest of Sarawak's ethnic groups. For the most part it was alluvial country, well-suited for growing sago palms which formed part of the staple diet for the Bisaya people. At one point we noticed a high staging built out from the riverbank over the water. This staging had a floor of split bamboo about six feet square covered with a loosely woven mat that was larger than the bamboo floor so that it lapped up on all sides. As we approached, two women began dancing on the staging, their feet moving rhythmically over the matting and their bodies swaying gracefully, as though they were performing a welcome dance.

Suddenly one woman lowered a four-gallon tin to the river and brought it up filled with water which she threw over the matting. They continued the dance. It turned out they were washing sago flour from the fibrous trunk of a sago palm. The palm was felled and split open, then rasped with a board studded with rows of short nails to extract the fibrous pith. This was then crumbled and thrown onto the mat on the staging over the river, where the sago flour was washed and trodden from the fibrous material through the mat and collected in a trough below. So much for a romantic dancing welcome!

We continued our slow journey upriver, covering about eleven miles, and stayed at a Bisaya house that first night. The Headman was reserved but received us courteously.

The next day we pushed on past a group of Chinese shops at Ukong, and soon afterwards we passed out of Bisaya territory. The land was low-lying, and so far we had not seen any site suitable for building. By evening we came to the first Murut longhouse. Not many people were around, but the few we met needed medical help for sores and ringworm. Since it was dark, we stayed there for the night.

The following day we found that the river had risen, which slowed our progress even more. Finally, we arrived at a well-built longhouse about three hundred feet long located at the mouth of the Medamit River. It was the home of the *Penghulu*, or chief of the district, a man named Belulok, but he was away.

Just before we arrived, however, some Ibans had come in a canoe from Tanah Merah, the next longhouse upriver. They had heard of our coming and wanted to take us to their longhouse, so we went with them in their canoe.

The Ibans, the largest tribal group in Sarawak, were mostly farming people living in the foothills and river valleys. They were sometimes known as Sea Dayaks, a name acquired during the 1800s when certain of their number accompanied the pirates who terrorized the northwest coast of Borneo. The pirates raided ships for plunder, whereas the Ibans wanted the heads of the victims.

The house at Tanah Merah was the longest house we had seen so far, and the best built. As we ascended the notched-log entrance, we were immediately confronted with several blackened human skulls hanging from the rafters in front of us. Along the length of the veranda we could see that each family apartment had its own collection of these trophies.

Headhunter Trophies

Despite this gruesome display, the people gave us a warm welcome and entertained us with a nice evening meal. In the morning they transported us back downriver to *Penghulu* Belulok's house.

Next we conferred with the leading people in the region, and they suggested we locate at Sungai Pranga about two miles downriver from where *Penghulu* Belulok lived. When we inspected the area, we found that it was comprised of three small hills rising fifty to sixty feet above the usual flood level, together with about twenty acres of flat land; the whole area was bordered by a small stream which formed a natural boundary. This seemed an excellent location for our first base and home site.

After arranging with some local Muruts to build us a small temporary house of bamboo and palm leaves at the base of the main hill, we returned downriver to the police outstation at Danau. From there I sent a report of our investigations to the Resident, who then came upriver, picked me up at Danau, and went on with me to see the site for himself and to find if there were any objections from the local people to our occupancy.

Not long afterwards, the Resident forwarded to us an official grant to the land at Sungai Pranga.

We had been in Sarawak only a few short weeks and had already met people from four different ethnic and language groups — Bisayas, Muruts, Ibans and Kelabits (although at that stage the Kelabits lived far beyond our reach). We also had our own plot of land and Rajah Vyner Brooke's official approval to build our first mission station.

CHAPTER 2

For the next two months we lived at the police outpost at Danau, forty miles upriver, which gave us valuable breathing space in which to take stock of our environment, our mission — and our isolation. Our clumsy *tongkang* had sunk. The river had risen rapidly in a sudden storm one night and the hull of the boat had apparently tilted and filled with water. It sank in about twenty-five feet of water and filled with mud and silt. With our limited equipment it was irretrievable. We had no other means of communication — no roads, no regular river traffic and, in those days, no radio or telephone.

During our free time, we disciplined ourselves to a regular schedule of study using a Malay grammar book and practical conversations with the two Malay policemen and other local people. We also had to devote more time than ever before to finding food. Some friends had given me a shotgun before we left Australia, and that now proved invaluable as I was able to shoot wood pigeons in the nearby jungle. In addition, we collected ferntips from the riverbank along with tapioca leaves to eat with our rice, and we bought cheap tinned fish from the lone Chinese trader in the nearby Bisaya village.

At the end of January we were able to buy a lighter and smaller canoe, so with one native accompanying us to steer from the stern, Frank and I set off downriver to Limbang town. It was our first journey using our own paddle-power on a big Borneo river, and with the help of the current we arrived downriver the same day. We were glad to receive the letters and a small bank draft from Australia which were waiting for us, and relieved to find that for a nominal rental we could stay overnight at a small government guest house.

When it came time to return upriver, however, our native helper did not want to come so Frank and I set out alone, this time rowing against the current. At nightfall we placed a little kerosene reflector lamp in the prow of the canoe to help us steer close to the bank and also to show us if there were any crocodiles at the surface of the water.

The light of the lamp reflected off the crocodiles' eyes with a sinister gleam, and we steered well away from them!

Eventually we pulled up to a small native house on the river bank, hoping for a rest, but the people were so astonished to see Europeans paddling alone on the river at night that they thought we must be outlaws and would not receive us!

By this time we were so tired that we forgot all about the crocodiles; we tied a line to a tree and lay down in the rolling canoe for a few hours' rest. Not until later did we realize how vulnerable we were to having our boat overturned by a powerful slap from a crocodile's tail.

After a couple of hours of much-needed sleep, we continued our journey. Our hands blistered, the paddles felt like lead, but we forged on through the rest of the night and the next day. The second night, as we were moving ahead steadily, with our little kerosene lamp at the front, we saw a spectral object, like a giant octopus, looming towards us. As it turned out, we were in the backwash of a huge whirlpool carrying us upstream, and what we saw were the white spreading limbs of a dead tree still upright and quivering in the river current. That sight was so eerie I still remember it more than sixty years later! Needless to say, we were relieved to finally arrive back at Danau late that night.

From our temporary quarters at Danau we visited the Bisaya houses nearby. Since the Bisayas were the ethnic group nearest to the Malays on the coast, they were familiar with the Malay language and culture. This was a great help, not only for us to practice speaking Malay but also to learn and compare the cultures of the two groups.

We were acutely aware of our need to continue learning in order to work effectively in this new environment. Notwithstanding the allowances required for dealing with different cultures, however, one of the first lessons I learned was that human nature and human emotions and feelings are basically the same, even though they may find expression in different ways. Cultural emphases may vary, individual temperaments may be extrovert or introvert, cheerful or sullen, but underneath these outward expressions is the commonality of human needs. This is reflected in the literature of the Bible and explains why that book, as an inspired record of God's dealing with the human race, is universally relevant. Mankind was created in the likeness of God himself, so his word carries its own powerful message to the human heart, irrespective of culture.

At the end of February 1929, we were able to move further upriver to our new homesite at Sungai Pranga, where the Muruts had completed our temporary lodgings. Although the hut was small by any standards, it was on land that we believed God had given us, and our daily lives were filled with a sense of purpose.

Original Bush Hut – February 1929

People started coming to visit us out of mere curiosity. Then, as they realized that we could assist them medically, they came asking us for help, for at that time there were no government clinics anywhere in the interior. We had brought with us a good supply of simple medicines, and Frank, Carey and I all had been given some training with the outpatient staff at the Royal Alfred Hospital in Melbourne.

When it came to our own daily lives, we soon learned to use the main native tools. The first tool we adopted was the *parang*, or jungle bush knife, used for clearing undergrowth and for general farming purposes — as well as for fighting. There were various kinds of *parang*, with the most common type having a curved blade about eighteen inches long and one-and-a-half inches wide. A more specialized type, basically meant for fighting, was cleverly designed so as to not get jammed when striking a heavy blow at a body. The cutting edge was straighter and the end tapered to a point; along its length the blade was forged with a gentle curve to accommodate either left-handed or right-handed fighters, and the side of the blade was carefully shaped so as to be slightly concave.

After the main hill of our property was cleared and burned off, I pegged out a contour line around the hill using a line level so that we could level the ground at the top in preparation for a building site. We cut about five feet from the top of the hill to provide a levelled area not less than 120 feet in each direction. To excavate the hilltop we used heavy steel hoes called *cangkuls* and carried the earth away in little two-handled baskets. We did this work in the morning or evening when the days were coolest, and most of it we did ourselves, as we did not yet have enough money to hire local laborers. It was hard work but it kept us in good physical condition.

The three of us shared the cooking duty, and we bought our supplies — such as soap, sugar, salt, flour and other kitchen necessities — from Chinese shops at Ukong, a day's journey downriver by canoe. Carey made us an oven from a five-gallon oil drum set in the midst of a pile of stones which stored the heat from the fire beneath. Using yeast he made from hops, Carey prepared dough and baked our bread.

We hunted for most of our meat. I often went hunting at night with the Muruts from across the river. One man would carry a kerosene-burning brass reflector lamp that would throw a beam of light as he waved it from side to side. We would stealthily creep along, watching for a reflected gleam of light from an animal's eyes in the dark jungle. Following close behind, with my shotgun at the ready, I would then aim between the eyes and fire. Mostly we got *plandok* or mouse-deer, about the size of a large rabbit, but occasionally I was able to shoot a full-size sambhur deer, and the smoked meat kept us and our fellow hunters supplied for a long time.

When we first came to Borneo, many of the people had guns, but these were mainly ancient muzzle-loaders which they packed with gunpowder and pieces of metal or nails, or even pebbles. In the daytime they hunted with dogs which would follow an animal and hold it at bay until the hunters could catch up and kill it with spear thrusts.

Among the people of Borneo, being a hunter was synonymous with being a man. No man could not be a hunter. And while the three of us enjoyed hunting, it was a means of survival for us more than a sport. In addition, it helped us build good relationships with the Muruts and Ibans, and assisted us in gaining fluency in their languages.

Three Hunters: Hudson, Carey, Frank

I certainly missed my share of opportunities when I hunted alone, but I do not think I ever missed a shot in those early years of night-hunting. As a result, when I later began travelling in the interior, I found that I had developed quite a reputation as a marksman — a reputation that was nice to have, but which undoubtedly exceeded reality!

Another sign of virility was the taking of heads, and the notorious practice of headhunting was at one time common to virtually all the indigenous tribes of Borneo. The more heads a longhouse possessed, the greater was its prestige. This practice not only led to endless intertribal warfare, but also discouraged travel and trade.

Just four years before we arrived in Sarawak, the famous peace-making had taken place at Kapit, midway up the Rejang River in the most central area of Sarawak. This event had brought together native chiefs from all over Sarawak, and even some from what was then Dutch Borneo.

> The officials were received by the Resident of the Division, with a guard of Sarawak Rangers . . . Then the warriors from over the border paddled in their canoes four abreast down the Rejang, raising their paddles in salute as they passed the Rajah's yacht. Other Dyaks and Kayans came in from neighboring districts. That evening there were more than four thousand warriors encamped round Kapit. The following day was spent in visiting and in feasts. The ceremonial peace-making took place on the 16th [of November 1924]. Pigs were sacrificially slaughtered in vast numbers; and the leading chieftains on each side rose one after another to pray that peace should be preserved and to curse those who should try to re-open the feud. Then the Rajah rose to thank those who had brought about the reconciliation and to warn his subjects that it must be maintained. The Netherlands Comptroller gave a similar warning to his people. Finally the Rajah made gifts to the leading chieftains on each side . . . The whole impressive ceremony ended with a genuine feeling of goodwill.[1]

Head-taking was suppressed, peace reigned, and the Rajah felt it safe to undertake a controlled program of transmigration. About 500 Ibans were allowed to migrate from the Skrang River in the heart of Iban country in the Second Division, where their increasing population was causing pressure on the land available for agriculture. These Ibans moved into the Limbang area, where the Murut

1. Steven Runciman, *The White Rajahs, A History of Sarawak* (Kuala Lumpur: S. Abdul Majeed & Co. 1992), 238, 239.

population had been depleted. Although the Ibans had given up headhunting, they brought with them over one hundred skulls taken as trophies in former years. These skulls were also valued for use in their pagan forms of worship. During certain rituals, their owners would keep them warm over a fire and place rice between their teeth, and at some ceremonies their spirits were invoked.

Iban War Dance

A large number of the Ibans from the Skrang area were living at Tanah Merah, the Iban longhouse we had visited during our first trip upriver in December 1928. After we settled at Sungai Pranga, they often came to us seeking medical help. Sometimes one of us would return with them to their longhouse; I well remember one such visit.

I had gone to Tanah Merah alone, taking my medical kit as usual. Several days earlier, one of the young men had fallen from a tree and struck the calf of his leg on a log. No bones were broken, but his calf was badly swollen from bruising and bleeding within the muscle. I felt it needed lancing to drain the inflamed muscle, so I used a hypodermic syringe to test where the fluid suppuration was nearest to the surface. I then lanced the swollen muscle, and immediately a mixture of blood, serum and pus gushed out, much to the alarm of his family who called out "*Mati! Mati!*" meaning "Death! Death!"

The Ibans nearby rushed in and eyed me suspiciously, but I remained calm and told them not to be afraid. After draining about half a pint of fluid from the infected area, I applied a poultice to allow further drainage. Of course we had no antibiotics in those days, but in about a week the man was better and the injury was healing.

Although the Limbang District was historically Murut territory, with transmigration the Ibans were already becoming prominent in that area. They were hard workers and good farmers, delighting in getting the maximum production from their farms by tediously hand-weeding their rice crops. When we employed them as workers, we found them diligent and friendly. They admired and responded to genuine friendliness, but were quick to reject anyone they felt had let them down. They were interested to hear the teachings of Jesus, but during our first few years of work there, the majority would neither accept nor reject any real commitment to its message. The Ibans were proud of their culture and identity, and on more than one occasion asked us if there were any Ibans in our country. When we said there were not, they immediately responded, "So no wonder you want to come to Sarawak, so that you can be with Ibans!"

In mid-1929, Hendy left us. Having introduced us to the Malay language and life in the tropics, he felt his job was done, and as he was about seventy years old, he wrote to the Mission council and asked to be withdrawn. We had appreciated his knowledge and experience and enjoyed his wry sense of humor and were sorry to see him go. From all that he said, he also had enjoyed our camaraderie and his interaction with the local people. For a few years he kept in contact with us from Australia, but eventually we lost touch with him.

Our work in Borneo certainly had small beginnings. Frank, Carey and I lived and slept in our miniature hut, built about seven feet above the ground, and had our meals at a split bamboo table positioned beneath the hut. We visited the coast once every two months, which meant a week's paddling there and back.

Our prayers were real, for our needs were great.

Once we had finished levelling the hilltop, we started constructing our headquarters building. My previous technical training was useful at this point, as I was able to draw up detailed plans for the building. The closest sawmill was seventy miles away on the coast, so we felled our own trees and hired a Chinese man to cut them into the desired dimensions using a pit-saw. We had brought carpentry tools with us from Australia, which enabled us to plane the floorboards and even tongue and groove them by hand. As more funds became available, we engaged local people who were expert at using their native adzes to hew the main hardwood posts. We also hired a skilled Chinese carpenter, which greatly accelerated the actual construction work.

Now that we were established at Sungai Pranga, the Ibans came to visit us more frequently, and as we had help with our building we had the time to increase our contacts with the people in their longhouses.

Longhouses were typically built about ten to fifteen feet above the ground and ran from fifty to five hundred feet, or more, in length. A longhouse consisted of a row of family apartments, each having a door opening out onto a long hall, about twenty or more feet in width, which ran the full length of the house. Some were built of timber hewn from the forest; others used split giant bamboo for walls and floors. The long main hall was used for general assemblies of all the people in the longhouse and for many other activities, and this generated an atmosphere of community. The character traits of all the peoples of inland Borneo were powerfully influenced by the nature of life in a longhouse.

Longhouse Interior

The role of the headman varied with the distinctive culture of the various ethnic groups, which ranged from the stratified class consciousness of some to the more open society of others. Among Ibans much depended on the personality of the headman. Typically he was a patriarch among free families, rather than a despotic chief. He decided matters of customs and had power to adjudicate in family disputes. Another role of the headman was to entertain visitors, and for that purpose he might call for assistance from other leading men of the longhouse.

My early impressions of the Ibans are summarized below, from a letter I wrote in 1929:

> A typical day in Iban life starts before dawn. They wake with the crowing of cocks which roost beneath the house. The morning meal in the Iban houses is usually over before six o'clock. During the farming season the men and women work on their farms from early till late, resting perhaps in the middle of the day. At other seasons, there is not so much work to do, and they can make boats, build houses or hunt in the forest. The old women do not go out to work, but weave cloth, make mats and look after the younger children at home. Weaving cloth is a special activity of the Ibans.

> Sometimes they spend months weaving and dyeing a single cloth, perhaps six feet by three feet.
>
> In the evening, after the day's work is done, people gather round for social chat and we find this to be the best time to visit with them. Though they do not make idols, their conception of a god is very primitive. They have not yet realized that God in his being transcends all that is human. Their thought is only in terms of human relationships in the mystical plane of the unseen. Their attitude is materialistic. They tend to think we are trying to teach them a better method of invoking the aid of unseen power; they have no thought of worshiping God as the creator of everything, but only seek to obtain material benefits in response to their petitions. Misfortune is attributed to the influence of *hantus* or spirits, and these must be placated by sacrifices of fowls and pigs.

None of the tribal people of inland Borneo belonged to any of the world religions. However, what we learned about Iban animistic beliefs was true of other ethnic groups on the island, though there were cultural variations. They believed that all nature was inhabited and animated by spirits, and they spent a large part of their lives evading the malignant activities of these spirits. The will of the spirits was interpreted by a complicated system of omens in which dreams and the flight and sounds of birds played a prominent part. The responsibility for interpreting omens and dreams belonged to the shamans; consequently, they had control over matters affecting the farming cycle and many other aspects of community life.

I remember instances when, because of the persistent cry of a certain bird, urgent farming work was delayed or abandoned. As a result, the proper seasonal activity was missed and for the next year food was scarce. On two occasions I recall a certain bird flying into a long community house and thus causing everyone, over 100 people, to flee from the house, carrying only a few essential articles with them.

Journeys were abandoned and house or boat building was interrupted because of adverse omens.

Moral and ethical standards were similarly affected. A young couple, recently and happily married, were compelled to divorce because a barking deer was heard in the forest. Sometimes the sick were not bathed and were denied the foods they needed. The smallest illness or misfortune was attributed to an evil spirit which would need to be exorcised or appeased by an elaborate ceremonial. Significantly, these ceremonies usually involved killing a fowl or pig and applying its blood to the person involved.

Aside from their animistic beliefs, the indigenous tribal peoples had many other traits in common. In the villages, most aspects of their lives were communal and major decisions were made by the people as a whole. Their economies, however, were not communistic; each individual had his own private property. In addition, the personal status of women was high. When it came to civil rights, the ownership of property and inheritance, the sexes were regarded as having equal status.

By our second full year in Borneo, 1930, Carey, Frank and I were settling in well, and the year saw several significant encounters and advances.

First, we were able to acquire a small outboard engine to power our longboat. This certainly made travel easier, although one day it almost caused a disaster. We were on our way to visit an Iban village on the Medamit River, a winding tributary of the Limbang. As we rounded a bend, a huge crocodile, sunning itself on the bank, hurried down to submerge itself in the river. Crocodiles in the interior were familiar with the click of longboat paddles and even a mile away would quietly submerge when they heard the sound of paddles, but they were not yet accustomed to the sound of outboard engines. On our return journey we encountered the same crocodile again. It had crawled back up onto a high mudbank, and apparently still did not associate the "put-put" sound of our engine with human beings. As we rounded the bend, this huge crocodile saw us only a few yards away and literally hurled itself into the river, almost landing in our boat!

That year we also received our first full-time recruit. George Aiken had applied to the Mission in January and, after some training at Melbourne Bible Institute, arrived in Limbang in September. He was a skilled carpenter and greatly helped in the completion of our headquarters at Sungai Pranga during his first few months there.

Timber House at Sungai Pranga – 1930

In late 1930, two Shell geologists, Dr. Trumpy and Dr. Irvine, visited us at Sungai Pranga. They were on a geological survey, and they continued on into the far interior — to the upper Limbang, the upper Trusan and over the international border into Dutch Borneo. On their return they told us of the large Murut population on both sides of the border. They described how those people lived on fertile highlands and had a relatively advanced system of irrigated rice cultivation.

Not long afterwards another expedition came our way, this time from the Sarawak Museum, to investigate the depletion of the Borneo rhinoceros population.

One of the earliest references to Borneo in ancient Chinese records concerns the export of rhinoceros horns to China, where they were powdered and sold as an aphrodisiac at fabulous prices. Traditional methods of hunting were sufficiently haphazard to ensure that the balance of the rhinoceros population was maintained, but by the 1920s and 1930s breech-loading shotguns became available, and there were reports that the rhinoceros population was being hunted to extinction.

To investigate these reports, the Curator of the Sarawak Museum, Edward Banks, journeyed to the highlands in the upper Trusan area and then travelled across through wild mountainous country to the upper Limbang, passing near the needle of stone, Mt. Batu Lawi. He was met there by the District Officer from the Baram district who had arrived by a different route. It had been arranged that *Penghulu* Belulok, the chief of our district, would take several large canoes upriver to meet these teams when they converged at the Medihit tributary of the upper Limbang, and then convey them down the Limbang. I took this opportunity to journey deeper into the interior. Accompanying Belulok proved a valuable experience and provided me with a number of good contacts, including *Penghulu* Malang, a distinguished chief from the Tutoh River.

Unfortunately, the canoes that Belulok had brought upriver proved insufficient for so many people to travel in safety down the rapids; however, by great skill on the part of the boatmen, the crowded boats survived the hazardous trip downriver.

On our arrival back at Belulok's longhouse, I witnessed an instructive sequel to this journey which was an excellent example of native diplomacy. When entertaining a prominent visitor, it was customary to toast him with liquor and, when presenting the glass, to chant a greeting or eulogy improvised for the occasion. Then the visitor could return the honour. Sometimes this custom was used to convey a poignant message without giving too much offence. On this occasion, *Penghulu* Malang chanted a diplomatically worded rebuke for the inadequate transport, but then apologized elaborately by suggesting that he himself was very drunk. It was a classic Asian resolution: everyone had a good laugh; Malang made his point; and, perhaps most importantly, Belulok did not lose face!

Carey, Frank and I were now well advanced in the Malay language and were learning Iban. We had a splendid Iban dictionary to work with, as well as the whole New Testament which had been translated into Iban by the Anglican mission. By the end of 1930, we were able to conduct daily morning Bible readings and prayers in the Iban language.

Now that our main building was completed and we had some understanding of the land and its people, the four of us began to spread out in various directions in active missionary work. Carey made a number of visits to several Iban longhouses on the Lubai River, and we each made visits to the settlement of Kelabits on the Medihit. I felt that we should also establish an outreach to the Bisayas, so we erected a temporary building at Limpasong, halfway downriver to the coast from Sungai Pranga. There, I lived among the Bisaya people for about ten months in 1931.

There was one other memorable development that year. Our Mission council in Melbourne felt that the time had arrived for a married couple to broaden the sphere of service in Borneo. I shared that view — I had been engaged to be married for more than three years!

Chapter 3

My own parents were married late in life. My father, Frank Elmer Southwell, was born in Swaffam in Norfolk, England, in 1849; he was the eldest son of William Castell Southwell, who was for over thirty years a manager with Gurney's Bank. After primary schooling my father spent six years at Christ's Hospital, the famous Blue Coat school founded by Edward VI, to which his uncle, Sir Charles Southwell, had a right of nomination as a governor.

My grandparents were devout Christians, as were all of their children. All of them, that is, except Frank. Although privileged and well-educated, Frank Southwell was adventuresome in spirit and would not settle into the staid career in banking for which he was destined. Instead, in search of adventure, he joined the Merchant Marine, and in 1866 set sail for Hong Kong. My grandfather's diary followed his movements around the world — New York, Calcutta, Singapore, Melbourne . . .

My father completed his naval apprenticeship and progressed well in his career as a seaman. In 1888, however, twenty-two years after leaving England, he suddenly lost everything when his schooner, *Ettalong*, was wrecked on a coral reef near Beacon Island while on a voyage from Sydney, Australia, to the Solomon Islands.

Three weeks later Frank and his crew were rescued by a passing ship which saw their distress signals. They were returned safely to Sydney where Frank decided to leave the sea for good. With nothing to show for his career, however, England was not the place to settle; after a brief visit to his homeland to see his parents, he returned to Australia, where the great depression of the 1890s was already developing.

Thus, at the age of forty, Frank Southwell started over as a travelling business representative, still very much a man of the world. A year later, through the influence of a stranger who came to his aid during one of his drinking binges, Frank had a personal encounter with God that completely changed his life.

Over the next ten years, wherever his commercial travelling took him, he sought out Christian gatherings, and his faith and commitment grew. It was during this period that Dr. J. Hudson Taylor, who had founded the China Inland Mission in 1865, visited Australia. Frank Southwell accompanied this distinguished visitor on his speaking tour and was both impressed and encouraged by the great missionary's unpretentious faith.

A faded letter dated October 25, 1898, from the Railway Hotel, Warracknabeal, revealed another interest in his life — Edith Rebecca Edwards, the daughter of a London watchmaker to the Admiralty who had emigrated to Adelaide, South Australia:

> Dear Miss Edwards,
>
> Now in offering myself to you, humanly speaking what are you receiving? A life nearly spent, a very uncertain income, no provision made for old age, four-fifths of my life a blank . . .
>
> Now, I have pleaded my cause and leave it in your hands . . .

Frank and Edith were married five months later, on March 31, 1899, at Talbot, Victoria. He was forty-nine. She was thirty-six.

I was born on June 28, 1900. Even before I was born my father and mother dedicated me to God for his service. Inspired by the missionary service of Hudson Taylor, they gave me the name Hudson. My other name, Charles, was partly in honour of my great-uncle and partly so that my initials would be the same as those of the renowned British preacher, Charles Haddon Spurgeon. So as Charles Hudson Southwell, I certainly entered the world with lofty expectations placed upon me!

The year I was born my parents were living in an old two-story stone house they had rented at Williamstown, the port area for Melbourne. My father travelled by train during the week on his commissioned sales, keeping in touch with my mother by notes hastily written on the back of invoices.

My brother Howard was born two years after me, and he was my great companion in those early years.

"The two boys, ten and twelve, are nice boys," a visiting English cousin wrote home in 1912, "but rather trying to their father and mother who are too old to enter into the youngsters' frolics."

And about my father he added, "The last time I saw Uncle Frank was at Swaffham nearly twenty-five years ago. The difference between then and now is simply marvelous, explainable only in one way, as he himself puts it 'by the grace of God.'"

Although as a family we lived frugally, my parents delighted in entertaining visitors, especially missionaries from all parts of the world, which stimulated my own interest in missionary work.

My father gave me a love for adventure and discovery, and he often told me tales of his travels. In those days Melbourne was frequented by the tall sailing ships, and I used to love to climb their rigging. My father taught me about the stars and read to me extensively. I was most interested in books on science, even when I was in primary school, and I soaked up facts about comets and meteors, fossils and dinosaurs.

My parents also taught me verses from the Bible, and I learned a verse for every letter of the alphabet before I went to school. For my birthdays my father adopted a rather unusual practice. As my birthday came round each year, my father would write me a letter in his classical copperplate handwriting, setting out his prayers and aspirations for my future, even though I would not understand some of them until I was older.

I made my first spiritual decision when I was nearly ten, and although it was sincere and real, I did not fully comprehend the step I had taken. My father's letter on my fifteenth birthday, the last of his letters that have survived, recognized my lack of commitment:

> My dear Hudson,
>
> Once again has this day 28th June come round, another milestone, and another year's work registered somewhere. Well! You are growing in knowledge and strength of body and mind. You know our greatest desire is that you will strengthen the purpose of your will to serve our God . . .

> D. L. Moody said about your age "I want to be the best man God can make," and from that moment he tried to please Him in everything, and succeeded too! . . .
>
> That is what we expect from our first born, and if you will trust Him, then, "The one who calls you is faithful and he will do it."[1] Try Him and you will never regret it. With much love and hunger for your soul's best interest.
>
> Your affectionate Father,
> (Signed) F. E. Southwell

I was also fortunate in my formal education. In 1912, the Victoria Education Department established the first suburban secondary schools for free education, and that year, at age twelve, I passed a qualifying test for entrance to one of these schools. By December 1914, I had completed the two-year course, gaining first place.

In 1915, I changed to an emphasis on technical education and was one of the first students at the newly opened junior technical school at West Melbourne. The school was staffed by skilled tradesmen who, with their outstanding craftsmanship, were able to teach us much more than merely the theory of their trades. Technical school taught me carpentry, tinsmithing and soldering, blacksmithing and forging, plane and solid geometry, building and engineering drawing, as well as the usual academic subjects, including general science.

The following year, 1916, was the darkest year of the First World War. I enlisted, at age sixteen, in the Royal Australian Naval Reserve, and for the next four years I was required to do about two months training each year at the naval base. In 1916, I was also offered a technical student teachership which entailed five years of academic training while doing part-time teaching, followed by four years on the staff of a technical school. I accepted and signed a contract that was to bind me for the next nine years.

Early in 1917, I commenced my contract with the Department of Technical Education and enrolled for a diploma in Chemical Engineering. Finding that my part-time teaching did not allow enough time for the comprehensive curriculum of that course of

1. 1 Thessalonians 5:24

study, I soon switched to a program in Chemistry at the Melbourne Technical College (now the Royal Melbourne Institute of Technology).

During the early years of my studies, my father's concern over my teenage attitudes certainly was not without basis. As 1915 rolled on into 1916, however, my views began to change, for it was then I came into contact with three young men who were planning to be missionaries in China. These three, J.H. (Robbie) Robinson, Norman Baker and Delwyn Rees, not only had a positive impact on my thinking, but became my lifelong friends.

The following year, 1917, I attended the annual meeting of the China Inland Mission. These gatherings had grown to be outstanding events within the Christian community in Melbourne and were attended by people from every denomination, many of them young people. The guest speaker that year was Rev. C.N. Lack, and he climaxed his account of the Mission's work in China with an appeal for young people to commit their whole lives to God for his service, wherever and whenever he should direct. Convinced that this was exactly what God wanted me to do with my life, I determined to follow this calling. It was a major turning point in my life, and I knew it.

However, this decision also presented me with a problem. Only a few months before I had committed myself to nine years of study and teaching. What was I to do?

I discussed my dilemma with several older people whom I respected, and they gave me what proved to be very sound advice. The two commitments were not necessarily inconsistent, they said, and suggested that since at that time I might be too young and untrained for missionary service, I should complete my contract with the Department of Technical Education. But they also said, "Don't lose your vision of complete commitment to serving God."

Unfortunately my father did not see this commitment fulfilled. In 1921, as I was preparing to take the final examinations for my Bachelor of Science degree, he contracted pneumonia. This was in the days before antibiotics were available, and the disease progressed rapidly. He knew the end was near, but had no fear of dying; rather, he looked forward to going to heaven to be with his Lord.

The day after I completed my examinations, I sat with my father from early morning on. His big frame looked gaunt and he had great difficulty breathing. Late in the afternoon he reached out to take my hand. I could feel his pulse fading. He whispered hoarsely the stirring words written by the Apostle Paul: "I know whom I have believed and am persuaded that he is able to keep that which I have committed unto him against that day."[2]

They were his last words. I am sure that I owe more than will ever be known to my father's prayers of faith for my future.

During my first three years with the Department of Technical Education, I received a wide range of training in both organic and inorganic chemistry, as well as geology, assaying, mining, metallurgy, mineralogy and even surveying. The next year I was trained in the chemistry and analysis of foods, drugs, fats, oils and waxes, leading to a Public Analysts Certificate. In my fifth year I gained one of four Commonwealth Scholarships to complete a Degree in Science at Melbourne University, majoring in chemistry. I was able to take physiology, biochemistry, physical chemistry, pure mathematics, as well as third-year chemistry, in which I gained First Class Honours in 1921.

Throughout those years, I also continued serving in a number of church programs, all of which provided valuable training.

In 1922, I was appointed to teach mathematics and science at the West Melbourne Technical School, and in the year following I was transferred to Castlemaine in central Victoria where I was placed in charge of the Science Department of the junior technical school.

I completed my nine-year contract with the Department of Technical Education in 1926 — and I was free! But such is the subtlety of the human heart that I then began pursuing a promising route of advancement in a science career and accepted a position as a research

2. 2 Timothy 1:12

chemist with a sugar refining firm. It was a profession I loved and, in addition, the company had offered to send me to the United States for further training.

A few months later, however, I reached a major crossroad in my life. Something had been bothering me, and I had been trying to avoid facing it. Although I was scrupulously honest in my dealings with other people, on a more foundational level I sensed that I was not living with total integrity. My younger brother, Howard, must have recognized this, because it was he who questioned me in a quiet way about the promise I had made to God nine years before. I knew that if I did not honour that promise now, I probably never would.

I agonized over this, and still vividly recall the inward conflict with which I struggled over a period of several weeks. In the end, I went to the general manager of the sugar refining company with my letter of resignation, explaining the reasons for my decision. To my surprise, he expressed a sincere respect for the choice I had made and asked me to stay on, if possible, for another three months.

To further my commitment, I entered the Melbourne Bible Institute at the beginning of the academic year in August 1926, and was fortunate to be able to secure a job as a part-time teacher at the West Melbourne Technical School, which paid my way through the two years at the Institute.

I shall never forget the opening session. During the prayers, it seemed as though Satan was saying directly to me, "What are you doing here? What a fool you are! Throwing away a career in chemistry that you worked so hard for and loved so much! What a foolish, impulsive thing to do!"

I felt utterly miserable but I was determined not to take a backward step. My heart cried out to God and then, as the prayers ended, an amazing thing happened. It was as though all the clouds had vanished and peace entered my heart. And I can truly say that never again, from that day to this, have I ever regretted making that commitment.

With this step, I assumed that my career in science was over. Little did I know how my technical training would benefit me in unexpected ways years later.

Chapter 4

I met Winsome Howell for the first time on a railway platform in Melbourne Station. She had accompanied her brother David to bid farewell to a mutual friend of ours who was returning to Sydney. At the time I was carrying a large map of Borneo under my arm, and many years later Winsome wrote, "That day Borneo and Hudson both came into my life, though I did not know it at the time."

During my second year at Melbourne Bible Institute, I lived at the institute hostel, and David Howell was assigned as my roommate. David's family lived near the campus, and he often invited me to his home and to play tennis on courts nearby. I came to know his family well and, after our initial meeting at the railway station, I was deeply attracted to his sister.

Winsome Howell – 1926

Winsome was close to her older twin brothers, David and Dick, a bond established from an early age, as described by David:

> Winsome, the only girl, was born eighteen months after us. She too was tall and dark, and as she grew she acquired Mother's charm, simple cheerfulness and faith. She was very much our playmate in the early years and we schooled together under governesses. We used to call her 'Miss' after the nurse who used to say, "Stop that, Miss, you naughty girl." She wore flouncy frocks and bloomers and our pet lambs would follow her, mistaking her for their mothers.[1]

Not long after Winsome's twelfth birthday, her mother was invited to Tasmania on a speaking engagement.

"As she set off in a taxi for the train station, I remember waving goodbye," Winsome recounts. "Then, I turned to a friend who was with me and said, 'She's gone.' And immediately I thought, *and she won't come back.*"

It was an extraordinary premonition, for her mother died the next day in a railway accident between Launceston and Hobart.

For a number of years afterwards Winsome stayed with her mother's sister, Mabel Beath. In fact, she was living with her aunt in a small house near the family home when I first met her. Winsome was twenty-three at the time and pursuing a career in music. She had studied under Sir Edvard Goll at the Melbourne Conservatorium of Music and already had a number of students of her own. Her tutors at the conservatory had encouraged her to continue her studies, as they felt she had the ability to become a concert pianist.

Our principal at the Melbourne Bible Institute, Rev. C. H. Nash, was held in high esteem by his students. He had trained for the Anglican ministry at Ridley College in Cambridge, England, and was not only a man of great scholarship, but had a profound knowledge of the Bible and of human experience. He also was a man of

1. David L. B. Howell, *Through the Long Grass* (West Sussex: Gooday Publishers, 1991), 6.

tremendous personality and character. In 1921, he had commenced teaching one student to prepare for missionary service, and five years later he had over 100 students.

Initially I did not know to what service God would lead me. I only knew that he had called me to prepare. Some people thought it would be China, since I had many acquaintances in the China Inland Mission and had been named after its founder. Mr. Nash, however, spoke often of countries that had not yet been reached by Christianity and one day challenged us by asking, "What are you young men doing about the islands to the north of Australia?" That struck a spark in my imagination, and by mid-1927 my thoughts had more or less focused on the largest of those islands, Borneo.

It was not that I knew a great deal about the country; in fact, we received no news in Australia concerning Borneo. It was simply that after studying and praying about the missionary situation, Borneo seemed to stand out. I believe that God directed my attention to it.

With my interest aroused, my first step was to visit the large public library in Melbourne and read everything available on the subject. Although Borneo is the third largest island in the world, it was not situated on any of the world's great trade routes and hence was largely unknown. The writings of the few explorers who had ventured into the interior fascinated me.

This isolated frontier was the home of the "wild men of Borneo," tribal warriors with a penchant for headhunting. It also was home to the large manlike ape, the orangutan, whose name comes directly from the Malay words *orang utan*, meaning literally "man of the forest." During my research, I found that some sources were confusing these large apes with the feared headhunters — a measure of how little was known about Borneo in those days.

I was also fascinated by the history of this mysterious island in the South China Sea and intrigued by the White Rajahs of Sarawak, whose unique and romantic rule had recently brought headhunting to an end.

As there was no large-scale map of the whole island available at that time, I set about producing my own map on the largest sheet of drawing paper I could find — about three feet by four feet. Although I had only sketchy British maps of Sarawak, the sultanate of Brunei, and British North Borneo, I obtained a much more detailed map of Dutch Borneo from the Netherlands Consulate in Melbourne. After assembling these, I used a pantograph to bring them to the same scale and filled in the rivers, mountains, and place names.

Many streams of information increased my interest in Borneo. For example, I read of Rev. R.A. Jaffray of the Christian and Missionary Alliance denomination who had pioneered work in Indochina. He had recently taken a journey on cargo vessels plying their trade from Saigon down through the straits between the southern Philippines and North Borneo, and between Borneo and the Celebes (now Sulawesi). With all my reading and research, I found no evidence that the peoples of the vast interior of Borneo had ever heard of the love of God as revealed in Jesus Christ. Gripped by the ambition that the Apostle Paul had, "to preach the gospel where Christ was not known,"[2] I knew that God had called me to Borneo.

It was during this same period in 1927 that two of my fellow students, Frank Davidson and Carey Tolley, also developed an interest in Borneo. So from that time on, the three of us concentrated on the challenge of this largely unknown island.

Following advice from Principal Nash, I wrote to the Worldwide Evangelistic Crusade and to the Southseas Evangelical Mission, asking if they would consider extending their outreach to Borneo. By February 1928, we had replies from both. Neither mission felt able to extend its activities to include a territory as large and as remote as Borneo.

Nevertheless, the three of us continued to pray together, and after another three months we all felt strongly that the time had come to take further initiative. The date was May 17th, and we decided to pray all morning specifically about Borneo. That afternoon the post brought a letter addressed to me from a man in the state of Queensland named Stafford Young, a friend of one of our fellow students. His letter contained the offer of a cheque for fifty pounds to "assist with preliminary enquiries and the sending of someone to Borneo." We felt this was God's answer to our prayers.

---

2. Romans 15:20

Fifty pounds was a relatively large amount in those days, but it was the timing and specific designation of this gift that were especially significant. When I told Mr. Nash of it the next day, he suggested I produce a letter advising people that we wanted to form a Borneo fellowship as a focus for prayer, for sharing information and as a centre to which gifts to support this movement could be sent.

By mid-1928, the interest was such that I began drawing up a provisional constitution for a proposed new mission. This original constitution was a simple document based on the principles and practices of the China Inland Mission, but adapted to our start-up situation.

From then on events moved quickly. Near the end of June, the three of us travelled to Yallourn, about a hundred miles from Melbourne, to meet with Alexander Henderson, an elderly Scotsman who had expressed an interest in assisting us. Henderson, or Hendy as we came to call him, had at one time been a timber trader in Dutch Borneo, and we were anxious to discuss with him what preparation and equipment we would need.

Hendy was full of stories, some of which, even to the uninitiated, sounded a bit fantastic. One classic was about the orangutans, which he said were very savage. He told us that a hut in the jungle should always be built with one end loose so that if an orangutan came in, you could just push the other end out and make your escape.

His tales and proverbs did not stop there.

"If you get sick in Borneo," he warned, "you are either better or dead in twenty-four hours."

And another one we heard many times over the next year was, "You always mash bananas — don't eat them raw!"

The Borneo Evangelical Mission was officially established on August 31, 1928, with a council of ten founding members: C.H. Perrin, E. Stafford Young, Mabel E. Beath, Harold Jeffrey, Mrs. R.S. Tregaskis, Rev. C.H. Nash, Carey W. Tolley, Frank T. Davidson, Alexander Henderson and myself. Our inaugural meeting was held on September 1st at the Melbourne Bible Institute, and the provisional constitution was adopted at a special meeting of the founding council on September 11th. The next meeting, held the following week, was of special significance for the three potential missionaries — Carey, Frank and myself.

It had not occurred to us that the other members of the council would question the certainty of our plans, but at that third meeting they asked each of us to go away alone for a weekend to consider our calling and give them an assurance in this regard. Were we offering to go to Borneo in obedience to a real call from God? And were we prepared to follow this call without reservation?

I did have one reservation, and it stemmed from my increasing interest in Winsome Howell. Her brothers, Dick and David, were preparing to go to Africa as missionaries, but she seemed to feel no such calling. Since I felt sure I would be going overseas, I carefully tried to conceal my interest in her from everyone, and particularly from Winsome herself.

Then came this direct challenge from the council.

I went away for the weekend to a place where I was not known and knew no one, and where I could be alone to think and to pray. It was September 15, 1928, and as I opened my *Daily Light*, a little book of daily Bible readings, the text that met my eyes was, "He is a double-minded man, unstable in all he does."[3] This was followed by, "No one who puts his hand to the plow and looks back is fit for service in the kingdom of God."[4]

That weekend I renewed my promise to God: I was prepared to obey him and go to Borneo, even if it meant giving up the prospect of Winsome becoming my wife. Paradoxically, I felt at peace with this decision, and I returned to face the council and give them my reply accordingly.

Carey and Frank both gave their own assurances as to their call and commitment, and Hendy also assured the council that, in assisting us as a team in Borneo, he would not use the occasion to engage in any trading or commercial ventures. Now confident that God had been leading us all in the rapid sequence of events of recent weeks, the council felt the way was clear to send us to Borneo with

3. James 1:18
4. Luke 9:62

the full blessing of each member, and a commissioning service was held two weeks later, on October 1, 1928.

After my weekend away and my subsequent interview with the council members, all my inward conflict had passed. It was as if God was saying to me, "Your commitment is irrevocable, so now you are free to declare your heart's desire regarding Winsome to her and to her family." So on the same day as the commissioning service, I met with her father, Samuel Howell. My asking for his daughter's hand took him quite by surprise, but he gave his approval. Winsome's aunt, Mabel Beath, was not surprised, however; she had seen signs of my feelings, though I had done my best to conceal them. She too approved.

The following day, Winsome and I went for a long walk in the renowned Melbourne Botanical Gardens, where I declared my love and asked her to marry me. The next day, October 3rd, we were engaged, and within less than two weeks I was bound for Borneo.

Now, more than three years later, I was scheduled to return to Australia. The Mission council booked my passage on the S.S. *Marella* to Sydney, and from there I caught the train to Melbourne. I arrived on Christmas Eve, 1931, and received an emotional welcome from my mother, who was then seventy; Winsome, who I loved and my mother adored; and members of the council.

The next few months were busy ones as Winsome and I prepared for our wedding and our return to Borneo. I also had a large number of speaking engagements in the states of Victoria and Tasmania where I was glad to meet so many of the friends who had prayed for us and supported us during the past three years.

Our marriage was celebrated on April 29, 1932, at St. Matthew's Church near the Melbourne Bible Institute. Our longtime friend and mentor, Rev. C.H. Nash, performed the wedding ceremony, and the church was full of family and friends.

During the years of separation, Winsome and I had corresponded regularly. Many of our letters were devoted to preparation for our service together, and by now Winsome was well qualified. She had obtained a certificate of midwifery as well as some general nursing training and had attended the Melbourne Bible Institute. Prior to my return, she had already applied to the council as a missionary candidate and been accepted.

At the time, some people felt that Winsome was too delicate to cope with the rigors of pioneering life in Borneo. Indeed, a few took the gloomy view that she would not survive more than six months! But I felt that God had shown his guidance and approval so clearly during the past three years that we should not fear to trust him for the future. Winsome and her father and her aunt, Mabel Beath, all shared my conviction.

Newlyweds at Sydney – June 1932

Within a few weeks of our wedding, on the evening of June 14th, we had a crowded farewell meeting in Scot's Hall in Melbourne. A new recruit, Roland Bewsher, had been accepted by the Mission, and he was booked to travel with us to Borneo. Although Roland was just twenty-one, he was a gifted speaker. At our farewell the three of us spoke briefly, and then Mr. Nash gave an impressive address of exhortation and advice.

My return to Sarawak, now with Winsome as my wife, was a joyful event. Travelling by steamship we called at several ports in Java, as well as Singapore, which gave both Winsome and Roland an excellent introduction to Southeast Asia. At Singapore we boarded a smaller Sarawak steamer which stopped first at Kuching and then steamed up the coast to the island of Labuan, just outside Brunei Bay. From there, a large launch carried us across the bay to the town of Brunei. In those days, before its large oil and gas reserves had been discovered, historic Brunei was picturesque and quiet, with its craftsmen known for making bronze gongs and delicate, handcrafted silverware.

Carey and Frank met us at Brunei, where we had a happy reunion. Carey had been given an outboard engine for his canoe, and he had brought this boat to take us up the Limbang River. We stayed one night at Limbang town, where the Resident kindly entertained us, and the next morning we set out on the seventy-mile journey upriver. We had almost reached the small Chinese bazaar at Ukong when the outboard engine broke down. All our luggage had gone on before us, so Winsome spent her first night in the interior without a change of clothes! The Chinese shopkeeper was very kind, however, and put his own bed and mosquito net at our disposal.

The next morning we pushed ahead by our own paddle power and reached Sungai Pranga about midday. Many of our Iban and Murut friends were there to meet us, including women and children who had come to see this new "Mem." At first, whenever Winsome met their eyes, they looked away in embarrassment. Soon, however, they ceased to gaze and whisper remarks to each other and progressed to friendly touches and pats, to see that she was really made of flesh and blood!

I was happy beyond words to have Winsome with me at last, and her presence also had a positive effect upon others. Her arrival in Sungai Pranga was an indication to the people that we had come to live among them permanently. In addition, she quickly transformed our jungle bachelors' quarters into a home.

In our Borneo newsletter dated September 1932, Frank wrote, "Hardly a day passes without the visit of both young and old women. All seem to have agreed together to teach her [Winsome] the Iban language as quickly as possible. They pick up or touch anything that is within reach, giving the native names, and all such words are put into a notebook for future study and use."

Everyone spoke Iban because, although there were many Muruts in our area, the Iban people had the kind of aggressive, extroverted nature that demanded attention in their own language. To begin learning the language, Winsome would write down the Iban words that she heard frequently and then later ask me their meaning. Before long, she was speaking a few Iban words herself. Since Winsome had a trained musical ear and a natural sensitivity to musical tones, she rapidly acquired the characteristic Iban intonation; this was even more appreciated by the people than an extensive vocabulary.

Because the women and children knew very little Malay, and since even the Muruts kept talking to her in the Iban language, Winsome, out of sheer necessity, learned to speak Iban first. She was probably the first European in history to speak Iban before learning the much more universal Malay language.

Part II
Awakening

Men go abroad to wonder at the height of mountains, at the huge waves of the sea, at the long courses of the river, at the vast compass of the ocean, at the circular motion of the stars; and they pass by themselves without wondering.

– Saint Augustine

There is a kind of happiness and wonder that makes you serious.

– C. S. Lewis

CHAPTER 5

The royal line of the Brunei Sultanate is believed to be one of the most ancient in Southeast Asia, extending back many hundreds of years before their conversion to Islam. It is unknown when these people of Malay stock first came to Borneo, but from Chinese, Javanese and local records a fragmentary picture of a truly ancient kingdom can be constructed. The first mention of the island of Borneo in Chinese writings seems to be in 414 A.D., where it is referred to by a different name:

> The island of P'oni or Po-ni, mentioned by several subsequent writers is almost certainly Borneo; and there is no doubt about the identification of Brunei with P'oni or Po-ni, to which references occur in the histories of the Sung dynasty. We are told that the King of Po-ni sent tribute to the Emperor of China in 977 and again in 1082.[1]

In the past, Brunei's political power extended far beyond its present boundaries. Indeed, the word "Borneo" is derived from the name of the kingdom of Brunei. When European sailors first came to the island in the early 1500s, they mistakenly thought that the name of the whole island was Brunei.

According to both traditional reports and historical evidence, the Murut people were the original inhabitants of this part of Borneo, predating the Malay migration.[2] When we first came to Sarawak, the Muruts were a relatively small ethnic group of less than 4000 people. They had once been the predominant ethnic group in this area, however, as witnessed by the many place names of Murut origin and

1. Steven Runciman, *The White Rajahs, A History of Sarawak* (Kuala Lumpur: S. Abdul Majeed & Co. 1992), 13.
2. The most commonly suggested derivation of the name "Murut" is from the name of the highest mountain in the Murut territory, known as "Murud." Since 1960, the Murut people have been officially known by the name "Lun Bawang," which simply means "the people of the country" as distinct from "the people of the sea" or "the people of the mountains." As most of the events in this book occurred prior to 1960, we have used the name "Murut" throughout.

the fact that their language was known over such a widespread area. It is believed that at one time they occupied the entire area from Brunei Bay across the mountainous interior and over to the north-east coast of Dutch Borneo (what is now Kalimantan).

An illustration of the antiquity of Murut civilization is revealed in the names given to one of the major rivers of this region. From its source at Mt. Murud and Mt. Batu Lawi, the Limbang River flows in a generally northern direction until it reaches a point only ten miles distant from the capital city Bandar Seri Begawan (formerly Brunei town). From this point there is a stream that continues to flow straight on in a northerly direction and gradually widens into a larger channel through the capital, and then empties over the rocky reef into Brunei Bay. In ancient times this was evidently a major riverbed, but floods and silting caused a dramatic change in course, and the main river now flows eastward past Limbang town. Although the main river is now officially known as the Limbang River, the local Murut population still refer to it as *Pa* Brunei (the Brunei River), a name that corresponds with the ancient river course and consequently has been passed down among their people over the centuries.

Physically, the Muruts are comparatively fair skinned and are taller and stronger than the Malays. Also, the Muruts, along with their related neighbors, the Kelabits, were unique among the peoples of Sarawak in having worked out an advanced system of irrigation for their rice growing. The Muruts lived in fertile territory, and whether the rice was grown in irrigated fields or by the slash-and-burn method where rice grain was sown in soil enriched by ashes, they normally had abundant rice harvests. With the suppression of headhunting and freedom from intertribal fighting, even greater harvest surpluses were achieved, and the surplus was invariably used to produce a form of rice beer, known as *borak*. Tragically, their own excessive consumption of this potent drink brought about the downfall of the Murut people.

When we first came to Borneo, the Murut people were regarded as an ethnic group on the way out, especially in the Limbang and lower Trusan and Lawas areas where they were considered to be apathetic drunkards. Their alcoholism had led to disease and infertility, and their houses were dilapidated and their living standards low. All these factors placed them at the bottom of the ladder among the ethnic groups in Sarawak, and because of that they tended to be shy and reticent.

A few days after Winsome's arrival, we paddled downriver about two miles to a large Murut longhouse named Rumah Chang, meaning "the house of Chang" — Chang being the Headman. The people were overjoyed that Winsome had come to visit them. We told them of the great God who had created all things. And we told them that even though mankind had chosen other gods to worship, God still loved all of us and sent his only Son, Jesus, into the world to save us from the power of evil.

"Yes," they said, "but does God love Muruts?"

When we told them that God did love them, their response was one of astonishment!

Next they asked, "But do you love Muruts?" And, "Does the Mem love Murut women?"

"Yes, that is why we came here," I said, "and also to tell you that God really loves you!"

They were totally amazed that anyone would care for them, particularly in view of their desperate condition as a people.

The next year, 1933, we started a school with one student, Kasa, who had been helping Carey in the Lubai area, but he stayed only a few months. Near the end of that year we started again, this time with several students, both Iban and Murut, between the ages of ten and fifteen. We used the Iban language for practical reasons, so the Murut boys improved their ability to converse in Iban and also learned to read and write. Until they became accustomed to writing, we used old-fashioned slates rather than exercise books — which meant far less consumption of pens and ink! They progressed amazingly, particularly the Muruts.

One day the Ibans said, "This is the season for farming. We want to go back to our longhouses to grow our rice," and they left school. But the Murut boys stayed on, and we taught them to write words and simple phrases in Iban, and then to write sentences from dictation.

By that time we had hired two Iban houseboys, Rompang and Undi, to help with the work at our base station. Both were married men, but we did not see much of their wives, as they were usually busy with farming work. Along with their household duties, Rompang and Undi also attended the morning sessions in the school, where I commenced every day with readings from the Gospels in Iban and tried to explain the meaning of the parables of Jesus. We often noticed Rompang's rapt attention as we read, but if we looked at him he would turn his head away, as though not listening. Undi, the older man, was the first to become a Christian, and some time later Rompang followed, proclaiming with characteristic Iban frankness, "It is not so much what you people said. But I could not resist that Book!"

The Murut boys who had stayed on at the school after the Ibans left, also responded. After several months we asked them to write a little composition, and to our surprise what they wrote amounted to a confession of faith. And they assured us that they really meant what they had written.

The response of these young people was indeed encouraging and in sharp contrast to some of the older people, such as the Iban shaman at Tanah Merah. On one occasion he sat next to me, and though he was outwardly friendly, I felt the power of intense demonic opposition coming through him. As I spoke about Jesus and the way of salvation, he made comments on what I said. Using veiled parabolic language which he thought I did not understand, he derided the crucifixion of Jesus. The atmosphere was tense, and I could see great inner conflict on some of the faces.

Carey had many similar responses from the older men as he travelled in the Lubai area. We shared these burdens of rejection and Satanic opposition as well as the joys of acceptance at our monthly meetings together at Sungai Pranga.

Though we were living many miles into the jungle, accessible only by river, things were seldom dull. One afternoon, soon after Winsome's arrival, we were chatting and drinking tea with several

Ibans who had come to visit us when we heard the loud squealing of wild pigs coming from the other side of the river.

"A python must be attacking the pigs," the Ibans said excitedly. "Hurry, let's go across the river and kill the python and get the wild pigs for ourselves!"

So they grabbed their *parangs*, dashed down the hill to their boat, and swiftly paddled across the river and ran up the muddy bank toward the sound of the disturbance. To their surprise, they found ample evidence of a fight — dozens of pig footprints everywhere. The pigs had all gone, but there was a huge python, dead, with its head almost completely severed. Apparently the snake had seized one of the pigs while it was rooting in the mud, wrapping itself around the animal's body, intending to squeeze it to death before swallowing it. But the other pigs had attacked the python and nearly bit its head off, rescuing their mate in the process.

Before long the Ibans came down the bank dragging this huge python and brought it across the river. I measured it to be twenty-two feet long. After I skinned it, the Ibans took the snake's carcass away to eat. I made a frame on which to stretch the skin, which measured twenty-two inches wide for almost its entire length.

On another occasion we were awakened in the middle of the night by a great commotion in the shed where we kept about thirty chickens. Taking my gun and reflector lamp, I went down to investigate and discovered a python strangling a chicken. I killed the python with one shot, but the bird was already dead. As I laid out the snake, which was only about nine feet long, I found that it had already strangled and swallowed another chicken before I got there. Hearing the shot, a crowd had gathered, so we divided up the spoils of battle. I took the hen that had been killed but not eaten, the Ibans took the one that had been swallowed by the python, and the Muruts took the python's carcass!

During those early years at Sungai Pranga, we also had some unique pets. One was a *lotong*, or leaf-eating monkey, which became very tame. Our Murut neighbors brought it to us as a baby; they had shot its mother while she was up a tree and she had fallen to the ground with the baby monkey clinging to her back. On another occasion, the Muruts brought us a young honey bear. How they killed the mother, I do not know, as a full grown honey bear is a very dangerous animal.

The baby bear, completely black in color except for a white patch under its chin, was about the size of a full grown cat when it came to us. It was still suckling its mother's milk, so I fed it with sweetened condensed milk from a feeding bottle, and it adopted me as a parent and followed me everywhere. It would even climb the leg of the table while we were eating our meals. If it got what it wanted it was quite happy, but if it was refused, the baby bear would fly into a rage and snarl and scratch with its sharp claws.

Unfortunately, one day its bad temper brought it to a sad end. We were burning off some jungle that had been cut and was tinder dry. The little bear followed me along the path, and when it saw the flames and heard the crackling and felt the radiant heat, it became enraged. It rushed in to attack the flames, and at quite a risk I grabbed it and pulled it away. But it scratched me and rushed again at the fire which it regarded as an enemy. This time I could not rescue it, and sadly it perished in the fire.

In early 1933, we began to hear strange rumors from the upper Trusan River and from Ba Kelalan. One example was a story that Jesus was coming soon and would take all the longhouses up to heaven with ropes and hooks!

On another occasion some Muruts arrived at our house and eagerly said, "We want to know about *Tuhan Isa* (the Lord Jesus); tell us all about him. We have heard that he is coming to earth again soon, and we want to know when and where." These words startled us; yet it was soon evident that it would be a mistake to read into them more meaning than was intended. "If he is coming soon we will not need to pay our taxes this year to the government" was the candid and very practical explanation for their curiosity!

Some days later we were visited by a crowd of Muruts from the Medihit tributary of the upper Limbang River, bringing with them a Murut from Ba Kelalan who said that he had met a white man who spoke about God. Though his account was mysterious and inconsistent, again there was a readiness to listen to a fuller explanation of this God about whom they had heard but knew so vaguely.

Since the time of our arrival in Borneo, elements of the gospel message had spread by word of mouth in the Murut language, which was widely known throughout the large area extending from Brunei Bay into the interior. Then, in 1932, a fresh stimulus was provided by the arrival of two Christian and Missionary Alliance missionaries on the other side of the Sarawak border.

In June 1933, Carey went upriver to visit the Muruts, both to correct the rumors that had spread among them and to teach them exactly what Jesus himself had said about his return. While he was still in the upper Limbang area, he met four young Murut men from the upper Trusan who were on their way to visit us at Sungai Pranga. They also were searching for the truth. So Carey travelled to the Trusan with these men, where he found that the people had indeed been stirred by reports about a God who was coming, but were troubled by the distorted accounts that had reached them.

Before Carey returned from his journey, we were suddenly visited by two longhouse Headmen from the lower Trusan. Raut and Lupong, with two followers, had paddled down the Trusan to Brunei Bay and then up the Limbang River, where at each longhouse they had asked, "Where is the man who can tell us about God?"

And at every longhouse they received the same reply, "Further upriver, at Sungai Pranga."

After seven days of travelling, they arrived and came up to our veranda, offering the customary greetings.

When I asked them where they had come from and what their purpose was in coming, they replied, "We want to know if you can tell us about God?"

"Yes, indeed," I said, "that is why we have come here."

"That is why we have come to see you," they echoed.

I have a copy of a newsletter I wrote nearly sixty years ago telling of that encounter, and the scene is still vivid in my memory.

Raut, a tall man with a clear open face and an earnest manner, said, "We have heard many vague rumors about *Tuhan Isa* and these reports have been upsetting all our people, and I want to find out the truth." He was intelligent and spoke excellent Malay, but could not read. He leaned forward to listen as I spoke.

I said that God had given us a Book which told us all about himself and *Tuhan Isa,* and therefore could settle all doubtful rumors. That appeared to satisfy him greatly.

Then I told them of God's majesty and power as Creator, and of his love for mankind whom he had made. I also told him about Satan, the chief of the evil spirits, and how he had deceived our first parents, Adam and Eve.

Raut and his companions knew nothing about God or that Jesus had already visited this earth from heaven, so they listened intently as I told them of his life and teaching and the miracles which proved that he had come from God. They gasped with wonder as I told them of God's love for us and that he was near us and that we could pray to him. I said that when we spoke to God we usually bowed our heads in reverence and closed our eyes to shut out other things from our minds.

As I prayed with them and asked that God would make things clear to them, Raut said emphatically in Malay, "Yes, that's it!"

After I had finished praying, he said, "I want to know more, to go back to my own people to tell them." I told him that even now he knew enough to believe in God. "I believe with my whole heart," he replied earnestly.

Raut wanted me to return to the Trusan with them, but since that was not immediately possible, he asked for a Malay New Testament, as he had a nephew who could read. He also asked me to mark key passages which would help him to understand the message better.

That evening we gathered for evening prayers in the home of Undi and Sema, the first two Iban Christians in our district. As our Murut visitors heard us sing together and then heard Undi and Sema pray in Iban, they were greatly touched. Raut was astonished that so few as yet had become Christians and followed God's teaching.

As he was leaving, Raut turned and implored me, "Remember me, *Tuan*. Write down my name and pray for me!"

CHAPTER 6

Carey returned from his visit to the upper Limbang and Trusan areas just before the end of July. He had been away about five weeks and had a wonderful story to tell.

He had first stayed several days with the Kelabits in the upper Limbang and its Medihit tributary, a few of whom we had met in December 1928 on our first journey upriver. Carey was able to correct their confusion about the distorted rumors they had recently heard. Then he set out for Ba Kelalan with the four young men who had been on their way down the Limbang to make their own enquiries of us at Sungai Pranga. Carey returned with them to the *bah* country, flat alluvial plains covered with irrigated rice fields — this was the same route that Spenser St. John, the first rajah's secretary, had followed in 1855, exactly seventy-five years before.[1]

"For three days we did not meet with any habitation," Carey wrote. "The country is mountainous and wonderfully beautiful. I do not know of anything more calculated to stir in one's heart and mind thoughts of God's power and majesty than to see stretched before one range upon range of magnificent mountains."

After fording the remote upper Limbang and following the Adang tributary to its source, Carey and his companions crossed the mountainous watershed and came to the Kelalan tributary of the Trusan River. At this point they met the leading Headman of the upper Trusan who wanted to take Carey to his own group of villages. Carey felt that he should visit the Ba Kelalan area first, however, so he continued up the Kelalan tributary and reached the source which lies on the watershed between Sarawak and what was then Dutch Borneo.

---

1. I have in my possession two rare volumes by Spenser St. John, titled *Life in the Forests of the Far East* (2nd Edition, 1862), in which he devotes six chapters to "My Limbang Journal." They are a detailed account of his journey up the Limbang and over to the Trusan and Ba Kelalan in 1855. From my own journeys in the same area, I can verify the accuracy of his observations and descriptions.

In this area many Murut longhouses were clustered among fertile areas of flat irrigated land at the bottom of the valley between two ranges of hills. Carey visited the main longhouses, and in each place people listened intently as he told them about God. Although this was our first visit to that area, the Murut people in the whole Trusan valley and beyond were favorably disposed because they had heard word-of-mouth reports from their relatives in the Limbang.

Another significant factor was the way the message of the gospel fitted into the pattern of their own mythology.[2] Even though the full meaning of their ancient myths was obscure to them, there appeared to be a God-inspired link between these and the biblical promise of Jesus coming from heaven, which stimulated their desire to hear the truth. Moreover, the evidence points to this as being a rather universal principle in the spread of Christianity among tribal peoples:

> Many social anthropologists studying primitive religions have concluded that tribal men did not acquire religion by their own thinking and research, but by oral tradition from their fathers and forefathers, and finally from the Creator. Nowhere do we receive evidence that these religions were developed to a higher degree of perfection by men through their own searching and finding, but, on the contrary, there is decline and deterioration.[3]

And so the Muruts gathered from far and near during Carey's sojourn. Evening and morning and throughout the day they kept coming and asking to hear more. Everyone, including the children, listened eagerly.

Some even crossed the border from Dutch Borneo. After these visitors heard Carey's message, they told him that two American white men (the Christian and Missionary Alliance missionaries) had told them exactly the same thing.

"Have you met these men?" they asked Carey. When he told them he had not, they were greatly impressed, and still more so when he said, "The story we bring to you does not depend on men. It is from God's Book which he has given to us all."

---

2. Don Richardson, *Eternity in Their Hearts* (California: Regal Books, 1981).
3. E. K. Victor Pearce, *Who Was Adam?* (Exeter: The Paternoster Press, 1969), 68.

After hearing Carey's report, we decided that I should leave immediately to visit Raut and Lupong's longhouses in the lower Trusan, so on August 14, 1933, I set off with three carriers. Rather than travel all the way downriver to Brunei Bay and then up the Trusan, we headed across country, fording the Lubai, Panderuan and Temburong Rivers, and then through virgin jungle where we lost our way and had to spend the night under a shelter made from palm leaves.

Travelling through Borneo jungle revealed less of its enormously varied wildlife than one might imagine. This is partly because a large percentage of it is either nocturnal or moving high in the forest canopy overhead. Many insects, birds and squirrels do not come out by day or rarely come down from the sunlit top layers into the shadows and dampness of the jungle floor. In addition, when anything strange enters the forest, warning calls are sounded ahead, signalling the various creatures that it is time to retreat or remain unseen.

Midday, on our fifth day out, we came to a Murut house on the Batu Apoi River. It was there we first found people who were interested to hear God's word. We pressed on, and by evening we emerged from the jungle just opposite Lupong's longhouse, the largest in the lower Trusan. Although it was dusk, the news of our arrival soon spread, and about sixty people came in from surrounding farms. My knowledge of Murut was still quite limited so I spoke to them in Malay, with interpretation, until about midnight, by which time my voice was gone.

Next day we went upstream to Raut's longhouse, and then further upstream to spend two memorable nights at the longhouse of Buaya Tadam. It was pathetic to see the sickness and disease among these people — many suffered with racking coughs and their bodies were covered with ringworm. By contrast, it was wonderful to witness their joy and eagerness to hear that God cared about them.

Raut and Lupong had been good forerunners with the gospel. About 150 people crowded into the available space where a few kerosene wick lamps provided the light. As with the others we had encountered, their chief interest was in the story of Jesus, the One who had come to this earth to die so that mankind might be reconciled to God.

"How can we pray to God?" was one of the first questions they asked.

Raut was a great help in explaining this, for he said that he prayed often since his visit to us at Sungai Pranga. One evening he prayed spontaneously in Murut, confessing sin both for himself and for his people, and asking that God would help them to live new lives. When he finished, there was a new light on the faces of many and a new hope in the hearts of some who were burdened by disease.

When I was ready to return home, six men volunteered to convey me back downriver and around Brunei Bay to Limbang town. From there we made the long walk back through the jungle to Sungai Pranga.

In October, Carey travelled to the middle section of the Trusan River, an area we had not yet visited, going over the same overland route I had taken to the lower Trusan in August. He stopped to visit Raut and Lupong, where he received a joyous welcome, and from there went over the Sepakoi mountain pass, known locally as the gateway to the interior.

People in this locality used the swidden (slash and burn) method of rice farming. After the jungle had been cut down and burned off, the men would make small holes on the rolling hillsides; then the women would follow behind, deftly dropping a few grains of paddy seed into each hole. The rice would quickly sprout and the hillsides would begin to turn green. Another staple in their diet, maize, would be planted in areas where piles of branches had been burned and the soil was specially fertilized by their abundant ashes.

As Carey passed through this farming country, the people responded with enthusiasm to the message of the gospel, just as those in both the lower and upper Trusan areas had done. Then, suddenly, their newfound faith was severely tested as influenza broke out among them. Some developed a pneumonic type of flu and many of those died suddenly. Carey's heart went out to the people, and he prayed for them and with them. Now, however, instead of the hopelessness of a death without regard for eternity, they had come to know God and the reality of his promises, and this sustained them in their sorrow. God had planted in their hearts the living presence of his Holy Spirit, and they did not turn to the drunken orgies that had followed the death of loved ones under their old customs.

The Muruts' tremendous response to the message of the gospel emphasized two big challenges that faced us: the need for education and literacy, and the need for a residential base in the Trusan valley. For the latter we required approval from the Sarawak Government. At that time, the Fourth and Fifth Divisions were amalgamated under the Resident of the Fourth Division at Miri, while the Limbang and Trusan areas were under a District Officer stationed at Limbang who was responsible to the Resident at Miri.

I requested that our Mission be permitted to extend its range of activities to the Trusan-Lawas area. But since the District Officer, Mr. Bruce, had not seen the profound changes among the Muruts, he still regarded them as a people degraded with drunkenness and disease. He was also mindful of the need for government intervention in the past, when heads were taken and houses destroyed, and he feared that harm might come to us.

When our initial request proved fruitless, I decided to go to Miri and speak with the Resident of the Fourth and Fifth Divisions, Mr. J.B. Archer. Citing the previous reputation of these people, Mr. Archer, too, said he was skeptical about our proposal of opening a new base among the Muruts in the Trusan.

"The Muruts are alcoholics, dying out," he said. "It's no use talking to them."

I told him of the amazing change that had taken place among them, but this made little impression.

"We couldn't let you live among them. They're dangerous. We wouldn't be able to guarantee your safety."

Extension of our work to the Trusan was closed, at least for the time being. But God was teaching me — as he did throughout my years in Borneo — that even though we might experience frustrations and seemingly closed doors, God is never frustrated; he always has other plans which he reveals to us in his own time. I asked that God would give me the sensitivity to see the door that would open.

Soon after the Resident's refusal to allow us to set up a mission base in the Trusan, we received a surprise visit from Stafford Young, the man who had sent us a gift of fifty pounds back in May 1928! Though we had never met him, he suddenly came to visit us in Sarawak. When he saw the response of the people to the gospel, he felt so impelled to join in the work that he stayed on and for some months helped Roland Bewsher, who was now working among the Bisaya people at Limpasong.

Frank's fiancee, Enid Gray, arrived in February 1935, and I had the privilege of performing their marriage at the Residency at Limbang. Around the same time in Tasmania, Carey was being married to Florence Roberts-Thompson, and he soon returned to Borneo with his bride. Stafford Young then went with Frank to the upper Limbang, where they prepared a bush house for Frank and Enid to live in while they worked among the Kelabits.

In September 1935, we heard that Rajah Vyner Brooke was to visit Limbang. Not wanting to pass up this opportunity, Frank and I travelled downriver to meet him. We met at the Residency with the Rajah and his Chief Secretary, and I reported what Carey and I had seen and experienced among the Muruts of the Trusan regarding the complete change in their attitudes and lifestyle. We told him that they were waiting for us to return to them as they wanted our teaching and medical help.

Rajah Vyner Brooke's own experience with the Muruts of the Trusan had not been positive. One confrontation dated back to his earliest years as an officer under the regime of his father, Rajah Charles Brooke:

> On May 2, 1900, a punitive expedition left Muara [on Brunei Bay] for the Trusan River, where the wily old chieftain Ukong had raised the flag of revolt. The Murut chieftain had killed a great number of men and had served notice that he intended to kill more. Some fifteen longhouses were in his

> possession, and he commanded perhaps three thousand armed Dayaks. The expedition consisted of four European officers, six hundred Dayaks, a hundred Rangers and a hundred Malays. They spent ten days marching over the mountains, climbing through jungles and along precipitous slopes, always in danger of attack from the enemy hidden in the forests. They were plagued by the heat, by mosquitoes, by long treks through swamps. Remembering the expedition many years afterwards, Vyner recalled how he was strangely lighthearted and excited throughout those intolerable days when danger lurked in the crackling of every leaf.
>
> Ukong had his spies in the forests, and watched their progress and set traps for them. When at last they came in sight of the longhouses, there was no sign of the enemy, but all the longhouses were surrounded with poisoned bamboo spikes. Twelve Dayaks were severely wounded by the spikes. There were occasional brief skirmishes, but no pitched battles. It was a curiously ineffective affair, for Ukong was in hiding, watching them while remaining himself unseen, and they never knew when he would suddenly emerge and fall on them. In the steamy heat they set about punishing him by removing whatever they could find in the longhouses, and by slaughtering his cattle. Then they burned the longhouses, and made the long weary journey back over the mountains to Muara.[4]

Rajah Vyner had also witnessed the subsequent ravages of alcoholism and he found it very hard to accept that the Muruts could have changed so radically. With the memory of their former condition in mind, he said he would fear for our safety if we went to live among them. The Rajah also took the pessimistic view that with the high death rate of the Muruts at that time, in a few decades they would become extinct and other ethnic groups would occupy the land.

I stressed that the Murut headmen and leaders realized their deep need and welcomed the message of hope that we brought. I also suggested to the Rajah that it would be better for them to be rehabilitated as an ethnic group with a long and interesting history

4. Robert Payne, *The White Rajahs of Sarawak* (Singapore: Oxford University Press, 1991), 151.

than for them to die out. But the Rajah had already made up his mind, and he emphasized that if we were to go against his decision we would be asked to leave the country.

Frank and I were disappointed to the point of being despondent. That same afternoon we left Limbang to return upriver. To relieve our great sense of frustration and our pent-up emotions we paddled far into the night by the light of a kerosene lamp placed on the bow of the boat. In addition to being discouraged, we also were hungry as during those years of the great World Depression our basic diet was salted fish and rice. Suddenly we saw a reflection from the eyes of a wild pig on the river bank. We shot it in the light of our lamp and immediately made preparations for an eleven o'clock dinner. It was delicious.

And God had another encouragement for us. Our selected reading for that night was, "Be still, and know that I am God."[5] We felt that this was God's word to us to wait for his timing. He was telling us that he had the situation in hand.

By this time Winsome and I had been in Borneo for three-and-a-half years, so we made arrangements to go to Australia on furlough. While there, we met with the Mission council in Melbourne to discuss administrative responsibilities for our operations. When the Mission was first founded, it had been fitting that the Melbourne council should hold that responsibility, rather than three inexperienced young men. Now, however, it had become obvious that our field council should have the responsibility for these decisions since we were the ones who best understood the situation in Borneo.

On our return from Australia to Sungai Pranga in 1936, we found that the Iban group nearest to us had moved their longhouse to a better farming area some distance away. So, seven years after building our first house and headquarters, we decided to make a journey upriver to find a new site nearer to a large longhouse. We found a

5. Psalm 46:10

good place near Nanga Meruyu where about thirty-six Iban families lived in a longhouse known as Rumah Kedu, which was over seven hundred feet long.

We decided to build a house near this big community of Ibans, but before settling in to this new work, I felt we should investigate a second opportunity that might be open to us.

During a stopover in Jakarta in 1932, Frank had met a Mr. and Mrs. Clemens who were botanists working in British North Borneo (what is today known as Sabah). The Clemens had numerous contacts with the Dusun (or Kadazan) people, and they later wrote to us recommending that we send someone to work among them. We were immediately impressed with the potential of this opportunity, although, looking back, we probably would not have pursued it if the Rajah had allowed us to extend our sphere of operations to the Trusan.

While our house was being built at Nanga Meruyu, therefore, we made arrangements for an exploratory trip through British North Borneo which, unlike Sarawak, was a commercial territory under Royal charter. Since Stafford was not yet committed to working with any of the ethnic groups — Iban, Murut, Kelabit or Bisaya — he seemed the best man to accompany me. We wanted to traverse the whole length of North Borneo, so we travelled first to Labuan, and from there found a Malay sailing *tongkang* which was leaving for Weston, a tiny port opening onto Brunei Bay. From Weston we travelled by train on a narrow gauge railway to Beaufort, located on the lower Padas River. We crossed the Padas River by ferry and then continued on the same narrow gauge railway up the huge Padas Gorge, with a steep towering mountain face on one side and the tempestuous Padas River on the other. After about thirty miles of magnificent scenery, the railway suddenly burst from the gorge onto the Tenom plain which was covered by a large rubber estate.

The geography of British North Borneo was quite different from that of Sarawak. Although many of the rivers were not navigable, its interior was more accessible in some ways than the interior of Sarawak. The large rubber estates meant the development of a transportation network; in addition to the railway and several roads, a system of bridle paths traversed much of the territory.

Having arrived at Tenom, the end of the railway, we were behind the Crocker range, a line of mountains running parallel with the coast, beyond which was a vast area of hilly country populated by the Dusun people. From Tenom we took a bus along some twenty miles of roadway leading to Keningau, the administrative centre, where there was a District Officer. From there we walked for more than a week, staying at rest houses or in Dusun villages. We spoke with many people before arriving at Ranau, a central town in North Borneo. Ranau lay in the shadow of Mt. Kinabalu, a magnificent black granite mountain rising 13,454 feet above sea level, making it one of the highest mountains in Southeast Asia.

Except in the central area around Tambunan where the Roman Catholics had a big mission, very few people we met knew anything about God. The last night before reaching Ranau we stayed at a place named Rendagong. As usual we presented the gospel, and as I spoke I noticed that the local chief and some others were especially attentive.

After reaching Ranau we walked up a steep path towards the spur of Mt. Kinabalu, which forms a watershed at the Tenompok pass, and from there we descended by a winding path for five days down to the sea at Kota Belud, a total of twelve days walk from Keningau. This large area was populated and farmed extensively by Dusuns. From our casual conversations with hundreds of Dusun people we found that they knew little or nothing about God, but they were quite open and willing to talk about him. This confirmed what Mr. and Mrs. Clemens had told us about these people. Thus, Stafford and I returned to Limbang feeling that North Borneo was indeed an open door and all of us agreed that we should commit some of our resources to this territory.

Around that same time, while Winsome and I were still at Sungai Pranga, a tragic thing happened. One evening at dusk we were standing outside our house when suddenly we heard a loud shriek from downriver. A few minutes later boats appeared on the river and people were shouting, "Someone has been taken by a crocodile and pulled under water!" I grabbed my gun and paddled in the direction of the commotion where I learned what had happened. The cousin of one of our schoolboys had gone to the river for an evening bathe, and when the lad jumped into the river he was immediately grabbed by a waiting crocodile. Lawai Asi, our student, had seen it all happen, and it was his shriek of horror that we heard at Sungai Pranga, nearly a mile away.

Instantly boats were launched and people began beating gongs and tins. This noise was designed to frighten the crocodile into staying submerged; then, when it finally had to come to the surface to breathe, it would stay there long enough so they could get a good shot at it and force it to release the body. They were not successful, however, and the remains of the body were not discovered until several days later.

Not long afterwards, there was another attack. This time one of *Penghulu* Belulok's water buffaloes was taken from the riverbank. A huge crocodile was seen frequenting the area and, certain it was the culprit, the Muruts were determined to kill it.

Their method for hunting crocodiles was ingenious. First, they would kill a monkey or a fowl to use as bait. Then they would sharpen a hardwood stick at both ends and tie it with light vines lengthwise to the body of the bait, and tie several strands of small but strong rattans to the centre of the pointed stick. These rattans were about ten feet long and would go between the crocodile's teeth so that it could not bite the stick in two. The other ends of the rattans were tied to a thick rattan fifty or more feet long. The bait was then suspended beneath the branches of a tree overhanging the river while the long, thick rattan was left floating on the surface of the water.

A few days later, early in the morning, I was told that the bait had been taken. I grabbed my rifle and hurried to the scene. The Muruts had already found the long, thick, floating rattan and taken it up the bank. Then they pulled gently, which loosened the ties binding the bait to the pointed stick, freeing it to move crosswise in the gullet of the crocodile so that it could not be disgorged.

Next the people on the riverbank pulled hard on the long rattan, now firmly stuck in the crocodile's stomach. As soon as the reptile came to the surface, the Muruts fired their old muzzle-loading guns, which were loaded with bits of metal and nails. This barrage produced a lot of smoke and noise, but not much damage to the crock's thick hide, so he simply wriggled and submerged again!

I asked them not to fire the next time he surfaced but to allow me to use my rifle. Slowly the crocodile came to the surface again, and as soon as the head appeared I fired my .44 calibre Winchester. One shot was sufficient. I shot it between the eyes and it flipped over, dead, floating belly up. It was a huge crocodile, over sixteen feet long.

We finished building our little bush house at Nanga Meruyu in March 1937. The simple structure was built entirely of native materials. The walls were made of bark stripped from trees, with prop-up windows and with split bamboo floors, except for our bedroom which had a board floor. We built the house high off the ground on an embankment about a hundred yards upriver from the Iban longhouse.

Moving into this house was quite a milestone in our relationship with the Iban people. This was the closest we had lived to an Iban longhouse, and we grew to feel part of their community. Winsome's training in nursing was in constant demand with the women and children; it gave an opportunity for demonstrating as well as speaking about God's love for them. It was a very happy experience.

Living at close quarters with so many people also presented some new challenges for us. One such challenge, particularly for Winsome, was river bathing. Neither the men nor the women would ever expose their bodies completely when bathing. In order to replace his loin cloth after bathing, a man would cover himself with his left hand while winding his loin cloth into position with his right hand. When a woman went to bathe, she would simply lower herself beneath the surface of the water by bending her knees and at the same time raise her sarong over her head and then place it on a rock or tree branch. Dressing was a reverse process. A native woman would hold the top end of the sarong in her teeth while she quickly changed her undergarments and then retied her sarong. Soon Winsome also became proficient at this.

Most evenings we went down to the longhouse and sat with various family groups and chatted with them while they wove mats, made fishing nets or did other handcraft work. During these relaxed times they began quite naturally to tell us about their problems and their fear of the evil spirits. They were always interested to hear something read to them in their own language, so we read to them often from an Iban New Testament. They were thrilled to hear that Jesus taught by telling stories or parables, for that was the way they also conveyed their opinions and communicated with each other. Indeed, when they wanted to drive a point home to a listener, they would speak in *jako karong* — by allusion or hidden language. For that reason, the Ibans regarded the parables in the Gospels with great respect. Then, too, when they heard about the miracles that Jesus did, whether acts of healing or his command over the storm on the sea, they understood that he was demonstrating God's authority and not merely that of a man. Reading these stories was more effective than preaching a sermon. Although only a few made a definite commitment during the two years we were with them, we heard years later, after the war, that many more had become Christians.

One day in August 1937, while we were still at Nanga Meruyu, four young men walked up the steps of our house. We could see at a glance that they were Muruts, but when we asked where they were from, we were surprised to find that they had come from the upper Trusan. They had walked from there to the upper Limbang and had then come down the Limbang with some Kelabits. We were delighted to see them, but happier still to hear the news they brought.

"We waited for you to come back to teach us," they said, "but then when you did not return, we sent messages over the border for some of our relatives to come to teach us. We are all Christians now."

We told them how we had longed to come back to teach them more from God's Word but that the Rajah had not allowed us to do so. We also assured them that we had faithfully prayed for them, and now we could see that God had answered our prayers.

The profound spiritual changes we had seen take place in these people four years ago had been permanent. God had changed them. Not only did they no longer fear the evil spirits, but God had given them power to overcome their habitual drunkenness. The very fact that these changes had continued in our absence showed that it was a miracle of God's grace, rather than something due to our influence.

Chapter 7

Not long after the visit of the four young Muruts from the upper Trusan, we received word that the Rajah of Sarawak was coming to visit the Limbang area again. We felt this was an answer to our prayers, and we were determined to renew our request for permission to extend our mission work to the entire Trusan area. I do not remember how we managed the problems of transportation but, in late October 1937, six members of our Mission were able to arrive in Limbang at around the same time.

We met again with the Rajah and his Chief Secretary at the Residency where we presented our written requests for permission to operate in all of the Murut areas, including the upper Trusan. We also asked for a remission of import duties on some radio communication equipment.

This time the Rajah was most cordial. Both he and his Chief Secretary seemed to have received good reports concerning the work of our Mission. After we had presented our proposals, the Rajah said, "Well, Mr. Southwell, we can't give you everything. The import duty, I'm afraid, must stand. But in all the other matters you have our favourable consideration."

We were ecstatic! Now that the Rajah had given his wholehearted approval for us to build a permanent base among the Muruts, our immediate need was for someone to visit the whole Trusan valley. Carey seemed the logical choice since he had already built a bush house as a base in the lower Trusan. But just as we came to this decision, he received word that his wife, Florence, and their baby, Elspeth, were returning from England where they had been with Florence's father for medical treatment. So Carey returned to Australia for furlough with his family. Owing to ill health, the Tolleys never were able to rejoin us in Borneo.

Frank and Enid needed to return to the Medihit, where they were fully involved in working with the Kelabits. Similarly, Winsome and I felt that we should return to our work at Meruyu among the Ibans at Kedu's longhouse. It was during that time a government physician, Dr. Finlayson, visited the Iban community. We arranged for the doctor to also examine Winsome as she had been experiencing abdominal pain; he recommended that we consult a gynaecology specialist at the earliest opportunity. So Winsome and I went to Singapore in November 1938, where Winsome had ovarian surgery. During her subsequent convalescence we stayed on at our large house at Sungai Pranga till December.

For these reasons, Stafford Young was really the only one free enough to visit the Trusan. He could not speak Murut, but I sent one of our students, Lawai Asi, with him as a translator. They left Limbang about mid-December and went all the way to Ba Kelalan. They were away for a month.

At our field conference in early 1939, it was agreed that Winsome and I should move from the longhouse at Meruyu to administer the operations of the Mission from a headquarters in Jesselton (later called Kota Kinabalu) in North Borneo. In addition to consideration for Winsome's health, we believed this move would be of strategic value. Throughout our initial years in Sarawak, we had faithfully presented the gospel to the villages near Sungai Pranga, including the big longhouse at Tanah Merah, but the people there were still largely resistant. Later, we invested nearly two years of concentrated work in the most densely populated Iban area in the Limbang district with only a limited response from their young people. Now we felt the new opportunities available among the Muruts of the Trusan and the Dusuns of North Borneo claiming our immediate attention.

Having received official permission from the Governor of North Borneo, we accomplished the move to Jesselton in stages. We left some of our goods at Sungai Pranga and some with Roland Bewsher at Limpasong. Stafford had already rented an old bungalow belonging to a retired government official. A few weeks later a veteran rubber planter, who planned to leave for an extended visit to England, offered us his furnished bungalow at a very modest rental. It was a beautiful home on a hilltop commanding a panoramic view over the sea to Gaya Island which sheltered the Jesselton harbour from the South China Sea. The servants' quarters provided dormitory space for our students, and the bungalow provided rooms for new missionaries who were soon coming to join us.

When Stafford returned from the Trusan he brought with him nine young men who wanted Bible school training. Five of these young Muruts stayed at Roland's school in Limpasong and four came with us to Jesselton.

Roland Bewsher and Assistant

Not long after our move we met Dr. John McArthur, a malariologist, and his wife, Kitty, who became a good friend to Winsome. The move also enabled us to co-operate with the Christian and Missionary Alliance missionaries, the Michaelsons, who had been working for several months among the Murut people near the Sarawak border.

As Winsome now had good living accommodations and friends to keep her company, I felt comfortable leaving her for a few weeks while I visited the Murut people on the Trusan River. This time I invited Einar Michaelson to accompany me.

Upon reaching Trusan town, the administrative centre, we were greeted enthusiastically by a party of Muruts. They had travelled all the way from the headwaters of the Trusan for trading and arrived just before we did.

A government party on its way to the interior also arrived that same day in Trusan town. The party was led by the District Officer, Mr. Barcroft, and the Curator of the Sarawak Museum, Edward Banks, who I had met in 1930 on a similar expedition to assess the status of the endangered Bornean rhinoceros. This time the government party had an escort of two armed policemen and Mr. Barcroft carried a pistol in his belt as protection against "the wild Muruts."

The Christian Muruts were so overjoyed at our visit that they offered to carry our goods without any payment, and next morning we set off for the interior. Our route took us through Tang Lapadan and over the Sepakoi pass and then through Tengoa, Brayong and Long Luping to Long Semadoh. The government party took a different route — to Long Tengoa, then up a valley through primary forest, and on to the same destination at Long Semadoh.

After six days' travel, our two parties arrived at Long Semadoh on the same day, and the museum Curator's first exclamation was, "Southwell, what have you done to these people? The last time I was here the house was rickety and filthy. Pigs were scavenging under the house, and there were drunken people everywhere. Now, they have a new house, quite clean, no *borak*, and you can walk anywhere under the house! What has happened?"

"I have not changed them," I responded. "God has changed their hearts. They have simply heard and believed the message recorded in the Bible. The teaching Jesus Christ gave to the world is so clear that they recognized it met their need, and they believed and acted upon it."

Mr. Banks was astounded with what he saw — and so was I — for these people really had been transformed. "You must write this up for the *Sarawak Gazette*," Banks said to me.

"No," I replied. "You write it up. You wrote an article telling about their extreme drunkenness, so now you should tell about the changes you have seen."

After returning to Kuching, Mr. Banks did indeed do so, but being an agnostic, he wrote the article in a rather cynical vein. He entitled it "Murut Morons" and remarked that one did not need aspirin for a bad hangover anymore when visiting the Muruts. Now one needed a Moody and Sankey hymn book. He did credit the fact, however, that the people were changed.

Einar and I visited several Murut villages; it was a real joy to be able to teach and encourage such responsive people. On our return journey we took the long route through the valley of the Adang tributary of the Limbang and visited the Kelabits on the Medihit River. Frank and Enid Davidson were not there at the time as they had gone back to Australia on home leave. From the Medihit we descended the Limbang to the Ibans at Meruyu and Tanah Merah, and finally visited Roland Bewsher at Limpasong before returning to Jesselton.

A few months later I again went to visit the Ibans and Muruts in the Limbang, and this time Winsome accompanied me. While there, we heard rumours that some Kelabits in the central highlands were wanting to become Christians, so we felt we should visit them to see if these reports were true.

By then Frank and Enid had returned to their station among the Kelabits in the upper Limbang, so Winsome stayed with Enid while Frank and I travelled to the remote highlands of the interior. This meant walking for nearly two days along a narrow ridge named Budok Lipi which in places was only a three-foot wide path with precipitous sides. We traversed ten streams flowing down from a towering rock face called Batu Iran and then crossed a pass leading to the Kuba'an River before following a long valley of moss forest with intertwining aerial roots several feet above the ground. This led to the prominent ridge known as Punga Pawang, which commands a glorious view over the whole Kelabit highlands. Some 1,500 feet below us, down a steep path, we could see the Bario longhouse.

At an elevation of over 3000 feet we shivered through the night in the longhouse. Next morning we were awakened by a persistent chipping sound and found two men working to open the circumference of a valuable old Chinese jar, about four feet tall. Alongside the jar lay a man's corpse, tied in a bundle with the knees under the chin so that it would fit into the jar, which was now being chipped open. The jar also had holes chipped in the base. In keeping with Kelabit custom, the jar and its content would be placed in the fork of a tree until only the bones were left, and these would then be given a secondary burial.

When we asked what had happened, we were told that the man had been drinking too much *borak* and when he went to examine his fish trap, he fell into the stream. His head became caught in the spiked entrance to the fish trap and he drowned.

There would be much more drinking of *borak* that day, so we continued on around the highlands to the longhouse on the Tarap River, near the border with Dutch Borneo. Here the Headman gave us a good hearing as we preached the gospel, but the people were not yet willing for a complete change from the old pagan ways. Clearly the rumours we had heard were premature. Somewhat disheartened, we set out to return along the same perilous route we had come.

By the time we reached the longhouse on the Kuba'an, however, we saw evidence of the working of the Spirit of God, despite the opposition of the Headman. As Frank told the gospel that evening, one man stood up, raised his arm, and with a determined shout said, "Even if no others do so, I will follow God." His name was Pun Abi, meaning "grandfather of all." His confession of faith was dramatic, courageous, and sincere.

Early the following year, Frank and Enid moved from the upper Limbang to the lower Trusan to teach the Murut people in that area. At first they lived in the little bush house which Carey Tolley had built but was never able to occupy. Eventually, however, they built a new house on a more suitable site a few miles below Trusan town. It was during the construction of this house that they were involved in a remarkable experience with a large python.

One day Frank and Enid had arranged for a work party to clear an area of land by the river bank on which to build a church. The land was covered with reeds and tall grass. The men would cut this scrub with their long jungle knives in one hand while in the other hand they held a hooked stick with which they flung back the cut grass. It was a rhythmic cut-and-fling action.

Suddenly one man saw a python about fifteen feet long crossing his path. With a shriek and a mighty swing with his knife he severed its head and then flung it backwards with the hooked stick. The man behind him heard the shriek and raised his head just as the python's head was flung straight at him! The nerve and muscle reaction of the python's severed head caused its jaws to open and then close again around the man's head. Although a python's bite is not venomous, its teeth curve inward and its jaws expand widely to permit it to swallow rather large animals. Everyone gathered around quickly to lever the teeth outward and soon had the man free — dispelling the horror he must have felt in suddenly finding his head caught in the grip of a python's jaws! It was one of those situations that was terrifying while it lasted but highly amusing afterwards.

Not long after that, Frank and I had a close encounter of our own with a very dangerous snake. Winsome and I were paying a final visit to Frank and Enid before going on leave, and Frank and I had been to inspect the construction of their new home. While walking back to the river through a small rubber plantation, we saw a large snake moving swiftly through the trees and waving its head from side to side about two feet above the ground. Its colour and markings and the swaying motion of the head, together with the hissing sound, were all unmistakably characteristic of the king cobra, or hamadryad, but neither of us had ever seen such a large one. It crossed the path in front of us at an angle of about forty-five degrees and disappeared into the trees so quickly that we could not be certain of its size, but both of us estimated that it was at least twelve feet long with a circumference about the size of a man's thigh. King cobras are among the deadliest of all snakes, and I have read that they will sometimes attack a man unprovoked, although during our years in Borneo I never heard of an instance where this actually happened.

From Frank and Enid's house, Winsome and I went on to visit the Muruts and the Ibans in the Limbang, and then returned to Jesselton and prepared to go on leave. Since we planned to make a detour through India on our way to Australia, we stayed a few days with our friends at the British and Foreign Bible Society in Singapore and then went on to Madras — thereafter travelling by train and bus south to Dohnavur in South India.

At that time Winsome's aunts, Mabel and Frances Beath, were both at Dohnavur where they were involved in an outstanding humanitarian project founded years earlier by Amy Carmichael. Frances had been working at Dohnavur since 1910, and Mabel had joined as travelling secretary in 1936. We spent two delightful weeks with Winsome's aunts and had the privilege of meeting with Amy Carmichael, who was then in her early 70s. We were also able to see for ourselves the multitudes of children and babies who had been saved from dedication to the service of pagan gods in the temples of South India.

Mabel Beath was a genteel lady, but she had great strength of character along with a touch of feistiness. One evidence of this was a clandestine plan she initiated to protect the life of a child named Muttammal:

> Amy went alone to court in the morning . . . the clerk floundered slowly through thirty or forty pages, the voice droning through the heavy heat till he came to words which stung like a whip-lash — Muttammal must be returned to her mother, all legal costs to be paid by Amy. At the moment of the verdict Amy experienced a sudden strange, triumphant joy . . . she could not explain it . . .
>
> What she did not know was that by this time Muttammal had disappeared from Dohnavur. No one knew where she had gone. Weeks of silence and uncertainty passed, broken only by an anonymous postcard with the words of 2 Chronicles 16:9,[1] suggesting that Muttammal was safe. It was months before she learned the story. A guest, Mabel Beath, to whom Amy had confided, had dressed the child as a Muslim boy and sent her out of the compound by a certain gate. Two

1. "For the eyes of the Lord range throughout the earth to strengthen those whose hearts are fully committed to Him."

> Indians met her with a bandy and by circuitous means she was taken to Colombo, Ceylon . . . For six months they did not hear of her whereabouts. In October came the letter saying she was safe.[2]

On leaving Dohnavur we went by bus and ferry to Colombo in Ceylon, and then by ocean liner to Australia. With the war escalating in Europe, we steamed at full speed with lights blacked out, arriving in Melbourne on June 6, 1940, just four days before Hitler's all-out blitz shocked the world.

While we were on home leave in Australia, the world stage changed dramatically. The Nazi war machine soon overwhelmed France, and the British expeditionary force was compelled to retreat to the shores of Dunkirk. Then, under the cover of eerie fogs and protective calm, a flotilla of small motor craft — hundreds of launches, tugs, barges and yachts — evacuated the outnumbered British Army. During the following months, Spitfires and Hurricanes fought off the aerial armada of German bombers in the Battle of Britain and thus enabled England to regroup for the coming battles in Europe.

During that time we received news from Borneo regularly, albeit belatedly, by mail. On one occasion we heard that the Rajah was planning another visit to the Trusan area, and in a subsequent letter we learned that on November 26, 1940, Rajah Vyner Brooke had this to say:

> I met your people Mr. and Mrs. Davidson at Lawas the other day, and have been very much impressed by the work of your Mission. My Secretary is writing an article on the Mission. I am amazed at the change in the Murut tribe. They used to be notorious drinkers, but when given arrack (Chinese whiskey) and cigarettes the other day they refused! They didn't want them. It's remarkable! Very remarkable! And they seemed much cleaner than I have ever seen them before. I believe you have done more good in a few years than the Government has done in forty.
>
> I think what impressed me most was the sight of that little lady [Enid Davidson] going away followed by forty or

---

2. Elizabeth Elliot, *Amy Carmichael* (E. Sussex: MARC, 1988), 209, 210.

> fifty Murut men and women and children following close at her heels. I've never seen anything like it before. Obviously they have the confidence of the people and a great influence over them. But the thing that surprises me is that your Mission does all this by methods of faith and by spiritual means.

This was an extraordinary acknowledgement from the Rajah who had formerly feared to allow us to work among the Muruts of the Trusan.

PART III
CLOUDS OF WAR

Sorrow and joy,
striking suddenly on our startled senses,
seem, at the first approach, all but impossible
of just distinction one from the other,
even as frost and heat at the first keen contact
burn us alike.

– Dietrich Bonhoeffer

CHAPTER 8

When the time came for us to return to Borneo in March 1941, the war in Europe had intensified greatly but the situation in Asia was still unclear. As the Foreign Affairs Department in Australia did not advise against returning, we travelled across Australia by train and embarked in one of the Blue Funnel coastal steamers at Fremantle, West Australia.

Many years earlier, Winsome and I had each acquired from our parents the habit of reading a little book of verses from the Bible selected for each day of the year. It is called *Daily Light*, and each day includes morning and evening selections intended for use in personal meditations and prayer. As I have followed these daily readings consistently throughout the years, I have often found that the verses selected for a given date were particularly relevant to some immediate personal need and seemed to be a message from God.

On that very day, March 25, 1941, the selected reading was, "I am with you and will watch over you wherever you go, and I will bring you back to this land."[1] Both Winsome and I felt this was God's specific message and promise to us.

We arrived in Borneo near the end of April and went first to Limpasong to get the office files from Roland Bewsher who had been acting as Field Secretary and Treasurer. Then we went on to Jesselton and found that the two most recent mission arrivals, Trevor White and Alan Belcher, were away in the interior. Alan had arrived in Borneo while we were in Australia, so Winsome and I went up the Padas Gorge and on to Tambunan, where he was staying with John and Kitty McArthur. It was while we were at Tambunan with the McArthurs that we heard Hitler's armies had invaded Russia.

1. Genesis 28:15

When Winsome and I returned to Jesselton, we found that the Sarawak Government had instructed Enid Davidson to return to Australia, as she was expecting a baby and concerns for security in Southeast Asia were increasing. Since Frank's health was not good and he was now alone in the lower Trusan, we all felt that Winsome and I should move there to work with him among the Muruts. Some two months later a new recruit, Brian Morcombe, arrived unexpectedly from West Australia, and he also joined us in the lower Trusan. With Brian there to help Frank, Winsome and I decided to visit the Ibans and Muruts in the Limbang area. I prepared our longboat and nine-horsepower Johnson outboard engine for a month's journey. We took only essential supplies and equipment with us, leaving behind most of the possessions we valued, little knowing that we would never again return to that little home in the lower Trusan.

We left on November 28, 1941, and travelled around Brunei Bay and then up the Limbang to Limpasong where we stayed for a few days to attend a conference. Less than a week later, as I listened to the early morning wireless news, I heard the startling announcement that the Japanese had, on December 7th, bombed Pearl Harbor in Hawaii! This immediately brought America into the war, and although we knew it would mean a major escalation in fighting, we felt it was so far away that it would not affect us. So we continued our journey up the Limbang.

How wrong we were! When we returned to Limpasong a week later with an Iban baby seriously ill with pneumonia, we learned that the Japanese had sunk the warships *Repulse* and *Prince of Wales* off the coast of Malaya.

Realizing the gravity of the situation, we decided to go downriver to see the Resident at Limbang. We had not gone far when we saw three Dutch bombers fly overhead towards Miri, and a few minutes later we heard bombs dropping, and gunfire, and saw fires burning — a distance of about seventy-five miles away. Several minutes later we saw only two planes return.

Suddenly Winsome turned toward me from the middle of the boat and smiled. She said something, but the engine drowned out her voice.

A little later when we stopped, she told me, "I had an amazing experience just now. When I saw the planes go overhead and heard the explosions, and then only two planes returned, I felt frightened. Then suddenly I heard a voice speaking on my right side. The voice said, *What are the Japanese to me and my power?* And immediately I relaxed, and I felt God's peace flow over me. It was wonderful."

Never before or since has either of us had such an experience. But on this occasion God had provided a message for a definite purpose. He knew what lay ahead and he graciously intervened to allay Winsome's fears.

On arriving at Limbang we went directly to see the Resident, Mr. J.G. Anderson, and learned that the Japanese had attacked the Miri oilfields and landed a naval force. Rumors abounded, including one that the Japanese might be in Brunei Bay. In light of this, the Resident advised that it would be unwise to attempt to return across Brunei Bay to Trusan.

"What do you propose to do?" he asked us.

"We feel it would be best to retreat into the interior," I said. "We want to continue our work among the people there, and we know we can trust them to help us."

Mr. Anderson told us that the Rajah had ordered all his officers to remain at their posts with a view to preventing bloodshed through an orderly surrender to the Japanese. Then, with grave concern in his voice, the Resident asked if we would be willing to take his wife with us into the interior. We readily agreed.

I was quite sure that with our knowledge of the secluded passages out of Brunei Bay we could have easily and safely slipped back to the Trusan, but we felt we should first check if there were other foreigners who needed help to evacuate. After spending the night with the Andersons, we returned to Limpasong where the Bewshers lived. Then, on December 22nd, Roland went back downriver for one night and invited several rubber planters including George Clifford and his wife and teenage daughter to join us. They arrived the next day on the big government steam yacht *Datu*, which was to be hidden as far upriver as possible.

As a first step, we decided to move everyone upriver to Sungai Pranga, so Winsome and I, along with Mrs. Anderson and the Cliffords' daughter, went ahead with the outboard to prepare for the others. The next day was a strange Christmas Day indeed. We were fugitives, with none of the atmosphere or trappings of Christmas, but we tried to make the best of it, with the help of Mrs. Anderson who was always good company. Her given name was Geraldine, but her close friends knew her by her childhood nickname, Dood, and soon this is what we called her too.

The *Datu* also arrived at Sungai Pranga on Christmas Day, but by then the planters wanted to continue on as far as they could, and they finally anchored just opposite the mouth of the Medamit tributary. Here a large sandbank studded with logs and tree stumps made further passage impossible for such a large boat.

The Resident had given us a *tongat terbai*, which in Iban custom constituted an order for urgent and immediate assistance to anyone bearing this symbol. The *tongat terbai* consisted of a burnt stick with a feather attached and a message indicating the action required. Ordinarily such a request would be obeyed immediately, night or day. But, given the circumstances, the Ibans knew there was not much power to enforce this command, and they were rather reluctant to help. It was a test of true friendship.

"If it weren't for you, we wouldn't take this party upriver," they said to us bluntly, speaking in Iban. "These planters don't care anything about us. But because you have helped us, we will help you."

After negotiating with the planters for high wages, the Ibans supplied several boats and men to transport the whole party upriver to Gani's longhouse, which was the last Iban longhouse before a long stretch of uninhabited and wild mountainous country. The planters were well-supplied with clothing, food and other household goods, and we also had the Bewsher's household things. It took us four days to get the entire party, together with many boatloads of goods, transported to Gani's longhouse. We stored about a third of all the possessions at Gani's before continuing on.

Roland and Mary Bewsher, along with the Bisaya twins they had adopted, went on ahead to the Medihit in the upper Limbang valley and got through quickly on low water. The rest of our party set out from Gani's longhouse on December 31, 1941, with four heavily laden Iban longboats, in addition to our boat with the outboard.

The journey upriver was a nightmare for the rubber planters, especially for old Mrs. Clifford. We spent the first night, an unforgettable New Year's Eve, in the forest below a huge limestone cliff at a place called Salidong. We beached the boats on a gravel bank and climbed to a bamboo grove, where the Ibans started to make a framework of bamboo for a shelter. Then the rain came down in torrents, and our party crouched under the incomplete shelter with only a leaky piece of canvas salvaged from the *Datu* for covering.

We were all wet and miserable, yet somehow we could not help but laugh at our situation! Then I remembered a roll of sisalkraft tarred paper in our belongings, and we cut off lengths for covering and groped around in the gathering darkness to improvise a shelter from the rain.

New Year's Day, 1942, dawned over our group of bedraggled fugitives huddled on the river bank — with the river roaring by, the deep forest behind us and a towering limestone cliff facing us on the other side of the river. The river rose sharply that day, and we had to stay in our crude shelter for three days and nights.

By January 3rd the river was still high, but falling, so we packed the boats and set out through a gorge where the rocks were fewer but the river was swift and deep. We had some heart-stopping experiences along the way and spent two more nights in primitive shelters, but we safely reached the mouth of the Medihit.

Each morning, before setting out, I prayed with the men in the Iban language, and both the Ibans and Europeans in the party remarked on how God had helped us to get through safely in the face of dangerous circumstances.

The Ibans, having brought us this far, now wanted to return to their longhouses, but first they built us a substantial shelter under a spreading tree on the upper edge of a wide bank of large rounded rocks. Behind this bank the jungle sloped gently upwards, so even if the river rose quickly we could escape to safety. On the opposite side of the swiftly flowing river we could see the mouth of the Medihit tributary flowing over gravel banks dotted with huge boulders.

Frank and Enid Davidson had lived about a half day's journey up the Medihit for five years, from 1935 to 1940, and their house was still standing there beside a small stream which the Kelabits had named Aroh Linoh, meaning "the stream of pleasant thoughts." It was a beautiful spot, with the rocky Medihit flowing in front and a cool mountain stream providing a constant water supply at the back door. This was where Roland and Mary Bewsher had headed and they were already there waiting for us. They soon heard of our arrival at the mouth of the Medihit through some Muruts who were living nearby.

Moving the whole party, with all the possessions, up the Medihit to Aroh Linoh was a slow job and took most of January. Meanwhile, I went back downriver with two men to Gani's longhouse to bring up some more supplies.

The Ibans of Gani's house were friendly, but lying in bed that night under my mosquito net, I heard them talking about a recent visit to the coast where they had met some Japanese. Then, using veiled parabolic language, they said that the Japanese were offering a reward of one *pikul* (about 130 pounds) of salt fish for any European head they brought in. Despite their friendliness, I felt I would be wise to get back upriver as soon as possible!

We all finally moved into the little house at Aroh Linoh. We had no idea how long we would have to remain hidden there, so all of us tried to conserve what we had. George Clifford carried this to an amusing extreme. Although he had brought an entire suitcase of cigarettes with him, he was determined to get maximum value out of each one. To do so without burning his fingers, he would smoke the butts of his cigarettes by holding them gingerly with one of his wife's hairpins.

Life at Aroh Linoh was not easy as the house was small for so large a party and everyone's space was restricted. In addition, some of the party did not adapt well to bush conditions and the atmosphere was often one of gloom and pessimism. But the saddest thing to me was that in spite of the way God had so clearly helped and protected us, there was no acknowledgement of him among most of our companions.

Winsome and I had always hoped we would be able to get back to our house in the lower Trusan by some overland route and then continue upriver into the interior. We were eager to get back, not only for the sake of the Muruts there, but also because we had heard absolutely nothing about Frank Davidson and Brian Morcombe. Also, anticipating a probable long isolation in the interior, we wanted to get food, clothing, footwear and some of our more valued possessions — assuming our house was still intact.

Thus, Winsome and I decided to try to make our way back to the Trusan, and Dood Anderson said she would like to come with us. I told her that our main objective was to return to active work among the Muruts, and cautioned her about the difficulties of the overland journey, but she seemed glad to join us.

We began by moving back to the base camp at the mouth of the Medihit and remained there for the rest of February, during which time the local Muruts and Kelabits were busy harvesting their rice. We often went to help them in their fields and soon learned to pluck the ears as quickly as they did.

Apart from the rice, which was plentiful, we often had little to eat other than ferntips or pumpkin. Then, after some trials, I learned the ways of the river fish, and they augmented the larder. I did have two rifles and a shotgun with me, but not many cartridges, so I used them sparingly.

During that time we also had a welcome visit from Kasa, the Iban lad who had helped Carey Tolley when he lived in the Lubai. One day while he was with us, we heard the call of a large sambhur deer from a thicket of giant bamboo on the opposite bank of the river.

"Hurry, Kasa," I said, knowing that he was an excellent hunter, "take my shotgun and go across the river — but first let us pray that God may enable you to get the animal, as we have not had fresh meat for a long time."

"Oh, no, don't mention its name," he said with great concern. "The spirits will hear, and it will run away."

"Remember that you believe in Jesus," I said. "He has more power than the spirits. It is right for us to ask him for the food we need." So I prayed in Iban that God would supply our need.

Kasa took my gun and paddled across the river and disappeared into the jungle. Minutes later I heard a shot, and then Kasa appeared, dragging the carcass of a big deer. After cutting up the deer, we gave some meat to the people around us, sent some to those at Aroh Linoh, and still had enough for our own use and a little to preserve by smoking over a fire.

When news from Frank and Brian finally filtered through to us around the end of February, we abandoned our plans for returning to the house on the lower Trusan. We learned that they had evacuated shortly after Christmas upon receiving urgent messages from Mr. McLaren of the Lawas Rubber Estates and from Mr. Willis, a planter who had already fled further upriver. Frank and Brian packed hurriedly and, along with Mr. McLaren, travelled to Kelasi's longhouse in a heavily laden motor boat. Brian had returned to the house with the boat at least once and recovered more of the goods belonging to Winsome and myself. We also heard that two of our friends in the area went to the house at night during the early days of January and saved a number of our cases of belongings. From Kelasi's longhouse, Frank and his party had travelled by boat to Long Briwan, and then Long Tengoa, and from there made their way overland to the Brayong and Tuyo Rivers where some good friends loyally helped them.

Then, on January 22nd, the Japanese came and ransacked the house, carrying off anything that was of value to them and destroying the rest, including our Mission files and records.

The local people had a bumper rice harvest which promised to keep them busy for many weeks, but we heard that the upper Trusan people had finished with their harvest, so toward the end of February we sent a message by Kasa asking for twenty-five people to come to help us travel overland to the upper Trusan. On March 6th they arrived, and it was grand to see them — there were thirty-two of them and they were all Christian. Their love and willingness to help and their keenness to know more about God encouraged us tremendously.

We told these Trusan people that we did not wish to be a burden to them and wanted to make our own farm, since after paying for our journey we would not have much money to buy rice for a long period.

Labo Upai spoke up for them all and said, "Just come and teach us more about the gospel, and we will give you all we can. You can live with us for the rest of your lives!" It was a warm-hearted invitation, and they were genuinely prepared to live up to it.

We left our Medihit base camp on Monday, March 9th, taking a route which led over Kap Labong, a particularly difficult mountain. Neither Winsome nor Dood had had much experience walking in the jungle, let alone such rugged mountain country, so I wondered how they would stand it, but they did splendidly. It was right at the end of the dry season, but we were able to complete most of the journey before the rains started. This was fortunate, for in wet weather the rocks and hillsides are treacherous, leeches are a nightmare, and big rivers like the Limbang and Trusan are unfordable — often for days at a time.

The tribulations of trekking through the Bornean jungle as seen through a woman's eyes can only be properly described by one who has had such experiences firsthand. A friend of ours who travelled frequently with her husband provides this perspective:

> Everything in the jungle bit me until my skin was raw, and I couldn't sleep at night for the scratching, and I said so. He was covered with leech bites and inflamed scratches, but he always slept as soundly as a crocodile on a sunny bank.
>
> I stumbled and fell often while walking in the jungle, and when I dragged myself up coated with mud, I thought he looked at me with silent disgust. At such times I hated his resilient step and his untiredness.[2]

---

2. Agnes Keith, *Land Below the Wind* (London: Michael Joseph Ltd., 1949), 255.

One truism of adversity is that it gives us a greater appreciation for simple pleasures. And no matter how bad things get, some women travellers can still dream of better times:

> We ate our dinners sitting over the smoking fires and each of us holding a shouldering torch in one hand, which we waved as we ate. The sand flies were uncontrollable. They were so small one could hardly see them individually, but they came in clouds and attacked every exposed portion of the body. The sensation was that of being stuck all over with pins. Within a couple of hours the bites swelled and itched more violently than mosquito bites did. For days after we were bitten the bites would itch every night at dusk. The sand flies were so small that they went through mosquito nets, and although we were using special double nets which were supposed to be proof against them, no net really was. When we got into bed that night the net was full of them, and I sat for twenty minutes holding smoldering sticks of wood over the bed until I got rid of some of them.
>
> I had a wonderful night's sleep, and dreamed that I was in a very smart shop at home buying beautiful clothes, and then I went to a beauty shop and had myself completely redecorated, manicured, shampooed and massaged, and emerged looking very nice indeed, so nice in fact nobody recognized me.[3]

We followed the bank of the Limbang for two days until we reached the Raya tributary where we camped for the night at about 750 feet above sea level. Next day we climbed straight up Mt. Kap Labong, over 5,000 feet high.

Ferns, giant creepers and orchids lined the track, and then, at the summit, a glorious panorama suddenly broke into view. Bright sunlight and fleecy clouds cast irregular patches on the forest below us, and we could see the whole country, way into the interior, spread out before us. But the most impressive sight was Mt. Batu Lawi. The valley of the Limbang led straight up to the main mountain peak, where the river branched into two tributaries. And there, from the centre, Batu Lawi pointed its majestic pinnacle up to heaven.

---

3. Ibid., 244.

That night we camped about an hour's journey from the other side of the summit. The fifth day brought us to a lonely Murut house situated across the Limbang near the Adang River. We were glad of the rest and stayed for a long weekend.

Our thirty-two carriers almost doubled the local population, and during our two-day stay they netted two huge catches of fish, about 100 each day, many of them being three or four pounds each and some larger. The people in the Adang were very isolated and were eager to hear the gospel. We taught them all we could while we were there and left them a good deal of medicine.

We trekked two more days up the Adang valley, rich farming country which had once supported a large population. After crossing the watershed, we made our way down the other side to the upper Trusan River, just below where it was joined by the Kelalan River. There the track came to a ford about eighty yards wide. The water was more than waist deep and flowing so swiftly we were nearly swept away. We got across, though, and camped on the foothills near Bukit Balud, an area which had gained notoriety at the turn of the century when sixteen Murut longhouses were destroyed during the Rajah's punitive expedition.

Since the first shock of the Japanese invasion and our retreat up the Limbang to the base camp at Medihit, we had felt like fugitives in hiding. The local Muruts and Kelabits were friendly and helpful, but they did not show much spiritual interest. The earlier signs of responsiveness to Frank and Enid Davidson's work seemed to have faded.

But as soon as our Murut carriers arrived in their own territory in the upper Trusan, the whole atmosphere changed. And now, having crossed the Trusan River, the warmth of welcome steadily increased from village to village. We were met with gifts of fowls, eggs, vegetables and fruit all the way up to the last village at the source of the upper Trusan.

When we arrived at Long Semadoh where *Penghulu* Ating Mugang lived, the people gave us a tremendous welcome. This was the village that had so impressed Mr. Banks, Curator of the Sarawak Museum, when I met him there four years earlier. Now, everyone flocked around us, stroking our shoulders and arms, and calling out, "*Boolih! Boolih! Boolih!*" which was the Murut way of expressing sympathy with our situation.

Dood had never experienced a reception like this before, and she turned to Winsome and me with a look of incredulity and said, "Is this really happening, or am I going mad?"

Although I had received similar welcomes before, the real significance of this one was that eight years had passed since these people had turned from pagan superstition to become followers of Jesus Christ. This was not a burst of enthusiasm as new converts; the gospel had really taken root in their hearts. They had received occasional visits from some of us, but no expatriate missionary had ever lived among them, and only a few of their young men had received brief periods of training at our mission stations. Without question they had entered into a new life relationship with Jesus Christ. It was not an emotional or even an intellectual change, but a supernatural heart change generated by the living Holy Spirit.

The last village upriver was named Punang Trusan, meaning "source of the Trusan," and Labo Upai, the young man we had brought out for training in early 1939, lived there. The Headman, Marong Ilan, and his people gave us a riotous and tumultuous welcome. We knew we were among friends; we felt we had come home.

Chapter 9

An emergency faced us soon after we arrived in the upper Trusan valley. On March 21, 1942, one of the Muruts returning from the coast brought back an anonymous letter informing us that the Japanese knew we had come overland from the Limbang and that they were coming up to get us. The writer advised us to hide deeper in the forest.

After we consulted with the local people, they decided to hide us on a low ridge beside the Payang, a beautiful stream in a secluded valley away from any tracks. It was at a high altitude and although we were only about 300 miles from the equator, it was cold enough that we could see our breath in the morning!

The people brought us wild pig and sugar cane, along with white, red and black rice. The red and black varieties were delicious and very nutritious. When cooked, the black rice was a deep chocolate color and had a faint fragrance of cocoa.

We were glad to have this period, hidden in a remote spot, to think and pray about future plans. All the villages on the upper Trusan had begged us to come and live near them. It was nice to feel we were wanted, but we wished to be able to help them in return.

We heard that John Willfinger of the Christian and Missionary Alliance was not far away across the border in Dutch Borneo at Long Berang, so I wrote to him saying that I would like to meet him, and the people brought him to our hiding place. Two days later Frank Davidson and Brian Morcombe also came to see us, and we all had a long talk with the Muruts, discussing our plans for the future. As a result, we agreed to have them build a house for us, with room for a school, at Punang Trusan.

After a fortnight, we learned that the rumour of Japanese soldiers coming to arrest us was not true, and we moved back to Headman Marong's longhouse (Rumah Marong) at Punang Trusan, a delightful spot with a lovely view extending about fifteen miles down the valley with a circle of mountains at the end. Behind us, but closer, was a similar circle of mountains which gave rise to the Trusan River. Nearby was a sparkling stream of water, and the soil had a fertility seldom seen in Borneo. The climate was cool and temperate. All of this was combined with the joy of living among a people grateful for their liberation from the fear of evil spirits, from their addiction to *borak*, and from the degradation and sickness that had resulted.

They built us a house with a bamboo floor and walls of bark sheets, with a room for Winsome and me at one end, and a room for Dood at the other; the space between served as kitchen and living room. After four months of camping and wandering in the jungle, we certainly were glad to move into this permanent residence. Also, the house was high enough above the ground to allow room for a school beneath, with bamboo seats and desks. We made a blackboard of white slabs of wood and used black charcoal instead of white chalk.

The fulfilment we felt in working with these appreciative people made us forget the difficulties and privations resulting from our sudden flight to the interior with only a few clothes and the bare essentials of daily life. And indeed God, who foreknew all these circumstances, provided us with the things we really needed. For instance, we needed simple medicines — and we found that just before the war the Sarawak Government had made three depots of medical supplies in the interior, one of which was quite near us. We needed salt — and were able to get it from salt springs at Ba Kelalan, where the local people evaporated the salt water in large iron pans and stored the salt in bamboo tubes. Also, Winsome and I felt the cold in our light clothes, but Dood had brought some skeins of wool with her, and she knitted woollen pullovers for both of us.

Dood fitted in splendidly. She endeared herself to the women and children and often assisted the women in pounding and husking rice. In addition, she was very courageous through all those months of separation from her husband when she did not know what had happened to him. In July she finally did receive news, and even letters in his own handwriting. He had been detained by the Japanese but was apparently well.

Our school was overwhelmingly popular, but our limited facilities restricted attendance to forty at any one time, so we had to select a few candidates from each village. School commenced on

May 18th and continued until August 5th, except for ten days when we went to Ba Kelalan. The students came for an early morning session, and then worked on their farms for several hours before returning for another session in the late afternoon.

Toward the end of May, John Willfinger felt compelled to leave his home in Dutch Borneo, as it was not sufficiently remote from the Japanese. Winsome and I immediately invited him to join us. He was an exceptionally fine man, an American with an engaging personality, black pyjamas and a saxophone — which greatly delighted the Muruts.

We made a good team. John had been in Borneo only about three-and-a-half years, but he was a gifted linguist and, having travelled extensively among the Muruts, had developed an excellent knowledge of their language. We immediately started work on translating, tackling hymns first, some of which are still in the Murut hymnal today. John had already translated the Gospel of Mark into Murut, and I was able to type out three copies on my typewriter using the Sarawak (or British) spelling of words, which differed somewhat from that in the Dutch territories. We then worked on a colloquial translation of the Gospel of Matthew and I typed that in three copies as well.

The weekly services in the little church near Rumah Marong were a special joy. On his trip to the Trusan at the end of 1938, Stafford Young had brought back several schoolboys from different houses for preliminary teaching since we had no one available to live and teach in this remote area. Four of these boys, Riong, Baru, Ukul and Labo Upai, had gone on to stay with Winsome and me at Jesselton. After their training they returned home, where each of these lads encouraged their elders to build small churches at their respective villages; the people gathered in these on Sundays, as well as two or three times during the week. These young congregations longed for teaching as they had only occasional visits from church leaders from the Dutch side of the border, and Frank Davidson had visited them just once in 1940 while he was living in the Medihit.

We were overjoyed with these opportunities, and I can truthfully say that, despite concerns about the war, I was never happier in any work or conditions in Borneo. Winsome's influence was also great and far-reaching among the women; she was the first missionary woman to live in the interior among them.

In early July, we decided to visit the Muruts at Ba Kelalan. While we were there, Dood went to visit Frank and Brian and the party of rubber planters who were with them at Tuyo, about three days' journey nearer the coast. When Winsome and I returned after a few happy days with the people at Ba Kelalan, we brought some medicines, including the new drug Sulphanilamide, from the Government's depot of medical supplies. We arrived back at Rumah Marong on July 16th and continued our teaching in the school.

Then suddenly, on August 2nd, the whole situation changed dramatically. A lad came running to us with the startling news that on Sunday, July 26th, a party of seventeen Japanese soldiers with one officer, armed with rifles and a machine gun, had captured Roland and Mary Bewsher and the rubber planters at Aroh Linoh. The Japanese had travelled upriver in seventeen boats commandeered from the Ibans and Muruts living on the Limbang. Apparently they had quietly surrounded the house while everyone was eating lunch.

The messenger told us that the Japanese had not treated their captives with undue harshness. They were allowed to sleep at Aroh Linoh on that Sunday night, and the next day the women were sent down to the main river in boats while the men were marched down overland, each one bound by one hand to a soldier. Roland Bewsher had managed to speak in Malay to this lad, asking him to come immediately to the Trusan to inform us that they had been captured.

The news of their capture soon spread, and that evening we held a consultation with all the headmen of the district, during which they discussed the possibility of collecting a force of men to be armed with blowpipes and poisoned darts and their old muzzle-loading shotguns! We restrained them from any thought of violence on our behalf and told them we were quite prepared to go down to the coast and surrender to the Japanese if necessary. The way forward was very unclear to us, and we wanted to ensure that we were following God's leading for each precarious step.

After prayer with the people, and further consultation, they all advised against surrendering. They then sent out messengers to gather more information. They also sent messengers to Frank and Brian and the planters with them. On hearing this news, the Muruts with Frank and Brian decided to prepare a secret hiding place in a lonely spot known only to a trusted few, and the whole party of Europeans went to this place at night. The Muruts at Tuyo with Frank advised that our Murut friends in the upper Trusan should do the same for us.

The consensus was that for the present we should continue to hide, as there was no indication that the Japanese had any definite information about our location, and we had not received any demand for surrender. Moreover, we did not know what form of authority the Japanese had established at the coast. Some of the stories we were hearing indicated the presence of rather lawless soldiers of fortune.

As we prayed about our situation, we remembered that we had often been invited to visit the Muruts on the upper Matang River, one of the source tributaries of the Padas River in North Borneo, only a day's journey away over the Trusan watershed. The Japanese could not reach the upper Trusan by river as they had done to capture the people in the Medihit. Since they would need to come overland through the villages, we knew that the people would give us ample warning of any danger from downriver. We therefore decided to visit the people in the Matang area for a fortnight, during which time our special hiding place would be completed.

Dood Anderson returned on August 12th from Tuyo and decided to remain at Rumah Marong rather than come with us. So John Willfinger, Winsome and I went over the watershed on August 19th and had ten days of constant travelling — teaching and preaching all the way down to Long Mio. The Muruts there were hungry for teaching, as they lived in a kind of no-man's-land, an isolated wedge of territory between Sarawak and Dutch Borneo that had little previous exposure to the gospel.

By August 28th, the three of us were back at Pengiran Langob's longhouse, the nearest village in the upper Matang to the watershed leading back to the upper Trusan. There, we found a letter waiting for us from Dood telling us that she had received a letter from the coast containing the ominous news that two coastal Muruts had been seen with three Japanese soldiers in the lower Trusan who said they intended coming up to arrest us in early September.

In light of this news, we decided to remain where we were. John immediately went down to Rumah Marong to get Dood, and the two of them arrived back the next day. The four of us stayed on at Pengiran Langob's longhouse, which was closest to our secret hiding place — just in case there was truth in this report.

The Muruts in this isolated spot on the Matang River were very kind. They were poor but they made nearly half of their house available to us, and they hunted animals and shared their food with us. I was glad for the sake of these people that we were compelled to stay there, for we were able to help them medically, and also able to give them more teaching from God's word. It was an example where "in all things God works for the good of those who love him,"[1] for if it had not been for that emergency situation, we would not have extended our stay by an additional three weeks in this most lonely part of the Murut territory.

Realizing that our time might be short, John and I also pressed on with our work of translation and typing during that three-week period from August 29th till September 21st. I recorded the intensive work that filled those days and still have my diary for this period. I also typed two copies of a letter to be left with trusted people — eleven pages of single-spaced typewriting — telling of our activities of the last seven months since we had come from the Limbang to the upper Trusan. I had started working on this letter several weeks earlier, after hearing of the capture of the Bewshers and the rubber planters at Aroh Linoh. Not knowing what the future might hold for us, I felt I should make a written record of ourselves and our activities and leave it with our Murut friends, Labo Upai and Laban Laput at Rumah Marong, with instructions that it was to be given to any of our people who might come to this part of Sarawak after the war. I still have a copy of this letter in my files. It began with these words:

1. Romans 8:28

> Dear Loved Ones and All Friends at Home,
>
> After some months of very happy experiences in service among the Murut Christians of the upper Trusan, it seems likely that we may be compelled to flee once more and disappear into the forests; we are therefore each leaving an account of the past months with a reliable friend, with instructions that if they know for certain of our death or unaccountable disappearance, it is to be sent as soon as possible after the war to the address given.

Eleven pages later, I concluded the letter as follows :

> We do not know what the future holds, or what other leading God may give to us. But I would like you to know that God has given us some glorious promises from His Word, and I can honestly say that we are quite calm and peaceful, through God's goodness and grace. If we do not come home we hope this letter will reach you safely, we know that many have been praying for us, and we feel that God has answered and will continue to hear and answer prayer . . .
>
> Then too I must add a further note as to Winsome's life here in the inland. She has always had a special love for these people, ever since Raut and his companions first came to see us and accepted Christ in 1933 . . . Then when we came to Trusan in August 1941 the women took her to their hearts, and of course Winsome just loved them. But the crowning joy to her, and indeed to us both, and the marvel of these past months, is that God should allow us to come up the Limbang and overland to these people in the Ulu Trusan, the more so that it is during, and even because of this time of war. It is difficult to imagine how we would have come here otherwise. God has given Winsome strength for these difficult journeys, and health beyond anything she has yet experienced in Borneo. To God be all the praise and glory, we certainly do praise and thank Him.

Then, the fateful hour came. On Saturday, September 19th, at around two-thirty in the afternoon, Labo Upai and Belawan arrived at the Matang River longhouse from Rumah Marong with the official demand for our surrender to the Japanese military in Brunei, failing which we would be subject to military law, which meant death for us and punishment for anyone who helped us. The document mentioned all our names.

Though not unexpected, this still came as a shock. We stayed where we were overnight so we could have a last Sunday service with the Upper Matang people. Then we hurriedly packed our things and left for Rumah Marong at Punang Trusan.

The next day we had a long talk with Native Officer Bigar who had come all the way from the coast with the surrender documents on behalf of the Japanese. Mr. Bigar was an experienced junior administrative officer under Rajah Vyner Brooke and the one man in Lawas who could speak inland languages. The Japanese had come to rely on him tremendously, but as later events would show, Bigar's loyalties were to the people of his country — and also to the Rajah who was now in exile.

The Muruts at Rumah Marong still urged us to go to a secret hiding place, and they devised a shrewd plan. They had demolished the house in which we had lived beside Marong's longhouse, and a few trusted Muruts had constructed a secret hideout in a remote place. Then, a second select party constructed a different hiding place unknown to those who had constructed the first one, and they planned to bring us secretly from the first hiding place to the second. If anyone other than those in the second select party were questioned they could honestly say, "We don't know where they have gone. They've disappeared."

It seemed ridiculously easy to hide in this mountain vastness with its trackless forests. But we also knew that to do so could result in punishment or even death for these people who had so selflessly helped us. In this situation, the vital thing was to find out God's guidance for us, and to this end, we prayed with open hearts for God to show us his will.

One of our Scripture readings at that time was an account involving Nebuchadnezzar, king of Babylon, and the prophet Jeremiah.[2] After Nebuchadnezzar destroyed Jerusalem in 587 B.C., leaving the poorer people in the land, the governor he installed was killed and the people, fearing his vengeance, petitioned the prophet

---

2. See Jeremiah 42

Jeremiah to ask God what they should do. God instructed Jeremiah to tell them to submit to Nebuchadnezzar. If they did so, their lives would be spared and they would be permitted to live in their land; but if they fled to Egypt, the war would overtake them and they would die there.

We felt this was God's direction for us to obey the command of the Japanese who were now in control of Borneo, and we gave up any idea of a secret hideout. Instead, we decided to pack our things and go down to surrender. We spent a very busy week preparing to leave the people and the home we had come to love so well. We left a good many things with them, including my typewriter and my shotgun and rifles, and packed only a few essential things that we still had with us. We also held final church meetings, and I baptized forty-five people from Rumah Marong and five people from the Matang longhouse.

Meanwhile, John had received a letter from some of his Murut friends in Dutch Borneo telling that one of his colleagues in the Christian and Missionary Alliance had taken off in their mission plane for Tarakan, with Japanese permission, but had not arrived there, and no one knew the reason. This aroused suspicion among the Japanese and no doubt contributed to the hostile reception which John received when eventually he surrendered at Tarakan.

Before leaving Rumah Marong, I typed a final postscript to the letter which I had prepared to be left with the people there. This final entry, dated October 1, 1942, was as follows:

> We had planned to leave here yesterday, but after our busy morning of packing, rain set in and as Winsome has malaria hanging about — and I also have not been as fit as usual — we decided it would be best to send a messenger saying that we would come next morning. So today we go.
>
> *Daily Light* for yesterday, both morning and evening, was a great comfort and assurance. May we trust and lean continually on him, come what may . . .
>
> Yours, until that Day dawns . . .

From Rumah Marong, the four of us went to Ating Mugang's longhouse at Long Semadoh where we stayed two nights, then went on to Long Luping as the next stage down to surrender. We also stayed two nights there, over the weekend, and had a service with the people on Sunday.

John had accompanied us to Long Luping, but he was in great turmoil of heart. Although his name was on the official Japanese list of those called to surrender, he felt strongly that he owed it to the churches in the Kemaloh River area, on the Dutch side of the border, to pay them a final visit and see to their needs.

Thus, on the morning of October 5th, John told us that he could accompany us no further. He felt the time had come for him to turn back and he would not be dissuaded, even though he sensed that great danger awaited him.

That morning, as together we read *Daily Light*, the verses selected[3] told of the assurances of God's presence, and John's spirit just soared in triumph and worship as he echoed David's trusting words, "though I walk through the valley of the shadow of death, I will fear no evil; for thou art with me."[4]

So we went our separate ways that morning with deep emotion, never to see each other again in this life. After the war we heard that John was executed some weeks after he surrendered at Tarakan and was buried in a shallow grave. They found his fountain pen, engraved with his initials — a gift from his fiancee — on his body. He had joined the select company of triumphant martyrs.

At each stopping place on our way down to surrender we had a final service with the people and interviewed those who wished to be baptized. Altogether we baptized several hundred people amid scenes of great rejoicing as well as tears of love and farewell.

On leaving Long Luping we met with two more messengers from the Japanese urging us not to delay; and, indeed, having made our decision to surrender, we hurried to keep to our schedule. After leaving Long Luping we stopped at Metallan, Merarap, Brayong and Tengoa, and then crossed over the Sepakoi pass.

---

3. Psalm 42:11; 116:1-4
4. Psalm 23:4

Winsome suffered a cut on her foot and the next day we had to walk through heavy rain. By that evening the wound was infected, but we had to go on, so some of the Murut carriers and I took turns carrying Winsome "piggyback" up the steepest hills on the path.

When we arrived at Tang Lapadan on the Trusan River in the late afternoon of October 10th, a boat was waiting for us with the message that we were expected to surrender at Sundar near the coast the very next day, October 11th — otherwise the Japanese would send soldiers to search for and arrest us. So we embarked in canoes and raced down the rapids in the rain and the gathering darkness to arrive at Kelasi's longhouse, where hundreds of our Murut friends met us with mingled joy and sorrow. Frank Davidson, Brian Morcombe and some rubber planters — Mr. and Mrs. Colina and their daughter, and Mr. McLaren — had arrived there ahead of us.

Next day, the nine of us were met at the town of Trusan by the *Ranger*, an old Shell launch now flying a faded Japanese flag, which carried us the last leg of the journey to Sundar where we formally surrendered to a contingent of two Japanese soldiers and an interpreter.

The soldiers immediately lined us up and warned us not to attempt to escape. We thought this rather needless as we had just travelled nine days voluntarily to turn ourselves in. Their attitude at first seemed designed to put a little "fear of the Japanese" into us, but we were not mistreated, and after their initial bluster, things settled down. In actual fact, I believe they were more than a little relieved. Now they would not have to face antagonized headhunters in the upper Trusan — at least not on our account.

The day we arrived at Sundar happened to be the Muslim holiday, *Hari Raya Puasa*, and the Malays there kindly gave us a meal of curry and rice. Next day we were put on board a launch and taken across the bay to Brunei town where we were placed under house arrest in vacated government bungalows. These places had been thoroughly ransacked, but were large and airy and had good water, electric light and sanitation. We were allowed to buy our own food from the town each day, and this, together with the food we had brought with us from upcountry, enabled us to live fairly well.

Several armed sentries paced around outside the houses, and a humorous test of nerves occurred the same evening that we arrived. It was already dark by the time Winsome went to have a shower in the semi-detached bathroom next to the room that was allotted to us. While she was showering, she heard the ponderous step of the Japanese sentry, and then saw a bayonet on the end of a rifle. The Japanese soldier appeared to be coming into the bathroom!

Winsome immediately called out to me, "Hudson, Hudson, he's coming in!"

The soldier backed out and came around the house to where I was. "Sorry! Not know! Beg pardon!" he stammered.

The sentries had evidently been ordered to treat us well. And all through our time in Brunei under house arrest we certainly were treated quite well, although we were often questioned by the *Kempeitai*, the notorious military police.

On one occasion they asked, "Why did you come down to surrender?"

Miss Colina replied quite naturally, "Because we believed what you said in your letter — that we had nothing to fear!" That appealed to their sense of honour and seemed to please them immensely!

One of the *Kempeitai* officers was a short burly man with a heavy dark beard. Based on his appearance, Winsome referred to him as "the Teddy Bear." From my observations of the man, however, I felt quite certain that his disposition did not match that nickname.

One day this particular officer called us in for questioning. We were standing, lined up against a wall. The officer was sitting at a table, tilting forward on his chair. Suddenly the chair slipped backwards on the polished floor and he skidded feet first under the table!

The atmosphere was electric, but we managed to keep our composure. "Very sorry, Sir. Floor very slippery," someone offered.

Incredibly, a few minutes later the same thing happened again! Thankfully, there were no snorts of nervous laughter from our side of the table, particularly from Winsome whose sense of humour usually preempted her respect for protocol. I shuddered to think what angry forces might have been unleashed at such a loss of dignity!

While we were under house arrest in Brunei, both Winsome and I showed symptoms of amoebic dysentery and were admitted to the Brunei hospital. Dr. Graham, a Canadian who had been the Medical Officer in Brunei and was now also under house arrest, was allowed to attend to us. We received the appropriate medical treatment, both by mouth and by abdominal washouts, and were completely cured.

How different the outcome might have been had we stayed in a jungle hideout! Amoebic dysentery is very difficult to cure completely, but we had excellent medication, and we never contracted it again. This was indeed another example of God's merciful care for us.

One other thing happened while we were under house arrest which I felt was profoundly significant. It involved a Japanese official translator named Takatomi. One day he came over to me and asked bluntly, "Have you got a Bible?"

"Yes sir," I replied.

"Give it to me," he demanded.

"My Bible is of great value to me," I responded. "I use it every day."

"Give it to me," he repeated impatiently, and so I did.

A week later he came back, and with the Bible open he said, "That is the best verse in the Bible." As I looked, I saw that he was pointing to Luke 23:34: "Father, forgive them; for they know not what they do."

Chapter 10

At the moment war broke out in the Pacific, Rajah Vyner Brooke was in Australia. Just before Singapore fell in mid-February 1942, he flew to Jakarta hoping there was some way he would be able to organize resistance against the Japanese.

> He asked to be flown into Borneo, but the Dutch were already preparing to abandon the large area of southern Borneo they once controlled. They said Vyner was too old to be a guerrilla leader, they had no planes to spare, and nothing was to be gained by an attempt to raise the Dayaks against the Japanese. Vyner argued, but in vain. He did not return to Australia until the whole Archipelago was about to fall into enemy hands.
>
> He flew to Melbourne, staying there for the next months, organizing a provisional government which was as powerless and ineffective as most of the provisional governments of that time . . . Towards the end of the year he sailed for England.
>
> All through the war years he was haunted by the helplessness of his country. He blamed the British for not putting up a token defence in Sarawak; he blamed himself for not being able to return to Sarawak and to die there. Nearly all his friends were in Sarawak, and he assumed they were all dead.[1]

In actual fact, nearly all of the Rajah's senior staff were still alive. Most had been placed in confinement at Batu Lintang, nearby Kuching, where the Japanese had established their headquarters in Borneo. Batu Lintang was the site that the Rajah himself had provided for his small army contingent and, in early 1942, the Japanese commandeered this facility to detain local Sarawak internees. Then, after Malaya and Singapore were overrun, about 2,000 captured British soldiers were shipped in. In the months that

---

1. Robert Payne, *The White Rajahs of Sarawak* (Singapore: Oxford University Press, 1991), 175.

followed, more civilian internees, including many European women, were brought in from both Sarawak and British North Borneo.

Winsome, Dood Anderson and I, along with Frank Davidson's party, had been among the last of the foreigners to surrender. After about eight weeks under house arrest in Brunei, the Japanese made arrangements to transfer us to Batu Lintang also. The relatively mild transition we had experienced under house arrest was over.

For the first leg of the journey, we were loaded onto the back of a small flat-bed truck along with our possessions. There was no cover and, shortly after we set off, low grey clouds blew in from the sea. Soon the rain came, not heavy, but relentless, as we bumped along over the rough dirt track, doing our best to keep from falling off.

Life was to grow increasingly grim, bringing into sharper focus mankind's capacity for cruelty — and also for kindness. Sometimes kindness came from unexpected quarters. On the day we were scheduled to leave Brunei, Winsome was still in hospital recovering from her bout with amoebic dysentery. She was quite weak and I was more than a little concerned about how she would handle the trip. Before we set off however, the Malay driver came, most certainly under someone's instructions, and gently guided her around to the cab of the truck. A third person was already inside. It was Takatomi, the Japanese interpreter who had borrowed my Bible.

At the town of Kuala Belait, we stopped at the Japanese army barracks. The "Teddy Bear" *Kempeitai* officer was already there, and to our surprise he gave us rice and boiled eggs and coffee! He also called me into his office and questioned me as to how we were able to live so long with the Muruts in the interior.

"How did you make them do what you wanted?" he asked. "Did you beat them?"

"We just treated them kindly," I responded. "We taught them about God, and helped them, and they also helped us."

He found this very hard to understand — an indication, perhaps, as to why the Japanese were never able to establish a real foothold among the native peoples.

On arriving at Miri we saw the crumpled, burnt-out oil facilities that had been destroyed by the British before they evacuated.

"Englishman no gentleman," one of our Japanese officers snapped. "Oil field not left in good order!"

At Miri we were put on board a small coastal steamer, where the only place to sit or lie down was the top of the hatch covering the cargo hold. That meant the nine of us, four women and five men, along with two Sikh guards, sharing an area of about eight feet by ten feet. We spent two nights on the open sea, miserable nights with the wind pushing a choppy swell, driving the rain and blowing the spray over us. On the second night the Malay captain took pity on those who were seasick and gave up his cabin.

What a relief it was to finally enter the relative calm of the Sarawak River and berth at the wharf in Kuching. After coming ashore, however, we were left standing on the wharf for hours, during which a heavy storm broke. Finally a truck came to take us and our belongings, which had also been sitting in the rain, to our places of internment.

We went first to an old convent building in Kuching, already crowded with Catholic nuns, where the four women were to be temporarily placed. As I kissed Winsome goodbye, the assembled nuns uttered a gasp of pity at our separation. They had no way of knowing the added poignancy of the moment. The date was December 16th — it was Winsome's birthday.

The Batu Lintang internment camp was about two-and-a-half miles from town, along a lonely road through a low swampy area. I shall never forget that first introduction: the guard room beside the gate; sentries with fixed bayonets at the entrance; another sentry at a central point; and guards pacing around the perimeter. Through the barbed wire I could see hundreds of men with sun-darkened bodies, most of them clad only in shorts. Barbed wire fences were everywhere, not only around the perimeter, but also dividing the camp into separate compounds.

On top of a broad hill with a commanding view was the Japanese administrative block and barracks. Then came the British officers' section which held about 120 men, the Australian officers' section with about 160 men, and a smaller section with a few Dutch officers.

The Japanese section and the officers' compounds were grouped around a central parade ground which was meant to serve as the hub of prison camp life. Here speeches, celebrations of victories and holidays, and also certain punishments, took place.

Dirt roads ran from the parade square to the other compounds in the camp. A garden space separated the officers from the civilian men's camp, which held about 250. Next to us was the large section of ordinary troops and NCOs, mostly British Tommies. Then came another garden block, followed by two sections with about 110 Catholic priests and 60 Indonesian soldiers. Finally, opposite these, was the section for women and children. When the group of women, which included Winsome, was finally transferred from the convent in Kuching, the numbers at Batu Lintang increased to about 160 nuns, 80 civilian women and 34 children.

Once we reached Batu Lintang, Frank Davidson, Brian Morcombe and I, along with Mr. McLaren and Mr. Colina, were taken to separate barracks in the civilian camp and each assigned a space. Most of the men had fixed up wooden beds for themselves, and after a few days I was able to scrounge some boards and do the same. The beds were no softer than the floor, but at least they afforded us some space underneath to store our belongings. Like everyone else, the area I was allocated measured just four-and-a-half feet by seven feet. And so commenced my life in internment.

A day or two after entering the camp, we were all called to be interviewed and questioned by the Japanese commandant, Major Tatsuji Suga. He was not a tall man but was powerfully built; his silver-grey hair was cut short, and he walked with a dignified bearing. He grilled us minutely as to our life, occupation and activities. When he heard that four of us were missionaries, he asked about our Mission and our beliefs.

"I know about Christians," he told us. "I studied in America."

From his reaction, it was apparent that he viewed us favorably, and once again we were amazed at the way God had undertaken for us. Everything seemed to confirm that our decision to surrender had been the right one. By contrast, many who tried to take charge of their own destiny met with disaster:

Early in 1942 a forester stationed on the Rejang River was making plans to escape into Dutch territory when he heard that some women and children from Kapit were also hoping to escape in the same way. He left his forest and came to Kapit, and began the desperate task of shepherding a crowd of fifty women and children in river boats up to the Dutch frontier, over treacherous rapids, and across the high mountains of Central Borneo. By a miracle the refugees reached the Dutch military post of Long Nawang . . .

Within days the Japanese learned that the refugees were in Long Nawang. They sent a small raiding party, captured the fort, lined up the women and told the children to climb into the trees. They machine-gunned the women and amused themselves by picking off the children one by one . . . The story of the children falling from the trees somehow symbolized the defenselessness of Sarawak. It haunts the imagination . . .[2]

Major Suga – Hiroshima, Japan

2. Ibid., 174, 175.

Although Major Suga (later Lt. Col. Suga) apparently did not condone the unconscionable torture that took place in some of the other concentration camps in Asia, Batu Lintang was governed by the harsh code upon which Japanese military discipline traditionally rested. In addition, cultural disciplinary practices were rigorously enforced within the Japanese army itself.

Bowing as a "salute" was a typical example: a stiff-backed bow of fifteen degrees, followed by a pause of three seconds before standing erect again. Any breach of discipline invoked an admonition in rapid Japanese, usually followed by a heavy slap on the face. Such discipline extended right down the order of ranks. A lieutenant could lecture a sergeant, and emphasize it with a slap. A sergeant could lecture and slap a corporal, a corporal could slap a private, and so on. And the one slapped was expected to say "thank you" for the discipline he received. Such practices were regarded as normal and proper.

As internees under the Japanese military, we also were subjected to their system of discipline. The Japanese guards usually did not exceed the practices accepted within the military hierarchy, but there was one sadistic exception; he would purposefully roam around until he found someone doing something he did not like, and then would brutalize that person.

The other guards we particularly dreaded were certain of the non-Japanese conscripts. Not content with slapping a prisoner heavily on the face, these guards would sometimes close their fists before impact, knock the person down, and then proceed to kick him viciously with their heavy army boots. This more violent treatment was normally reserved for the POW soldiers, but occasionally civilians also were treated very roughly.

Apart from being brutal, some of the less disciplined guards were extremely unpredictable, flying into a rage at the slightest indiscretion. All of this kept us on edge, creating an atmosphere of tension throughout the camp.

When I first arrived, I was assigned a place between two Dutch men. I could not speak Dutch but I was interested to learn, particularly because of our involvement with the Muruts living on both sides of the international border. I began immediately to study the Dutch language and was able to build up a reasonable vocabulary.

Within a few weeks, an Englishman in our barracks died and I was moved into his place at the English-speaking end of the building. My new neighbor on one side was Reginald Rutter who, at the time of the Japanese invasion, was the senior Resident in the civil service of North Borneo. On the other side was a young rubber planter. Near the end of my bed was another prominent officer of the civil service named Harry Keith. Irrespective of our background or station in life, however, internment was a great leveller. We all received the same limited rations — and the same humiliations.

Many of the local civilian men in Kuching had been arrested by night and thus had only a few personal effects with them. Others, like those from North Borneo, had been able to bring several suitcases of clothing and personal possessions. Winsome and I had very little with us, so we had to improvise.

When I first entered the camp, for instance, I had only one packet of five stainless steel razor blades, but I kept them sharp by rubbing them on the inside of a glass jar. This technique was well known to many during the years of the Great Depression and I used it to good advantage. With regular sharpening, one Gillette blade kept me clean-shaven for an entire year!

As prisoners, each of us reacted in our own way to being deprived of our individual freedoms. Mr. Rutter was not at all happy about his confinement and he tended to keep to himself. He had a short temper and a sharp tongue, but I generally got on quite well with him. One day, however, with the tension of camp life building up on everyone, a disagreement developed. He snapped at me in a caustic manner, I retaliated, and the battle was on. He stayed in his assigned space, and I in mine, but we really had it out verbally.

A certain decorum is expected from those who consider themselves gentlemen and, undoubtedly, some recognition of that was weighing on both our minds. Also, I think we both realized we had pushed things to the absolute limit. In any event, our disagreement ended. Abruptly. We did not utter another word to one another for about three months. Although our bunks were only a couple of feet apart, we each went on about our lives as though the other person did not exist.

Then one day an incident occurred which required some communication between us. I addressed Mr. Rutter in a completely natural way, and he responded similarly. From that point we resumed normal communications as though nothing had ever happened. Not a textbook method of resolving conflict, and not one of my prouder moments, but we each managed to preserve some element of dignity. Given our circumstances, perhaps we did not do too badly.

Everything we did, day or night, was tightly controlled by our guards, who were suspicious of anything that seemed to be an unusual activity which might lead to an attempt to escape. During our first year, for example, they refused to allow more than ten persons to gather together for lectures or educational courses. This restriction was relaxed for regular Sunday church services or for an occasional concert, but otherwise was rigidly enforced.

Their restrictions were not totally effective, however. Among the British soldiers were a number of signals corps engineers, and by amazing ingenuity they improvised a wireless set capable of receiving BBC radio broadcasts.

Interestingly enough, one of the key elements was a hearing aid. Among the people brought in from North Borneo was a civilian who was nearly completely deaf and required a special hearing device. The electronic equipment used to amplify sound for him included a thermionic valve which he carried in a hand-held box. This equipment found its way into the hands of the British soldiers who then built a miniature generator and other ancillary parts from materials salvaged or stolen by men on work parties.

To power the generator, the soldiers fashioned a flywheel from a round tabletop cleverly set on a pivot so that it could rotate. By spinning the tabletop on its pivot, they generated enough electric current to run the sound amplification equipment and could clearly receive radio signals in Morse code from the BBC broadcasts.

A careful guard was set so that those operating the radio were given warning of approaching prison guards. When not in use, the equipment was hidden in various places, one of which was the false bottom of a soldier's mess tin.

Although communication between the camps was forbidden, the soldiers were able to relate news bulletins through the barbed wire to a trusted member of the Sarawak Civil Service who had a phenomenal memory. He would then come to the various barracks in our camp, sit on one of the beds, and casually tell us the British version of the latest war news. We all listened eagerly. For almost the entire period of our internment we received regular BBC news updates. We learned later that the Japanese suspected that war news was being received from some source, but they never discovered our secret.

The radio was a great morale booster for all of us — a symbol of our soldiers' indomitability and resourcefulness. It was also a symbol of their courage, for if discovered, those involved almost certainly would have been executed.

Food rations were poor but edible the first year. In the civilian camp we started the day with *bubor*, or rice gruel. At midday and evening we each had a mugful of cooked rice and two or three marble-sized morsels of salt fish or pork once a day. As civilians, we were able to supplement our rations with what we were allowed to grow in our own vegetable gardens. The land was rather poor, and by experience we found that the only way to get any productivity was by using nightsoil from the pit latrines as a fertilizer. We grew tapioca, sweet potatoes, beans, spinach and papayas. These gardens undoubtedly saved many lives, especially as the war raged, years passed and rations dwindled.

Life was much harder over in the soldiers' camp. One twist of Japanese military culture was that soldiers or officers who surrendered thereby forfeited respect as human beings. Thus, the soldiers were forced to do hard manual labour for long hours, had poor food and were regarded as expendable.

The soldiers were in a section of the camp just next to ours separated only by strands of barbed wire about six inches apart; we watched helplessly as month by month their bodies became more emaciated from hard work on insufficient rations. Yet their discipline and morale remained high. Every night at nine o'clock a bugler sounded the Last Post, while everyone stood to attention. As we listened, the words set to that magnificent bugle call echoed through our hearts and minds:

> Day is done, gone the sun,
> From the sky, from the hills, from the West.
> All is well, safely rest, God is nigh.

As the months passed, death came with increasing frequency. The cemetery was within the camp perimeter, and the Last Post was sounded over each soldier's burial. It was a most moving experience, and a tribute to our soldiers' strength of character.

Many stories of heroism and of tragedy are told of the war in Asia and some of those involved touched our lives personally. One such was the Rajah's Chief Secretary, C.D. Le Gros Clark, who chose to stay in Sarawak though he easily could have escaped when the Japanese first invaded. Mr. Le Gros Clark was assigned to the same barrack as I was. He was a particularly fine gentleman. In the early days of his internment he wrote:

> For long I have been appalled at the calamity gradually approaching this innocent people of Sarawak. By the inexorable march of circumstances, forced on a people who had little or no say in their development, war has come to Sarawak with all its sufferings and hideous results.
>
> With these people of Sarawak, among whom I have spent many years of my life, I have determined to remain and to share with them their sufferings during this period of trial.
>
> I do not regret this decision. I am proud to share with my companions in captivity this honour of hardship during a war which affects the lives of millions throughout the world.
>
> I could not have it otherwise.[3]

C.D. Le Gros Clark was accused by the Japanese of being involved in a plot to escape and was executed during the last months of the war.

---

3. Ibid., 174.

After being separated from Winsome in Kuching, I did not see her again for some months. When she was eventually transferred from the convent to the women's camp at Batu Lintang we were allowed, for the rest of that year, to visit for an hour or so once every two or three weeks, under the watchful eyes of the guards. These visits were usually timed to coincide with some notable occasion, such as a Japanese military victory or the Emperor's birthday.

Life in the women's camp was difficult, to be sure, but the discipline was less severe than in the other sections. As a general rule, the women internees were not slapped for failing to bow appropriately, for example. The guards were under orders not to brutalize or molest the women and these orders were generally followed.

Like Winsome, Mary Bewsher was confined in the women's camp. She and the twins bunked next to a woman named Agnes Keith and her young son who was not yet three years old when they entered the camp. Agnes was my neighbor Harry Keith's wife and she attracted considerable scrutiny from the Japanese. She was an American, she was outspoken, and she was a very talented writer.

The other members of our Mission were scattered around various parts of the camp. Alan Belcher was asked to become one of the cooks, and worked in the kitchen. Trevor White developed the art of cutting hair and became the camp barber. Frank Davidson and Brian Morcombe lived in one of the barracks not far from mine and I usually tried to meet them at meal times when we lined up for our rations. Roland Bewsher was assigned to duty in the camp hospital. He lived near the hospital complex in a separate section of the camp, so we saw little of him.

One day, in late 1943, I received a note from Roland that had been passed through the wire. It was written on the only paper he had available, the back of a cigarette package, and constituted his letter of resignation from the Mission. In it he advised me that he could no longer accept the tenets of the Christian faith.

Receiving this letter was a tremendous disappointment for me. I felt sick inside. Roland was a good worker in the Mission and our workers were few. But more to the point, he was a good friend, and I was sure that he was making the biggest mistake he could possibly make.

Although we were controlled by our captors in a treadmill of daily routines, we also had a great deal of time to think. I thought deeply about many things. I thought a lot about the basis for my faith. And I thought about what it meant to really trust when everything seemed to be falling apart.

Frank Davidson's health was not good, and during 1944, as food became more scarce and we received almost no protein at all, his condition gradually deteriorated. The cooks tried their best to prepare food for him that was both nourishing and digestible, but their supplies were extremely limited. On one occasion, by a miraculous contact with people outside the perimeter fence, we were able to obtain a large quantity of fresh eggs for him and, in an effort to get maximum nutritional value, Frank forced himself to swallow each one raw.

I became acquainted with the Japanese medical officer, Dr. Yamamoto, and I asked him to examine Frank. He palpated Frank's abdomen, then in a loud voice solemnly pronounced his verdict.

"Liver," he exclaimed, "liver," heavily accentuating the last syllable each time. One of the internees, also a doctor, had recommended a certain drug for Frank's greatly enlarged liver, and I asked Dr. Yamamoto if he could procure this for us. He was able to do so, and it was given to Frank by injection, but it was already too late.

Frank's abdomen became more and more swollen, but he preferred to stay in his bed in the barracks rather than go to the camp hospital. Conditions there were no better, and in the barracks he had our companionship. He read his Bible constantly and managed to read it through twice in the latter months of 1944 and early 1945.

On April 27th we realized the end was near, and that night I went to watch with Brian, who had nursed Frank carefully and faithfully during those last weeks. It was pitch dark, with no moon nor any artificial light.

About nine o'clock Frank whispered hoarsely, "I'm thirsty." So I felt about for a bottle of water and a glass, and put it in his hands.

"From an old friend," he said gratefully.

A little while later he said, "I'm going." They were the last words he spoke before going into presence of the Lord he loved.

Next day, Frank's fellow missionaries were permitted to accompany his body to the cemetery. There we solemnly and sorrowfully read the comforting words of John 14 and 1 Corinthians 15 as we laid his body to rest.

After the war, Frank's body was reinterred in the Anglican cemetery in Kuching, where today a wooden cross bears the words "With Christ which is far better." Frank Davidson's name — and that of his wife Enid, who still survives him — lives on with the descendants of those among whom they sowed the seed of the gospel so many years ago.

CHAPTER 11

Tatsuji Suga was born in Hiroshima, Japan, on September 22, 1885, the second son of a Buddhist-Shinto family. His older brother converted to Christianity, became a protestant missionary, had a church and founded the YMCA in Hiroshima. This older brother had a profound influence on the young Tatsuji who, as a teenager, even played the organ in his brother's church.

His mother was an outspoken, articulate and educated woman who instilled in Tatsuji-san a sense of the value of women as well as a feeling of loving-kindness, even chivalry, toward them.

In 1907, Tatsuji-san graduated from the military academy in Tokyo as a Second Lieutenant and was posted to his home province. His parents promptly arranged for him to marry a beautiful woman named Tern, who bore him two sons and four daughters. Together they cherished and educated all six equally. In a day and age when only five percent of Japanese went beyond the fifth or sixth grade, the Sugas saw to it that all six of their children, both sons and daughters, went to college.

Suga was an affectionate and demonstrative father who cuddled his children when they were young, and carried them on his shoulders. He was also a firm disciplinarian who let no one put anything over on him, but never held grudges against his children or turned them away from himself.

He loved *kendo*, the Japanese art of fencing with wooden swords, and was an expert horseman, who enjoyed riding often through the outskirts of Hiroshima. He told his children that to subdue and tame any horse, he needed only to control the horse's mind with his own mind.

Suga's military duties took him to Siberia at the end of World War I, then to Korea, Manchuria and China. In 1924, he took early retirement as a Major and decided to do what he really loved — teach English. He sailed to America, leaving his pension behind for his family, intending to support himself abroad without depriving his dependents. Once in the United States, Suga took on such jobs as dishwashing and fishing while he studied to become certified as a teacher of English as a second language at the University of Washington in Seattle and the University of California in Sacramento.

Tatsuji Suga – Passport Photo 1924

He then taught English in Japan, Korea, China and Manchuria before being called back to active duty in the Sino-Japanese War in 1937. In October 1941, ill with diabetes, he once more retired from the military and returned home to his family.

Then came Pearl Harbor and the rapid Japanese advances throughout the Pacific, at which time military retirees were invited to volunteer for positions in the rear lines. Major Suga volunteered to be a prison camp commandant, believing that his language ability, experience and skills would prove useful. He also believed that he could run a good camp and still serve his country with loyalty.[1]

1. Resource material for the profile of Tatsuji Suga was obtained from Mrs. Khattiya Jalayanateja, a friend of the Suga family, and is based on her personal discussions and correspondence with surviving members of his family.

This proved difficult, however. Duty and conscience were often in conflict, and wartime military policy, coupled with the prevailing mood of hostility, fueled dangerous accusations against those who showed compassion to the enemy.

The rations of rice issued in the camp at Batu Lintang started to decline around the middle of 1944, and from then on we seldom received even a morsel of salt fish or meat. We heard grim stories of people catching rats and mice to eat. The Japanese officers told us the ration scale was set by Tokyo and that they merely carried out the orders they received.

To meet the need for foods and medicines, Col. Suga decided to enlist those in the civilian camp who had expertise in producing substitute foods or medicines and thus could help to alleviate the shortages. An official statement to that effect was published by one of the Japanese officers on July 20, 1944. Two days later, we in the civilian camp received the following notice from the Camp Master:

> The Japanese authorities have called upon us to submit the names of persons who have knowledge and experience of medicines and foodstuffs obtainable from plants and herbs to be found locally. They also require the services of persons with laboratory experience who can utilize such local knowledge in the setting up and operation of stills, etc. An assurance has been given that persons who offer their assistance will work within the Camp boundaries, and for the benefit of the Internees and Prisoners of War. Any persons willing to offer their services should hand in their names to the Hut Master before 9 a.m. tomorrow (Sunday) July 23rd.

I volunteered immediately, along with about fourteen other civilian internees. It had been years since I had studied, trained and worked in the field of chemical science, then given it up to go into mission work. I had not anticipated re-entering my old profession, and certainly not in this way! However, through the Japanese military, I was now being presented with a wonderful opportunity to relieve the tedium of internment camp life and at the same time do something worthwhile. The fact that I loved this work was an added bonus!

The Japanese, with characteristic thoroughness, checked the qualifications and suitability of each volunteer. They assigned Dr. Yamamoto to this task.

Dr. Yamamoto was about thirty years of age. He was taller than the other Japanese officers and had sharp, angular features. His manner of speaking was formal and rather curt but not unpleasant, and his command of English was reasonably good. I described my education and practical training to him in some detail. While he seemed pleased with this, he informed me that he wanted to check my qualifications further.

Later that same week he took me into the town of Kuching to a pharmacy where there was a Japanese chemist. This man knew essentially no English and I knew only a few words of Japanese. We communicated well, however, in the international language of scientific symbols, formulas, and equations. There was much nodding and smiling and exclamations of what seemed to be approval in Japanese. By the time we left to return to Batu Lintang, I had passed Dr. Yamamoto's test and had established some valuable personal rapport with him in the process. As a result, I was appointed the chairman (in Japanese, the *hanchõ*) of our newly formed group, known simply as the "Science Party."

I drew up a proposed program of work and submitted it to the Japanese authorities. That suggested program has been lost, but one of my progress reports survived. Here are excerpts from it:

> On July 20, 1944, Lt. Col. Suga informed our Camp that a state of emergency had developed and that henceforth Kuching could not expect to receive further supplies of medicines and foodstuffs from outside. The Camp Commandant and Dr. Yamamoto therefore asked the civilian internees for volunteers from among those who had specialized knowledge, to form a party to meet the emergency. The plan suggested was that these volunteers could do this by devising and making substitute medicines from plants and other materials available locally . . .

> The Japanese authorities provided poles, palm leaf thatch and rattan for building materials, some oil drums and "compo" pipe, sheet metal, a flange and some water pipe, and in addition the members improvised tools and equipment from various other sources. The members constructed their own building, also made bricks, and built fireplaces for boiling and distilling. They made a distilling apparatus with fractionating column, and an oil press. [The members] also laid on a water supply, and have planted a garden of medicinal herbs . . .

Although we were never allowed to provide help on a scale large enough to relieve the great malnutrition in all the camps, the Science Party was able to produce some much-needed medical substitutes and food supplements for the sick in the hospital and for the children in the women's camp. Some of these products are described as follows:

> *Derris root extract,* a lotion which we supplied to the hospital for skin infections.
>
> *Red palm oil,* extracted from palm fruit growing locally. It was rich in Vitamin A and was a valuable tonic for tubercular patients, for the women and children, and for cases of malnutrition.
>
> *Palm nut kernels,* which we cracked and pounded by hand and distributed to the women and children.
>
> *Shark liver oil,* a concentrated source of Vitamin A. The liver from one large shark was enough to supply the needs of all the camps for a fortnight.
>
> *Calcium phosphate,* produced from calcined bones. After complete calcining, the bones were powdered finely and sifted through muslin and then distributed to the hospital and various camps as a tonic source of calcium and phosphates.
>
> *Alcohol spirit,* distilled from fermented potato peelings, sugar cane refuse and waste fruit skins.
>
> *Lemon grass oil,* produced from lemon grass grown in the vegetable gardens. The oil was extracted by distillation in steam.
>
> *Citronella oil,* obtained by similar means using citronella grass. This was used as a mosquito repellent.
>
> *Kaolin powder,* used for medicinal purposes and produced from fine clay by filtration, settling and heating.

> *Herbs and other medicinal plants* obtained from various sources and cultivated in a garden area near the Science Party's premises.

In making my report to the Japanese authorities, I made it as plain as I dared that greater co-operation by the Japanese, along with a larger supply of readily available raw materials, would enable us to produce much more cooking oil, sugar, salt and medical substitutes for imported drugs. The report ended on this note:

> We appreciate the interest that Lt. Col. Suga, Lt. Nagata and Dr. Yamamoto have shown in the needs of the camps in the present emergency, and we appreciate the facilities already given to us, but we feel that much greater use could be made of the experience and specialized knowledge of the members of the Science Party. We would respectfully point out that the members volunteered to meet a state of emergency in the hope that full use would be made of their knowledge and experience, and that raw materials that can be obtained locally would be made available to us. The production of foodstuffs such as nipa sugar and coconut oil was included in the suggestions originally made to us, neither of which we have so far been able to produce. Under the present conditions of further restrictions of rations which has recently been made, the increase in the supply of coconut or other oils is an urgent necessity.
>
> The members of the Science Party are prepared to cooperate with the Japanese authorities to help alleviate the present serious shortage of oils and protein in the camp diet, which in our opinion largely contributes to increasing ill health and more frequent deaths . . . We appreciate the interest of the Authorities so far taken in the welfare of the Camps, but we feel that a much greater degree of cooperation to supply urgent needs can yet be attained.
>
> C. H. Southwell
> Leader of Science Party
> January 1, 1945

In order to produce the substitute medicines and food supplements, we had to make most of our own tools and equipment. The first thing we built was a simple forge patterned after one I had seen in the interior of Borneo. The bellows for the forge consisted of a long wooden box with a square cross-section, and a square wooden piston lined with feathers glued to the edges with rubber latex. At each end of the long box we attached little valves made of sheet metal which flapped open and shut. As we pumped the piston in and out it delivered a blast of air to a charcoal fire.

The Japanese provided us with lengths of spring steel from an old motor car which we were able to heat, to red-heat, in the forge and then hammer on an anvil made of angle iron nailed to a block of wood. With this native-style forge, we were able to make cold chisels for metal work, carpentry chisels, plane irons, simple auger drill bits and various kinds of knives for working on oil palms. The Japanese kept a watchful eye on us but they seemed to enjoy seeing our improvisation.

From a personal standpoint, the Science Party provided a stimulating escape from the daily grind of life behind barbed wire, along with some side benefits. For instance, in our workshop we were able to cook up extra tapioca for our lunch. And before calcining bones, we always reboiled them — in that way getting extra soup for ourselves.

In addition, as chairman of the Science Party, I enjoyed a position of some privilege within the camp. Our workshop was located outside the fence of the civilian men's camp in an area near the camp hospital, a distance of about a hundred yards from our compound gate along a dirt pathway. Once the Science Party was established, I made this trip almost every day except Sundays, passing a sentry post near our gate.

My routine was always the same. I would stop in front of the sentry post, set down my basket of tools, bow to the guard, flip open the cover of my basket so he could see inside, bow again, and then continue on. From time to time the guard would come out of his sentry post to check the Japanese logbook in which I was required to keep a record of attendance for the Science Party.

Occasionally the POW soldiers would send a message to us, asking if we could produce things for them. Once some antiseptic was urgently needed, so I carefully packed a bottle of alcohol spirit inside my canvas army bag and tucked it in the side of my rattan tool basket, using the flap of the army bag to cover my tools as usual. It was a calculated risk, but I had done it before without incident.

This time, however, when I stopped in front of the sentry post, the guard unexpectedly launched into a tirade. He was one of the conscript guards, a huge fellow. His outburst was in rapid-fire Japanese, quite unintelligible to me, but I set my basket down as usual and gave him a particularly correct bow.

When he finally ended this harangue, I reached down and pulled back the canvas cover, exposing my tools. Suddenly he came down from his post and began rummaging through my tools and fumbling with the canvas bag — a little disconcerting, to say the least. Amazingly, the only thing he uncovered was my Japanese logbook. He flipped through it and, finding it up to date, shoved it back to me. Then, growling to himself, he stomped back to his post.

During my entire time in the prison camp I was never beaten up or even slapped by the guards — one of a relatively few in the civilian men's camp who was not. However, if the bottle of antiseptic had been discovered that day, I might not be here to tell about it!

Trading between separate sections of the camp was rigidly forbidden. Anyone caught trading through the barbed wire was beaten and sentenced to serve time in the guardhouse, where he was beaten again and fed on rice and water. Despite this terrorism, venturesome people did a brisk business in contraband. Profits were good but the risks were great.

As food rations diminished, contraband buying and selling increased. Work parties outside the camp were often able to make contact with the local Chinese or Malays, but the punishments inflicted for these breaches were so brutal that direct trading essentially ended and, instead, the guards themselves became the intermediaries. Internees who had extra clothing or jewellery sold these items to obtain additional food. Eggs, shrimp paste, coconut oil and dried shark meat were the main contraband foodstuffs, but the prices were fantastically high.

One day the guards caught my neighbor Harry Keith communicating with soldiers through the barbed wire. He was immediately accused of involvement in clandestine activities, was treated very roughly, and then locked up in the guardhouse. His cell was a wooden cage measuring about four feet in each direction, directly exposed to the hot tropical sun by day and to the damp and the mosquitos by night. The guards told him to squat in this confined space and think about his crimes. They left him there for over three weeks.

When they released him, Harry was really shaken.

"Hudson," he said to me during one of the darkest periods of our internment, "we'll never get out of here."

Life behind barbed wire had a way of teaching us when to listen and when to offer a response. We learned to choose our words carefully and to say what we meant. On this occasion, I knew I had something meaningful to say.

"I believe we will, Harry," I told him. "The very day we left Australia, God gave my wife and me the assurance that he would bring us back. And I believe that God will keep his promise."

Chapter 12

By early 1945, conditions were becoming increasingly harsh in all the camps, and we were down to starvation rations. Rice was now so scarce that each morning our "breakfast" was a mugful of sickly gruel made of sago. It looked and tasted like wallpaper paste, and even though we were so hungry, we could hardly get it down. The fish we were given was often crawling with maggots, but we realized we must have proteins, so we would wash it and deep-fry it in oil until every microbe that might have been left was certainly killed.

In the soldiers' camp next to us, the situation was desperate. Every morning at six, POW work parties were marched out to do hard manual labor on the airfield and the railway. The food they were given was pitiful, and during the final months of the war the soldiers were dying at a rate of ten to fourteen every day.

Rumors were rife, and the atmosphere became more and more tense. Japanese military victories were increasingly infrequent, and those of us who were married were allowed to talk with our wives only about once every two months.

The first American planes flew over on March 25th — the fourth anniversary of the day Winsome and I had left Australia to return to Borneo. Our reading from *Daily Light* that morning was the promise we still claimed, "I will bring you back to this land."[1] To see those two planes making reconnaissance passes high overhead that very day seemed like a message of encouragement sent directly from God.

Then came the air raids on Kuching. We could see the bombs dropping on the waterfront. American Liberators bombed the airfield repeatedly and the soldiers from our camp were marched out afterwards to fill in the craters.

We were forced to dig slit trenches and, when the air raid signal sounded, we were herded out into the trenches while guards stood over us with fixed bayonets and hand grenades. The Japanese were

---

1. Genesis 28:15

determined that we would not be set free by commandos dropping from parachutes as had happened in Manila.

Meanwhile, as we would learn later, the Allies were secretly establishing a foothold deep in the interior of Borneo. On March 25th, a Liberator flew over central Borneo carrying four commando paratroopers. As the plane reached the mountains, it flew into nearly complete cloud cover. Although they could not see any landmark, those four commandos bravely dropped through the dark morning clouds. As related by their officer-in-charge, Major Tom Harrisson, they soon found that they had parachuted into the Kelabit highlands:

> This was the third dropping sortie, the thirty-second hour of flying over Japanese-held territory, in my final effort to get in. If it was ever to be done, this must surely be it. For worse or for better, after two circling searches, four bodies shot through the Liberator's camera hatch in quick succession and joined their gently falling parachutes to the general pattern of downy blobs drifting with softness over the Plain of Bah.
>
> In a few minutes these had fallen through the cloud and materialized upon the Kelabit earth, as the bodies of three Australians and an Englishman. I was the Englishman, with the doubtful privilege of being the first white man to touch down and thus to return after the years of Japanese occupation.[2]

The commandos quickly came in contact with the Kelabit people and were taken to the longhouse at Bario. Before the day was out, Headman Lawai Bisarai had pledged that he and his people would support this "Z" Special Unit, as it was called.

The Kelabits were astounded to see these paratroopers drop from the sky. They must have seemed like men from outer space, for the Kelabits lived in one of the most isolated areas of the entire great island of Borneo. During the whole of the war, the Japanese never

---

2. Tom Harrisson, *World Within* (Singapore: Oxford University Press, 1990), 137, 138.

penetrated the Kelabit highlands. When Frank Davidson and I visited this area in 1939, perhaps only two or three Europeans had ever been there, and none of these had known anything of the Kelabit or Murut languages.

Tom Harrisson – Photo taken in an airplane, 1944

Following those first commandos, many others parachuted into other parts of Sarawak and North Borneo, where they enlisted the local people into irregular but effective fighting forces. Everywhere they landed, the Allied commandos were welcomed by the people of Borneo, including those Muruts of the upper Trusan among whom we had lived so happily in 1942.

Our loyal friends at Rumah Marong gave the commandos the letters we had left with them, and those letters were flown out to Australia while we were still in the grim circumstances of the internment camp. Included in this package was the last letter I had written with the directive that it was to be sent to Australia "if they know for certain of our death or unaccountable disappearance." This letter was reprinted in mid-1945 in *New Life,* a Christian newspaper published in Melbourne. Understandably it created quite a stir among our families and friends in Australia.

Although the Japanese soon learned of the presence of the "Z" Special paratroopers and the cooperation of the people of Sarawak and North Borneo, they did not know how many commandos were involved. They apparently thought "Z" Special was a considerable military force, rather than what was primarily intended to be an intelligence operation. Because this mission was secret, no mention of it was made by the BBC news bulletins which were being received by the POW signals corp in our camp. Hence we knew nothing of its activities.

The next big development was in June 1945, when the Australian army invaded and captured the island of Labuan. From a base established on Labuan, they bombed and captured Brunei and Limbang, and then began their advance along the coast of Sarawak.

While we knew nothing of these recent advances, we did notice the Japanese guards becoming increasingly nervous, and Dr. Yamamoto actually told me that they expected the Australian army to attack Kuching on June 27th, which greatly surprised me.

By late July and early August, the BBC news became so sensitive that the men operating the secret Morse code receiver felt any indiscretions in relaying the news to sections other than the military POWs might precipitate a crisis reaction. At that point, the signals corps stopped relaying the BBC bulletins to us, but it was obvious to us from the new vigor among the soldiers and their hardly suppressed elation that momentous events were indeed taking place. By early August, rumors of peace became more frequent, and the POW soldiers began removing boards from their barracks to make fires to cook their advanced rations!

On August 15th, our expectations were realized. That morning, the married men were allowed outside the civilian section of the camp to meet their wives for about half-an-hour. Then, later in the day, we were assembled in the big central parade ground, where Colonel Suga announced that Japan had accepted the Potsdam Declaration which involved an unconditional surrender.

Colonel Suga then told us, with great emotion, that the Americans had used an "atom bomb" that had killed hundreds of thousands of people in Nagasaki and Hiroshima.

"It is peace for you," he said, "but I have lost everything. I sent all my family to Hiroshima, and they are all dead."

It was indeed an emotional moment. His world had fallen apart. We knew he was dying inside, yet he was doing it courageously, showing amazing restraint and self-discipline.

We found out later that the Japanese surrender came just three days before the date on which their military authorities had planned to liquidate us all. Documents to that effect were found after the war. And although officially the war was now over, doubtless many of the Japanese soldiers would have willingly vented their anger on us, but for Colonel Suga's restraint. They had the weapons; we had none.

Realizing how delicately poised our situation was, we contained our sense of jubilation. We maintained our self-discipline, we continued to bow to sentries, and we kept up the camp routine.

Four days later, Sunday, August 19th, planes flew over our camp dropping thousands of leaflets announcing Japan's unconditional surrender and encouraging us with the assurance that help was on the way. Still we restrained our emotions. The Japanese guards were fully armed and in control, so we carried on as usual. We had learned by experience that the guards were unpredictable, and we tried to be careful not to provoke them. Despite that, one of the guards who was noted for his brutality, arrested an elderly civilian internee and beat him severely, apparently for picking up one of the leaflets.

But events were moving fast. Towards the end of August the light mosquito bombers made frequent passes over the camps, sometimes diving over the barracks and just skimming the roofs. On August 29th, they dropped newspapers and leaflets containing messages of cheer. And the next day they dropped parachutes loaded with bags of freshly baked bread, tins of butter, ham, milk, chocolate, biscuits — food which we had not seen for years!

The surprise and delight to hungry people receiving such delicious food can only be imagined. I saw it as a gift from God, and later that same day Winsome and I, in our separate camps, both opened our *Daily Light* booklets to the evening section for August 30th and read, "They said to each other, 'What is it?' For they did not know what it was."[3]

The timing could not have been more incredibly appropriate. I laughed out loud, oblivious of those around me. The verse for that very evening was about God's gift of manna falling from heaven!

Two days later we learned of another positive development, as recorded in the Batu Lintang camp official documents for August 31, 1945:

> The senior British Military Officer in the camp, Colonel Walsh, took the initiative, by the third week of August, of addressing a meeting of camp representatives. He informed them that in view of existing circumstances, and the difficulties that would arise if control of all camps by the Japanese authorities was removed before the arrival of the Relieving Forces, the three senior Military Officers had requested Col. Suga to continue his administration of these camps until the arrival of the Relieving Forces. Col. Suga had agreed to do so, and had expressed his intention to relax existing regulations as far as was consistent with the safety of all camps. They were satisfied that Col. Suga had their best interests at heart.
>
> Col. Suga accepted the advice of the three senior Military Officers, and would continue his administration as requested by them. After pointing out the dangerous situation still existing outside, owing to the presence of large bodies of Japanese troops who were still armed and in their positions both in Kuching and up-country, he said that he agreed that some measure of control was necessary for our safety. It was requested that freedom of movement be allowed between all camps forthwith. Col. Suga said that all Japanese guards were now removed to the perimeter fence.
>
> Colonel Walsh emphasized the point that existing Camp regulations must be followed, subject to any relaxations approved by Col. Suga from time to time, and stated that any

3. Exodus 16:15

person leaving the camp area without official permission would render himself liable to extreme danger and would be reported to the O.C. Relieving Forces.

These records illustrate the delicate situation in the camp, and also the foresight of Colonel Walsh and the senior Allied officers. They indicate, too, the admirable attitude of Colonel Suga, despite his own personal grief over his family and his country. Under God, I believe that his presence resulted in our survival.

On September 1st, Colonel Suga officially handed over the administration of all the camps to our senior officers. The transfer was amazingly smooth, and from that date the Japanese guards were stationed on the outer perimeter fence only, a symbol of authority protecting us from the Japanese troops — young, fanatical, unsurrendered, and 5,000 strong — who were still in Kuching and the surrounding area.

Although Colonel Suga had made his dramatic announcement on August 15th acknowledging Japanese defeat, the document of surrender was not signed in Tokyo until September 2nd, and relieving forces from the Australian army did not land at Kuching to accept surrender of the Batu Lintang camp until September 11th. During those four weeks of transition, the daily routine stayed much the same, though the atmosphere was more relaxed. In view of the tension that had pervaded the camp up until then, it is remarkable that few serious incidents took place.

The relieving force of Australian troops under Brigadier General Eastick came from Labuan to Kuching on an American destroyer commanded by Captain Jennings. This small force of about 500 men marched in a circuit around the streets of Kuching several times to create the impression that there was a large body of troops in the town, and then a small contingent marched into Batu Lintang.

About mid-afternoon on September 11th the message came. "Assemble in the parade ground. The troops have arrived."

Within seconds the barracks were deserted — everyone was on the road, surging toward the square. Behind us we could see the women and children pouring out of their gate, and the soldiers, many of them moving slowly and laboriously. I waited for Winsome, spotted her quickly, and we pressed on together.

Just then a staff car pulled up, and a big, heavily built officer got out. There was a spontaneous gasp of surprise at his size.

"Sir, we have not seen so much meat on bones for years!" someone said.

"Oh," he laughed. "Wait until you see General Wootten tomorrow."

Many of the POW Australian officers already knew the big man, and they pushed forward to greet him. They told us he was Brigadier General Eastick of the Ninth Australian Division. He had come to take the surrender of the camp.

This was the moment we had longed and prayed for. We were walking on air. It was as though we had been freed from all human limitations and entered heaven. Our feeling of elation was beyond description, but the words of Agnes Keith certainly capture a sense of that moment:

> While Brigadier Eastick is speaking, we in the crowd come a little nearer to realizing that we are free. We are beyond words, our hearts hammer and bang, our pulses throb, our throats ache, we weep and we cheer. We strike each other's backs and clasp hands. The children are held high in the air. But they are quiet now, for our tears astound and frighten them. Harry attempts to lift George to his shoulder, but he is still too weak; a friend lifts George up instead.
>
> Then over this sea of hysteria Captain Jennings speaks. Here are his words:
>
> "Today is my first experience of this sort. It is worth many a battle, and many a long, hard night on the sea. This is what we have been fighting for."
>
> It is the one perfect speech that I have ever heard, it is the only speech I ever wish to hear, but it finished composure. Captain Jennings himself . . . ended his words in tears.[4]

After the liberation ceremony, I was still outside the civilian men's camp, when suddenly I saw our friend Alan Begbie striding

4. Agnes Newton Keith, *Three Came Home* (U.S.A.: Little, Brown and Company, 1947), 281, 282.

along towards me shouting, "Hullo, Hudson, how are you? Where's Winsome — is she still alive?"

Alan had been a fellow student at the Melbourne Bible Institute and was now Chaplain of the Ninth Division. I was thrilled to meet him again. Later that same day we were all given a sheet of Red Cross paper and informed that we could write a letter to our relatives and friends, and these letters would be dispatched immediately.

The next day, the whole camp assembled again for a service of thanksgiving for our deliverance. It was conducted by our friend, Division Chaplain Alan Begbie, and the Anglican bishop of Kuching also took part. The service included this prayer of petition for spiritual healing:

> Eternal God, the Father of all mankind, we commit to you the needs of the whole world. Where there is hatred, give love; where there is injury, give pardon; where there is distrust, faith; where there is despair, hope; where there is darkness, light; through Jesus Christ our Savior and Redeemer. Amen.

We enjoyed about a week of freedom within the camp perimeter, but did not go outside the gate into the town. We were so psychologically conditioned to bowing to the Japanese that we often found ourselves bowing to the Australian soldiers! What a pleasure it was to talk with them about life outside Batu Lintang and to hear of their experiences. Again, Agnes Keith's perspective has a ring of authenticity:

> These men came into Kuching with blood on their hands, from heavy fighting in Borneo and the Celebes. They were soldiers known for their toughness, taking no prisoners, observing no laws; yet never did we hear from them a word of impatience or anger, a rough speech or a curse, or see an unkind or unpleasant action. To us who were weak and were helpless they were gentle as angels from Heaven.[5]

5. Ibid., 282, 283.

And these men surely did treat us kindly. One of the soldiers noticed that Winsome did not have a wedding ring. When we told him that it had been left with a Murut woman in the upper Trusan, he immediately went to work and skillfully made Winsome a new ring from a silver shilling.

That week we also gathered up the few possessions we still had. Since the camps had been subjected to frequent searches by the guards, we soon learned to hide or bury under the barracks those things which might be confiscated. I had brought with me a copy of the translation of the gospel of Mark into Murut and had entrusted this to Winsome's safekeeping. When the women's camp was searched, Winsome adopted the practice of hanging the precious translation on the clothesline and then hanging clothes over it! Safeguarded in this fashion, it survived all the camp searches, and after the war it was printed and published by the British and Foreign Bible Society in London. Those original pages that were hidden on a clothesline in the Batu Lintang camp are now in the archives of the Bible Society in London.

God also watched over the translation of Matthew's gospel, which I had kept with me. It had been found and confiscated during one of the searches. However, after the surrender, piles of papers and documents were thrown out of the Japanese offices. I searched among all this rubbish and found every one of the sections I had typed — the whole gospel in the Murut language — providing a continuing memorial to John Willfinger, the original translator.

On Tuesday, September 18th, we were flown to a rehabilitation camp on the northern coast of Labuan where we had excellent medical and dental care and full army rations. It was wonderful, and after five weeks I was back to my normal weight.

During that time in Labuan I was able to go across Brunei Bay to visit Lawas, and from there I set off along the two miles of muddy track to the Murut village at Gaya. As I walked, I pictured the faces of the people of the lower Trusan area in my mind — some of whom I knew quite well dating back to our first memorable visit from Raut and Lupong in 1933.

By the time I reached Gaya, it was mid-morning and, being Sunday, the Murut people were in church. When I walked in, the surprise, the welcome and the mutual joy were overwhelming. They had heard nothing of us and thought we were all dead. Yet the reality of their living faith — quite apart from us — was clearly evidenced by the fact that after three years of silence and the destruction of their church building, there they were, meeting on the Lord's Day for worship!

There was also one tragic footnote to our stay in Labuan. During our time in the internment camp, Colonel Suga had often come into the church services in the women's section and sat near the back. Once he told Winsome directly, "I'm a Christian." This was a startling admission for a Japanese officer to make to a prisoner during wartime.

Now, with the end of the war, he awaited a military tribunal. His country had been destroyed; his army defeated; his family lost. And, apart from the despair in his heart, the *bushido* tradition, the code of the Japanese warrior, had deep roots.

The fateful day came on September 16th, one week before his 60th birthday, traditionally a time when a family would gather around in celebration. Colonel Tatsuji Suga believed he had no one left to gather around; and he had no desire to see that day alone.

He took a knife from his mess tray and slipped it into his water canteen which he had filled with sand. He had planned carefully. No one noticed the canteen and the sand prevented the knife from rattling as he returned to his cell. Once inside, with his two faithful Chinese orderlies beside him, Colonel Suga took the knife and cut his own wrists. Next, he attempted to cut his throat, but the knife was blunt and with his bloodied hands he could not get a firm enough grip. Finally he asked for his orderlies' help. Then, while he held the knife point to his jugular, one of the young men slammed the heel of his palm against it full force and drove the blade deep. It took thirty minutes for him to bleed to death.

The two young Chinese wept as they buried him there at Labuan and planted flowers on the grave, in loving memory of his passion for flowers and nature. Afterwards, they carefully packed up the Colonel's personal effects including his insignia, his photo albums (some of which pictured him with prisoners — men, women and children — from Kuching), drawings by Agnes Keith and a booklet he had used for his daily meditations, *Vital Force: The Power of Soul*. They had made a deathbed promise and now they were determined to travel to Japan and search for survivors amidst the devastation in Hiroshima.[6]

The final episode in our liberation began on October 24th when we were flown to the RAAF Base at Morotai Island where we spent the night. We took off the next day in a DC-3 wartime transport plane with canvas bench seating along the sides of the fuselage. After climbing quickly to over 13,000 feet to cross the high mountains in Dutch West New Guinea (now Irian Jaya), we followed a course across the Arafura Sea direct to the Cape York peninsula, the northernmost tip of Australia.

Emotions were high, and I was eagerly watching to get the first glimpse of Australia. Suddenly we passed through a rain shower, and then a completely circular rainbow appeared. And there, right in the centre of the rainbow, I could see the tip of Cape York.

"Look! A rainbow!" I said excitedly to Winsome. "The sign of God's promise! He has kept the promise[7] that he gave us at Fremantle."

Shortly afterwards we landed to refuel at a wartime emergency airstrip near the northern end of Cape York. It was late afternoon, but we took off again because the aircrew wanted to reach Townsville.

---

6. Resource material for the account of Colonel Tatsuji Suga's death was obtained from Mrs. Khattiya Jalayanateja, a friend of the Suga family.

7. "I am with you and will watch over you wherever you go, and I will bring you back to this land."

Winsome and I took out our little *Daily Light* books and opened them to the evening selection for October 25th. "The end of all things is near," we read. "Therefore be clear minded and self-controlled so that you can pray."[8]

Suddenly I heard a strange sound. I craned my neck around, and through the window behind me I could see that the left-side engine had broken down — we were flying on only one engine! I looked around us. With the background noise inside the old DC-3, not many others were aware of the danger, although I could see that Roland Bewsher had noticed it. I mentioned the problem to Winsome and we quietly prayed, "Please, Lord, bring us through this emergency."

Our *Daily Light* booklets were still open in front of us, and we continued reading, "God is our refuge and strength, an ever present help in trouble. Therefore we will not fear."[9]

We were flying across Princess Charlotte Bay now, and the crew radioed the airstrip at Cooktown to prepare for an emergency landing. With a heavy cloud cover over Cooktown and mountains in the vicinity, the crew put the plane into a high-altitude circling pattern, burning up excess fuel while looking for a hole in the clouds.

The break came after about half-an-hour, and suddenly we could see the emergency flares on the runway far below. Our pilot, a Battle of Britain veteran, quickly brought us down below the clouds, compensated just right for the failed engine, and touched down with near-perfect alignment.

As we emerged from the aircraft we saw the ground crew dressed in asbestos suits, with fire equipment ready, in case the landing had ended in disaster. God had granted us another deliverance!

We had a magnificent meal in the officers' mess at Cooktown, slept the night there, and next morning another aircraft took us on to Townsville, where we had our first experience of shops and shopping in years. The next day we arrived in Brisbane where Winsome's aunt, Mabel Beath, was staying with friends. Finally, on October 31st, we reached Melbourne, and there was my dear mother, 83 years of age, and my brother Howard. What a wonderful reunion!

8. 1 Peter 4:7

9. Psalm 46:1,2

I do not consider myself a mystic in the sense often given to that term, but I do believe in the sovereign power of God acting to fulfill his purposes of grace. Indeed, looking back over the years since I consciously dedicated my life to God for any service that he might choose for me, I have often felt like an onlooker, seeing God in final control. I have seen God at work, and I have experienced his power as I obeyed his word.

Moreover, I am convinced that this power often becomes available to us through our prayer and the prayers of God's people.

Of all those who prayed for us faithfully during the war years, perhaps the most diligent was Mabel Beath. Many years later, after her death, we were given her Bible and her *Daily Light* devotional book. In it we found a small photograph of Winsome and myself taken in March 1941, just before we left Australia to return to Borneo.

On the back of that photograph, in minute handwriting done by a mapping pen with Indian ink, were recorded the promises which she had claimed by faith from God during the Japanese occupation. She had recorded eleven promises in all, each with a small note accompanied by a date.

On September 23, 1942, she had written, "Felt they are not in enemy hands." This was, in fact, true. Although we had, a few days earlier, received the official demand to surrender, we were still with the Murut people at Rumah Marong on that date.

On October 11, 1942, she wrote, "Assurance of safety claimed anew, Psalm 91:15." This was the very same day on which we had surrendered to the Japanese soldiers after racing down the Trusan River rapids the previous night to meet their imposed deadline.

Looking back, the words of that Psalm text certainly took on a special reality for Winsome and me:

> He will call upon me, and I will answer him;
> I will be with him in trouble,
> I will deliver him and honour him.

Part IV
New Foundations

The man who knows God hears his step in the tramp of daily events, discerns him near at hand to help, and hears his answer to the appeal of prayer in a hundred happenings outwardly small and insignificant, where another man can talk only of remarkable coincidence, amazing accident, or peculiar turns of events. That is why periods when the life of faith is strong, and men have enthusiastically surrendered themselves to God, have also been times rich in miracles.

– Walter Eichrodt

Chapter 13

The great euphoria at the end of the war was followed by months of readjustment as people everywhere attempted to pick up the pieces of their lives. My impression, having lived through both World Wars, was that the period of shock and readjustment was greater in 1945 than in 1918. The end of the Second World War brought unprecedented pressures for change. And nowhere were those pressures greater than in Borneo where indigenous people, whose way of life had seen little change for centuries, were soon to be confronted with a world of jet airplanes, computers and television.

Rajah Vyner Brooke returned to Sarawak in April 1946, after four-and-a-half years' absence. The Dayak chiefs, the Malay nobles and the Chinese merchants greeted his homecoming with a royal welcome. Once the ceremonies were over, however, the aging ruler discovered something of the toll those years had taken:

> Vyner entered the *astana,* which he once thought he would never see again. During the war the Japanese Governor of Sarawak had taken up residence in the *astana.* Nearly all of Vyner's books, nearly all his possessions had perished. Hundreds of letters and documents written by Sir James Brooke had vanished in the flames.
>
> For seventy-five days Vyner ruled over Sarawak. He met his old friends, decorated those who had served bravely in war, and briefly examined the collections of Japanese heads amassed by the Dyaks. He sauntered through the streets of Kuching as he had done long ago. He was at home again.

The Rajah had come home, but the world had changed. Governing involved new international complexities and required vast sums of new capital. Vyner now felt that no one man could effectively rule a country as large as Sarawak in this modern age. He was seventy-two, and he sensed it was time to go.

---

1. Robert Payne, *The White Rajahs of Sarawak* (Singapore: Oxford University Press, 1991), 180.

In February 1946, before leaving London, he had issued a proclamation urging the people of Sarawak to enter the British Commonwealth. The decree of cession came into effect on July 1st of that year, and Sarawak became a British crown colony. The era of the Rajahs had come to an end.

Rajah Vyner Brooke

Meanwhile, in Australia, Winsome and I were particularly glad just to be alive and free from Batu Lintang. It had been a wonderful experience to be welcomed back home and reunited with relatives and friends. People were keenly interested to hear of our experiences, which gave us great opportunities to tell others of God's faithfulness to his promises and also to share with them the vision we had for the future. We met many young people who had seen military service in the islands to the north of Australia. And now, after the war, some were considering returning in other kinds of service.

Winsome and I still carried vivid memories of the year we had lived among the Murut people of the interior and of their responsiveness to the gospel and the effect it had on their lives. Convinced that the postwar period would provide opportunities greater than any we had seen, early in 1946 I published a booklet entitled *Days of Opportunity in Borneo,* telling of the challenges of reconstruction and extension work. It reflected my intense burden for action.

In view of the pioneering type of work that would be required to reopen the Mission, I felt that I should go back alone to assess the situation and prepare a base for the others. Doctors also advised that Winsome needed more rest, both physically and emotionally. I had hoped that Alan Belcher could accompany me, but he had recently become engaged and had plans to be married before returning to the field.

With the end of the war, there were suddenly huge demands for transport, so it was difficult to get a ship back to Borneo. In the end I was able to get a berth on a cargo vessel, the M.V. *Suva,* due to leave Sydney on June 16th with relief supplies for ports in the Solomon Islands, New Guinea, Hong Kong and Labuan Island.

The journey was tedious and rather depressing. At each of the ports of call the people appeared listless and weary in the aftermath of war. Hong Kong, especially, was devastated. We spent a fortnight there while the crew unloaded flour and sugar for hungry people. During that time I made my way up to the renowned vantage point on Victoria Peak and looked out over a city of windowless houses, holed by gunfire. Who would have imagined that in just a few years that same horizon would be filled with skyscrapers.

From Hong Kong we sailed south. Five days later, on August 16th, we landed at Labuan, where we found the town badly damaged by war. During our time of rehabilitation there the previous year, Bill Clack of the YMCA had collected medical supplies, tents, folding tables, camp beds and equipment to help with the reconstruction of our Mission. Now to my dismay, I found that all this store of goods had been plundered. A large number of conscript laborers who had not been repatriated were still on the island, and lawlessness abounded.

Three days later, I was able to load some of my personal goods on board a military launch and travel to Limbang on the mainland. There I discussed my plans to reopen the work of the Mission with the Acting Resident, Mr. Snelus. All of our mission buildings in Sarawak and North Borneo had been destroyed during the war, so we were forced to make a completely new start.

Next day the launch went on to Brunei town which, like the Limbang bazaar, had been completely destroyed by bombing. From there we continued on to Lawas where a letter from Winsome was waiting for me. She had written the letter on my birthday, June 28th, and even though I did not receive it until eight weeks later, it brightened up my day tremendously:

> Well darling, my treasure, today is your birthday and I feel so disgusted with myself that you haven't a letter, but I will send you a telegram. I have been praying for you and will be thinking of you all day off and on. I do thank God for you darling. I think I have always loved you; at least when I first met you I thought, "that is a particularly nice type of man." And then later I thought, "it would be very nice if that man felt he loved me." You rather appealed to me as my ideal of what a man should be. You were so gentle, and so sincere; those were the first two qualities I admired, and you were so nice to look at and so clever, and yet not conceited. And oh darling, I don't know how I let you go to Borneo now without me. I can't believe it sometimes. But yesterday I saw a poster, and it was the name of a film or a play, *Because of Him*, and I thought that is your and my daily motive really isn't it? . . .

After three days in Lawas, I caught a Chinese launch back to Labuan to pick up the balance of my personal goods. While in Labuan, I stopped in at the army base to see the commanding officer. Only a few military personnel remained on the island so Brigadier Goss generously offered me a large supply of surplus material such as tents, folding camp beds and tables with folding legs — the very kind of things we needed to start the mission base and a bible school. He then put me in contact with the military hospital, and the medical officer gave me a good supply of bandages and other basic medical supplies, all of which helped to make up for the supplies that had been stolen. Upon my return to Lawas I was able to store these new supplies safely with a friendly Chinese shopkeeper.

Sunday, the first day of September, was a most memorable day, for it marked my return to the Borneo I knew best. I walked through the jungle to Gaya, about two miles south of Lawas town. Tangled roots, muddy paths, a log or two over a creek and the sounds of the jungle all brought back old memories to me.

At Gaya, nearly two hundred lower Trusan villagers crammed somehow into the little temporary church building. I read to them in Murut from the book of Matthew and gave a short talk, and together we praised God for his goodness and deliverance. Exactly twelve months had passed since Colonel Suga had relinquished control of the Batu Lintang internment camp. Right next door were the blackened ruins of their church building, burned to the ground by the Japanese. But that day the war seemed like a faded, distant memory.

After the service I walked a few miles further to *Penghulu* Itai's house. I was there only a short time when another guest suddenly appeared. It was Labo Upai, our trusted friend with whom we had left our letters and other personal effects before surrendering to the Japanese. *Penghulu* Ating Mugang and Riong Awa were with him. Upon learning that I was back in Sarawak, they had set off on a six-day walk from Rumah Marong in the upper Trusan where we had lived as fugitives four years before. We had a grand reunion.

Later we talked about possible sites for our new base and settled on the Lawas area, since this was the gateway to the Muruts of the Trusan River, who at that time formed the nucleus of the Christian groups. Lawas was the established trading centre for this part of the coast; it was a major outlet for products from the interior, with a history of international trade and commerce dating back more than a thousand years to the time of the great T'ang Dynasty of China.

Rangat, a local Murut, provided us with some land about two miles upriver from Lawas town. Known as Budok Ngeri because of its magnificent *ngeri* hardwood tree, this tract of land sloped down to the Lawas Damit, a tributary of the main Lawas River.

When Stafford Young and Trevor White arrived in Lawas on September 11th, I showed them our new site and briefed them on developments before they proceeded on to Jesselton to recommence working in North Borneo where they had been involved before the war.

Now I was faced with two urgent tasks. I wanted to visit the people of the interior whom we had not seen for four years. But I also needed to start building a base.

I contracted people from the Lawas area to clear the site at Budok Ngeri and placed orders with them to prepare a quantity of round timber and large bamboo. I also ordered a thousand pieces of nipa palm *atap* for roof thatching. We then transported my stores of materials to the building site. Once these things were in place, I felt free to launch into my first priority.

I left Lawas on October 1, 1946, and walked the sixteen miles to Trusan town along a rather muddy track. I had five carriers with enough stores, clothing and medical supplies for just one month, not anticipating how much time would actually be taken up in individual counselling.

From Trusan town, we went on to Kelasi's old house where Frank Davidson and Brian Morcombe had left some of our possessions before escaping upriver in January 1942. Nearly all of Frank's and Brian's things and one of my steel trunks were still intact, but all the other trunks belonging to Winsome and me had been lost. They had been stored in a hut in the jungle, and when the Japanese retreated into the interior, they found the hut, broke open all our boxes, took what they wanted and burned all the rest. Unfortunately Winsome's engagement ring had been left there and was lost.

We continued on up the Beriwan valley to the Sepakoi pass. From there we went down to the Tengoa valley, crossed the river, and went on to the house at Long Lutok, where we learned that many of the people there had suffered on account of an American Liberator plane which had crashed near Telahak. Nine Americans had survived the crash and had been able to make their way through the jungle to the Trusan. Unfortunately, they had thrown away their empty cigarette cartons beside the track, and when Japanese soldiers found these, they accused the Muruts of helping the Americans to escape. They arrested nine Muruts and took them down to the coast and tortured them. At least three of them, including *Penghulu* Sakai, died at the hands of the Japanese without revealing anything about the Americans.

The next village was Brayong, where Frank Davidson and his party had stayed for a time, and we spent an extra day with Baru Agong, the Headman who had hidden Frank and the others. Fortunately the Japanese never discovered this.

Many of the Muruts of the Trusan had assisted in other ways during the war, and those who served under the "Z" Special Unit forces had readily earned the respect of their commanding officer, Major Tom Harrisson:

> One of the things that the small proportion who by that time were already Christian definitely had not lost was the martial quality and the aggressive trait. If anything, I would say that the Christian Muruts were just an edge better than the pagan ones in fighting. They were certainly better in special jobs where they did not have to use firearms and yet had to take great risks, show energy, responsibility and daring. For instance, we used Christian Muruts, mostly from the villages on the middle Trusan, extensively as super-speed runners carrying messages between the coast and the interior; as guides moving fast and often unarmed ahead of larger parties (unarmed so that they appeared harmless if they contacted any enemy point); and as special agents and spies percolating into the coastal areas to bring back specific information.[2]

---

2. Tom Harrisson, *World Within* (Singapore: Oxford University Press, 1990), 250.

After we left Brayong, it started raining, and the path became so slippery that I had three falls, one of which was absolutely spectacular. My bare-footed carriers, who rarely so much as stumbled, whooped and cheered as though they had witnessed an Olympian performance. We eventually reached Long Lapukan and Long Luping and the people welcomed us warmly. It was here we had last seen John Willfinger. We then pressed on and reached the upper Trusan, stopping at Long Semadoh and then further upriver at Rumah Marong, where we had spent so many happy months in 1942. It was a great experience to again be among such real friends. They had looked after everything we had left behind with them.

Although the Japanese had exerted some measure of control in the lower reaches of the Trusan, it was a very different story when they ventured further into the interior. As Vyner Brooke had found more than forty years earlier, jungle fighters in the remote and rugged territory of the upper Trusan were almost impossible to pin down. With guns provided by the "Z" Special commandos and intelligence reports supplied from the coast by Native Officer Bigar, the Muruts and Kelabits were a terrifying fighting force, as Major Tom Harrisson confirms in his description of the first military incursion by the Japanese into the upper Trusan:

> It was unfair, really; too unsporting. For, through Bigar, we had precise information about the plan, programme, personnel and equipment of this force before they had started inland . . .
>
> The Muruts and Kelabits let the Japanese patrol get about seven days up the Trusan before we set an ambush where the path climbs steeply out of a creek bed above Long Semadoh. It had to be a one-sided ambush. For not one of the local guerrillas would consider being left out . . .
>
> [This] our first operation went one hundred percent. No one escaped down-hill to tell the tale . . .[3]

After a day at Rumah Marong, we crossed over the high watershed and on to the longhouse on the Sia stream. It was a very long walk. The people at the Sia longhouse had built a big church,

3. Ibid., 249, 252.

and that evening I had discussions with them about many problems, and forty-two people asked to be baptized.

Next morning, I was up before dawn and had another long day's walk back to the source of the Trusan, returning to Rumah Marong. It would have been great to stay longer with these people, but I felt it necessary to press on. After stopping again at Long Semadoh, we continued on to Long Beluyu, where I stayed with a respected teacher, or *guru,* named Pantalusang. He had written to me before I left Australia, and part of the translation of his letter is copied below:

> I wish to introduce myself with this letter. I used to be a teacher in the area where Aris Doemat was in charge, but now I have been moved. Since July 1945 my family and I have been living in the upper Trusan ministering to the church at Long Beluyu . . . I have only good to report concerning the people of the upper Trusan. True, in some other parts there were some who during the war went back from their belief in the Lord, but the people here in the upper Trusan remained faithful . . .
>
> I am also the teacher at the Government school which was opened in February, so now I am in charge of both the school and the church at Long Beluyu.
>
> All the churches of the upper Trusan are awaiting your return. Truly, *Tuan,* we are just longing for your return. Our hope is that you will come to us quickly and minister to the needs of the churches here . . .

Guru Pantalusang had trained a very good choir which played flutes made locally from a small species of bamboo. I spent the Sunday there, preaching and counselling.

The next day, we travelled up the Beluyu River, crossing and recrossing the river twenty-six times. Midway, we climbed around some steep rocks by means of notched logs. The Muruts had ambushed a party of retreating Japanese soldiers at this point the year before, and I saw one skull perched on a sapling as a stark reminder of that encounter. In pagan days it would have been added to the skulls hanging in the longhouse.

About an hour further on, the path levelled off at the junction of the Kelalan River with a branch stream called the Pala. We spent the night there in a large hut specially built for travelling parties. From this point the path led on to the broad valley floor and the irrigated rice farms known as the *bah*.

After about two hours walk along the valley, we reached the knoll where on October 31, 1945, Major Tom Harrisson and the Japanese Envoy had called on the last company of about five hundred Japanese soldiers to surrender. Many were in a pitiable state, having exhausted their salt rations as they struggled through the jungle from the upper Limbang. They did not know that they were only a few hundred yards away from the famous salt springs of the Kelalan valley, which had sustained the mineral needs of the Murut population in this remote and isolated place for generations.

I spent two days at Ba Kelalan and then went up to the watershed at the source of the Kelalan stream. In order to circumvent the precipitous peak between the upper Kelalan and the Kelabit highlands, we crossed the international border into what was formerly known as Dutch Borneo; with Indonesia's declaration of independence from the Netherlands at the end of the war, this became Indonesian territory. The population here was much greater than on the Sarawak side of the border, with twenty-seven longhouses on the Belawit *bah* alone. At Belawit, I stayed with Aris Doemat, a Christian and Missionary Alliance pastor from the Celebes (later called Sulawesi) who had played a big part in holding together the Murut church throughout the Japanese occupation.

While I was at Belawit, I received a letter from Mr. Jacks, the Sarawak Government District Officer at Marudi, who was travelling on the Baram River. He was making his first postwar inspection visit and had arrived at Lio Matu, the last Badang Kenyah longhouse, which was at the limit of navigation in the upper Baram. Above Lio Matu, the Baram River pours out of the Kelabit highlands through a series of gorges and cascades.

During their military service with the "Z" Special Unit, the people living in the upper Baram had come in contact with the Muruts of the Trusan River and had seen the great changes that the gospel had brought to their lives. The Badang Kenyahs of Lio Matu and some Penan people at Long Akah wanted this same freedom from fear of the spirits, and they had asked Mr. Jacks to write to me, saying that they wished to become Christians too.

While he was still at Lio Matu, Mr. Jacks heard through the native travellers' "grapevine" that I was visiting the Muruts in the upper Trusan, so he dispatched a letter to me. Remarkably the messenger reached me, after eight days of hard travel, at the very time I was staying with Aris Doemat at Belawit.

I was elated to receive the District Officer's letter but it presented me with a real dilemma. Should I extend my journey down to Lio Matu on the Baram River, seizing the opportunity to open up a whole new territory? Or, should I return to Lawas, to construct a base to accommodate additional mission workers?

The opportunities seemed boundless, yet I could only respond to one at a time. To complicate matters, I was feeling really ill, and for awhile I thought I might again have amoebic dysentery. How I wished it were possible to get in touch with Stafford Young and Trevor White in North Borneo, but I had no way of contacting them.

I longed to be able to meet the challenge of this new opportunity in the Baram but, in the end, I decided that I should first try to complete my undertaking to build a base. So, as soon as my fever subsided, I left Belawit and began retracing my steps to Lawas, still wondering if I had made the right decision.

CHAPTER 14

My return to our new building site at Budok Ngeri marked the end of a journey that had taken just a day short of six full weeks. Upon arrival, I found that the lad I had employed to care for the stores and equipment had neglected his job. The medical supplies had been damaged by flood water and the stores were in a disorderly mess. After surveying the damage, I walked out to Gaya for the Sunday church service, and afterwards told the people about my journey.

I also told them about the great need to move forward with the construction project. I explained that men were needed to work each day and that large quantities of round timber were required. My plan was to build a main mission house that would accommodate six to eight people and another smaller house for Brian Morcombe and his wife and baby. The houses were to be of simple construction, using bamboo and round poles tied with rattan cane. I also wanted to build timber platforms near the riverbank upon which we could erect tents to lodge students.

At the beginning, six men came to help, and we soon constructed a workshop equipped with a carpenter's bench and a tool store so that we could work even when it was raining. Then the palm-leaf thatching that I had ordered from the Malays began to arrive. As more men came to work they brought some round timber, and we built a hut where I could live and which we could also use as an office. Next, we burned off the dried timber and undergrowth which had been cut down over a month before to prepare a site on the hill for the main house. By the end of the first week after my return, we had made a good start. The next two weeks saw more progress as I designed and laid out the plan for the mission house; then another party of Muruts arrived bringing additional round timber, and they built a temporary hut so that they could live on the site and give continuous service.

Along with supervising the building project, I was kept busy attending to correspondence and counselling work. Some of the

Murut leaders asked me to draw a Christian code of conduct. Though they had become Christians before the war, they had not received any pastoral care and counsel for over four years. It was a healthy sign that they earnestly desired to live in accordance with God's will, so after discussions with the church leaders, I drew up a simple code of biblical principles and typed it out.

On Sunday, December 1st, we held our last church service at Gaya. The people felt that the time had come to build a new church, replacing the one the Japanese had destroyed, and since the headquarters of the Mission were being built at Budok Ngeri, they decided to move their church there also. The next week, along with the ongoing work on the mission house, we began building the new church. Unfortunately, I could not assist much as I was ill with nausea and a fever.

That same week I received news that our old friends, Jim and Dood Anderson, had come to visit Lawas, as Jim had recently been reappointed as Resident of the Fifth Division. I sent a note to them explaining that I was ill and could not come to see them, and the next day they both came upriver to visit me and offered to take me back with them to see a doctor. I gratefully went with them, first to the Residency at Limbang and then to Brunei, where the doctor told me that I was a bit run down and needed some rest. Relieved that there was nothing radically wrong, I continued on to Labuan to pick up more surplus military equipment.

While I was away, good progress had been made with the building at Budok Ngeri, and we were now at the stage where we needed planks of timber for flooring, and for making doors, windows and furniture. At that time, sawn timber could only be obtained from a sawmill at Tagai, about two hours journey by launch, and the necessary hardware, like nails and hinges, had to be purchased at Limbang, Brunei or Labuan, all of which had been devastated by war.

It was a tremendous job to build a new base in the jungle with unskilled labor and few tools. We rested only on Sundays and on Christmas Day, and the local Murut Christians continued on the job right until the end of December, when they had to leave to start harvesting their rice. By that time we had erected the framework of the main house, installed the thatched roof and laid the floor with freshly sawn planks, roughly nailed to allow taking up again after shrinkage.

In those early postwar years, airmail communication was not reliable as there was no regular air transport between Australia and Sarawak, so I sent a telegram to Australia, saying that I hoped to be ready for Winsome and new missionaries to arrive by early March of the new year, 1947.

I was eagerly awaiting Winsome's coming, but the house was far from ready. With my Murut helpers now busy with their harvest, I worked alone during January and the first half of February, racing against time. The outside walls, as well as the internal dividing walls, had to be covered with palm leaf matting. Then I made the doors and windows, stairs, cupboards and some simple furniture. I also built a water storage system and set up the water tanks.

By the middle of February the harvest was ending and my helpers started coming back again. Also, visitors came from the upper Trusan, and some of these helped me in finishing the house and would not accept any payment. Around that same time I was able to contract some Malay workmen to construct a building for the bible school, and this was a great help.

"This is my last night in the hut," I wrote in my diary on Tuesday, February 25th. "Thank God for this place. It has been an excellent temporary home, and many thoughts and plans have taken shape here."

Acting on the telegram they had received from me in early January, Winsome and the Morcombes left Australia on the S.S. *Marella* on January 24th and arrived in Singapore in mid-February. There they were delayed about two weeks, waiting for a ship to go on to Labuan, and at last they were able to book passages on the S.S. *Marudu*, hoping to arrive on March 7th.

I closed up the house and went over to Labuan to meet them, but when I arrived, I learned that the *Marudu* had been delayed and would not reach Labuan till March 12th. Meanwhile, some bulk supplies sent from Melbourne by cargo ship had arrived, so I took delivery and left by launch to transport them to Lawas. Some of the boxes had been broken open and things had been stolen, so I was glad to get what remained into safe storage.

By the time I got back to Labuan, I found that Winsome and the others had already arrived and left for Lawas that very morning. After months of anticipation, I felt intensely disappointed at not being able to meet Winsome as planned. In the end, however, I caught up with her at our new base where we settled in with a real sense of happiness and thankfulness for being together again.

Another visitor had arrived during the time I was in Labuan also. Trevor White came over from North Borneo and spent about two weeks with us at Budok Ngeri. He and Stafford Young had received a great welcome from the Dusun people at Ranau, and it appeared that the need for more workers was no less pressing in North Borneo than it was in Sarawak.

The first week of April was Easter week, and we had big attendances in the new church at Budok Ngeri. Then, on the Monday after Easter, our calm was shattered.

A party of Muruts from Long Lapukan, on the Luping River, had walked six days' journey down to Lawas, bringing four Kelabits bound with rattan to be turned over to the District Officer, Mr. Meikle. The story they told was grim.

A party of sixteen Kelabits, including a Headman and his wife, had come from their longhouse in the centre of the Kelabit highlands, down the Beluyu River, to the longhouse at Long Lapukan. According to the native custom of hospitality, they had been entertained to an evening meal. At dusk they were all sitting in the communal covered veranda when suddenly, so the Muruts said, four young Kelabit men had sprung up, drawn their long jungle knives, and slashed around indiscriminately. Utter panic broke out, and everyone fled. In those few seconds of total confusion, three Muruts were killed. One other was seriously wounded with an arm severed, and four others were badly cut.

All the Kelabit visitors fled from the house, but the Kelabit Headman and his wife and two young men surrendered later that evening to the Muruts. These four Kelabits, now in custody, told a different story. They said that one man, Lawan Arun, was the attacker, and he had fled with the others.

Mr. Meikle immediately arranged to go up to the Luping with a party of Malay police to hold a preliminary inquiry. Since he had only recently taken over administrative responsibility for the Lawas and Trusan District, he asked me to accompany him to interpret as I knew the language and the people.

We all felt this emergency offered us an opportunity to be of service to both the people and the Government. Winsome and the Morcombes had by this time settled in at Budok Ngeri, and they were able to handle the ongoing requirements at the new headquarters and open the bible school.

We also felt that since I would be travelling that far into the interior, I should continue on to the Kelabit highlands and then try to respond to the request I had received six months earlier from the Badang Kenyahs at Lio Matu and the Penans at Long Akah. Now that our base was operational, I could hardly wait to take up this invitation to the huge Baram area where we had not been before. So, I hurriedly packed my travelling gear and prepared for an extended journey.

Our party left Lawas on April 9th and travelled up through the Sepakoi pass. After six days we reached Long Lapukan.

The house was a tragic sight. Three new graves had been dug nearby, and inside there were blood stains everywhere — on the floor and on the walls. One of the wounded was in a bad way, with bone projecting from her arm which had been severed above the elbow. The District Officer, Mr. Meikle, ordered her to be carried to the coast for hospital treatment, but I doubted that she would reach there alive. In addition to those who were wounded, several people were ill with malaria, and one woman died from dysentery the morning after we arrived.

After talking with the Muruts in the house, I was convinced that the attack had been entirely without provocation. Mr. Meikle found this hard to imagine, especially when the Kelabits had brought women and children with them; but as he questioned the witnesses one-by-one and recorded their statements, he too concluded that the Kelabits had not been provoked.

The Kelabits put all the blame on one man, Lawan Arun, who had escaped, but the Muruts insisted that four Kelabits had attacked, though the witnesses, including the wounded, were rather confused in their identification of who actually had attacked them.

After two days, Mr. Meikle had completed his inquiries and headed back to Lawas. A few days later, a large party of Kelabits from the highlands, fully armed and escorted by Sergeant Boland, the government upriver agent from Bario, passed through the Kelalan and upper Trusan district on their way to Lawas. They had with them all the Kelabits who had been involved in the original attack, including Lawan Arun who was handcuffed and had a rattan halter around his neck.

Sergeant Boland was from Manado in north Celebes; he had been in Dutch Borneo during the war and knew John Willfinger quite well, and actually saw John when he surrendered at Tarakan. Later he served under Tom Harrisson and was now in charge of the police at Bario.

This group of Kelabits also blamed Lawan Arun entirely for the murders, and although their stories were not consistent, they all seemed to agree that he was mad. Lawan Arun claimed that the real murderers were among the captives already sent down to Lawas and that two more were still to be captured.

I talked with Lawan Arun; he seemed quite sensible and his story of what had happened sounded credible. "They all say that I did the killing," he said softly, "but why would I do such a thing?"

After the others had left for Lawas, I stayed on at the longhouse for a few days to try to be of some comfort to the bereaved, and then set off on the long trek to the Kelabit highlands. Almost every evening on this journey I wrote a letter to Winsome in the form of a journal, letting her know what was happening, and sent these by personal messenger whenever I could find someone going to the coast.

On April 19th, I reached Rumah Marong in the upper Trusan where our old friends were keenly interested in more teaching. From there, I continued on to Long Semadoh and Long Beluyu. People were distressed by the murders at Luping and several asked for counselling. Then someone asked me to pray for a woman who was having difficulty in childbirth.

When I went to visit her, I found a middle-aged woman who was having labor pains with no result. She was an enormous size, and I tried to find out by palpation if there were twins. The woman was afraid that she was going to die. I gave her a drink of hot water with some sugar to revive her strength and prayed with her. I also boiled plenty of water, scrubbed my hands and prepared some antiseptic solution. They had the woman lying on bare boards, so I made them get a mat and hoped that my methods of cleanliness would be an object lesson to them. Then I tried to help when the pains came. Suddenly she gave an extra effort, and in a second the baby was born — a fine big boy!

I cleaned up the baby and tied the cord before cutting it.

"Oh!" they said. "We never tie the cord, and it always bleeds."

Before leaving, I gave them some soap and cotton, and they washed the mother.

"I tried hard to remember things I learned from you," I wrote to Winsome, "and I quoted you as my authority."

We went on to Ba Kelalan, and there I had some amusing times counselling young girls who had been married but who refused to live with their husbands. One girl was adamant, but another was hopeful that eventually she would settle down with her husband. The problem was that they had been pushed into marriage far too young.

A young man who had followed me from Long Beluyu told me that he was engaged to one of the Ba Kelalan girls and wanted to marry her. When I interviewed the girl, however, she said that she did not really want to marry him but had been talked into it. I commended her for being frank and advised her to break off the engagement. This took all the wind out of her sails, and not long after she sent me a message saying that she wanted to be married after all. So I went to see her again, and she told me directly that she wanted to marry the young man. I advised her to wait until a later date, but no, she wanted to be married now. So I married them.

"I told her bewildered husband that women always reserve the right to change their minds," I wrote in my letter to Winsome. "Next morning, as I passed her house, she came out and beamed at me, so I think everything will be fine."

From Ba Kelalan we crossed into Indonesian territory. After a short visit with Pastor Aris Doemat at Belawit, we returned to Sarawak and went straight on to the Tarap house situated on the northern end of a circuit of longhouses around the perimeter of the Kelabit highlands. The people here were friendly enough but offered little spontaneity and warmth, and it was only after the second meeting that a few stayed on to ask questions and discuss problems. The attitude of the questioners, and the general feel of the place, was that they had made up their minds to listen and show interest but to go on with their habitual drinking.

I learned that following the visit Frank Davidson and I had made to this area in 1939, Tama Bulan, who was then Headman of Tarap, resolved to trust God. He was a powerful Headman and was still spoken of with great deference and respect. Tama Bulan gave up drinking and spirit worship and gradually influenced others, until in 1943 the people sent messengers to Aris Doemat in Belawit, inviting Aris and others to come and teach them. The people gave up all the old taboos and learned some hymns and how to pray, but though their drinking decreased, they never gave it up entirely.

Aris Doemat and others wanted to visit them again, but the Japanese military became too active. Then, early in 1945, the "Z" Special commandos commenced their operations, and after the war some of these commandos stayed on, disarming and disbanding the many hundreds of Kelabits and Muruts who had been enlisted as irregulars attached to the "Z" Special Unit.

The universal story of the people was that the "Z" Special commandos, and chiefly Major Tom Harrisson, encouraged them to drink again. Their influence was most harmfully felt at Belawit where the Muruts had given up their drinking habits entirely, but were led back into it again by the commandos. This was not merely social drinking of a glass or two, but orgies of drunkenness. Several told me that Tom Harrisson had taken them by the hair and forced their heads into a bowl of rice beer, particularly when he was drunk himself.

Tom Harrisson had a tremendous reputation among the Kelabit and Murut people for his physical feats, and there is no doubt that he was a help to them in a number of ways. However, many of them, particularly the younger people, found it difficult to understand why he was so eager for them to return to the drunkenness which had plagued them.

From the Tarap longhouse, the path led in a generally southern direction, and for several days we walked at between 3,000 and 4,000 feet above sea level. Some of the young Kelabits carrying my loads told me that their bodies felt ill and out of sorts after drinking *borak*, and they would be glad to give it up. They said that, in fact, many of the younger people wanted to give up drinking, but the older men and Headmen insisted on retaining the drinking custom and ritual. As we walked, I could not help but feel that this silent body of opinion among the younger Kelabits would one day make its presence felt.

Meanwhile, in Lawas, the investigation into the longhouse murders was proceeding. Three young men and Lawan Arun, who was perhaps fifty, were being held in custody, awaiting trial. Also, the witnesses from the Luping River all stayed in Lawas for some weeks.

One day before the trial the four accused were being given exercise while handcuffed and under guard. They were walking along the road beside the Lawas River, when suddenly Lawan Arun broke away from his guards and jumped into the river and drowned himself.

Shortly afterward the remaining three were called to trial, found guilty and condemned to death. They were then sent to Kuching for execution by firing squad.

During the time that the three young Kelabits were in detention awaiting execution, Tom Harrisson arrived in Kuching. After his discharge from the "Z" Special Unit he had returned to England, but now had come back to Sarawak as the Curator designate of the Sarawak Museum.

Tom Harrisson knew the three young men, and when he visited them, they told him their story. They insisted that Lawan Arun alone was guilty of a lightning attack on their Murut hosts. On their behalf, Harrisson made an appeal for a retrial. At the hearing of the request for a retrial, the former commando gave a dramatic demonstration in court of the damage that one active man, with a long jungle knife, could inflict on an unsuspecting group of people. Tom Harrisson, like Bornean people, was very athletic, and his demonstration was so convincing that a new trial was ordered. The Resident of the Fifth Division, Jim Anderson, was instructed to conduct the retrial at Lawas.

At the second trial, Harrisson gave another graphic performance. In addition, the witnesses' testimonial evidence was inconsistent and Mr. Anderson, as judge, felt compelled to overturn the conviction and declare the three men not guilty.

The final verdict was indeed correct. Subsequent to the trial, we learned that Lawan Arun had been subject to fits of paranoia in which he imagined he was being attacked. Ten years earlier, he had travelled with a party of Kelabits down the Baram as far as Long Akah. There they had stopped to bathe in the river and Lawan Arun was sharpening his *parang* on a stone at the water's edge. Suddenly he had an illusion that he was being attacked, and he sprang up and fled into the jungle, taking only his long knife with him. A fortnight later he arrived back at his longhouse in the Kelabit highlands.

The improbable proved to be true. Tom Harrisson had shown that one man could indeed have killed three people and seriously wounded four others in a sudden crazed attack. In doing so, Tom was clearly instrumental in saving the lives of the three young Kelabits on trial. Years later, the story took on an another twist of irony that seemed positively providential. Although it likely was not something Tom would have intended, one of those young men decided to become a pastor to his own Kelabit people.

CHAPTER 15

At the turn of the century, Charles Hose was the Resident of the Fourth Division in Sarawak. His administrative centre, Fort Hose, was built in Marudi on the Baram River in 1901. In order to stimulate communication between ethnic groups and provide for peaceful competition as a counter influence to headhunting raids, Hose initiated the Baram Regatta at Marudi. For many years this event was a celebrated attraction as long canoes, manned by sometimes more than sixty paddlers, engaged in highly contested races.

At one of these early regattas, Hose noticed some strangers speaking a language he did not know. Through an interpreter he asked them where they came from.

"From Long Labid," they answered.

Hose misunderstood their reply and wrote it down as "Kelabit," and thus originated the name by which these people came to be known. As an ethnic group they were known in their remote homelands as Lun Daye, which simply means "people of the interior," but since no European had yet been to the central highlands of Borneo, the name Kelabit stuck.

In physical appearance, the Kelabits mostly closely resembled the Muruts living on the other side of the spinal mountain ranges and with whom they were related by intermarriage, customs and language. Whereas the vocabulary of the Kelabit language was perhaps ninety percent identical to the Murut, the dialect and pronunciation were about as different as that of a Londoner and a Highland Scotsman.

The Kelabit highlands were so remote and isolated that the people living there had to be hardy to survive. Their lifestyle demanded and developed toughness. Indeed when it came to calf, thigh and back muscles, it was difficult to find anyone who could match a well-developed Kelabit for strength and endurance. The Kelabits' lifestyle also developed resourcefulness. Speaking generally, the Kelabits were thorough in all they did, whether making finely woven mats or baskets, or other craft-work in wood or metal.

There are only a few practicable ways of getting out of the highlands on foot. The encircling mountains, which rise in places to over 7,000 feet, are impossibly precipitous, their approaches cut with tortuous gullies. The Kelabits thus found themselves in a position of strength. They could go out through almost secret passes, but few could get in, and those who did were vulnerable to ambush along narrow gorges or at river fords.

When Frank Davidson, Carey Tolley, Hendy and I met the band of Kelabits on the lower Limbang River shortly after our arrival in Sarawak in late-1928, little did we know of their secluded homelands, or of the ways in which our lives would become intertwined with theirs.

At the time of our first meeting, the Kelabits numbered less than two thousand people. However, high in the Tamabo Mountains bounding Kelabit territory, there is evidence that in ancient times fertile pockets of land had been farmed, as well as the highlands themselves, indicating there was once a much greater population than there is now.

Today the Kelabits are still one of the minor ethnic groups, but their influence in the Malaysian nation is out of proportion to their number as they hold positions in the medical and legal professions, in commerce and in government.

After leaving the Kelabit house on the Tarap on May 6, 1947, I continued my circuit of the highlands. In addition to several carriers, who sometimes were replaced by others at longhouses along the way, I was accompanied by two Murut helpers — Kading, who had been with me since setting out from Lawas, and *Guru* Riong, who had joined us at Ba Kelalan.

Upon arriving at the Umur longhouse, we met some Kelabits returning from the coast and bringing letters from Winsome. After two nights there we went on to the house on the Bangar stream. At both places, some of the people were responsive and open, and I felt sure that God spoke to many.

As we travelled, we passed through some rich river flats, quite suitable for irrigated rice farming. The track we followed ran essentially due south along the eastern fringe of the Kelabit highlands, and we passed several *ngabang*, large trenches cut across the ridge of a hill to commemorate special events. Some of these must have been dug ages ago.

We forded the Dalih stream and came to the Kelapang which is the principal source of the great Baram River. The Kelapang was a big stream at this point, and a high suspension bridge, made of rattan and giant bamboo, had been built across it. *Penghulu* Miri was chief of the southern Kelabits; he was out on the track as I approached the Dalih longhouse and he escorted me to his house. Miri was quite young, in his early thirties, with a magnificent physique and a strong personality. He was clever and spoke several Baram languages.

In the evening I spoke to the people, discussing what it meant to be a Christian. Afterwards, *Penghulu* Miri organized some entertainment for me. He had a talent for playing the *sapi*, a native guitar used mostly by the Kayans and Kenyahs, and that evening he arranged for some of the young men and girls to dance in the graceful *ngarang* style, using fans and feathers on their fingers. The performance was skillful and demonstrated their well-developed aesthetic values.

The next house was Batu Patang, and after that Ramudu. I had good meetings with the people at both places and, as was my usual practice at all of the longhouses we visited, I gave out medicines.

From Ramudu, the most southerly point in the highlands, we headed north to the longhouse on the Mada stream. As this was home to the people who were involved in the murders on the Luping River, I had considered going straight on to the house at Mein, but the people implored me to stay the night. It was a big house with many young men, despite the fact that ten of their number were being detained at Lawas, awaiting the murder trial. That night I spoke plainly about the danger of following God half-heartedly. After the service, however, they went away to drink, and next morning I saw them preparing more rice for *borak*.

When I eventually arrived at Mein, the centre of the Kelabit highlands, I was welcomed warmly by *Penghulu* Pulu Ribuh. The longhouse here was truly long. There was also a teacher's quarters for *Guru* Paul and a big school with desks made from boards. As it was Sunday, we held three services, and after the evening service most of the older men stayed behind to chat. They asked intelligent questions and made comments that showed they were receptive to the Christian message. Giving up *borak* was a big issue for them, although they recognized how harmful it had become, both physically and morally. Some people questioned the need to give up *borak* when becoming Christians, but most acknowledged that drunken orgies, which led to fighting and immorality, could not be reconciled with the teaching of the Bible. A number of the Mein villagers told me that if everyone agreed to give up *borak*, many would welcome its going.

Although this longhouse was in fact situated near the source of the Mada stream, it still retained the name of Mein, as the people had formerly lived close to the big salt spring near the Mein stream from which most of the Kelabits got their salt. This salt spring flowed quite freely, and natural gas bubbles rose from it continually. My carriers told me that when a bamboo tube was thrust into one of the crevices, the gas would support a continuous flame.

The vegetation around the salt spring was luxurious, and I saw some huge wild tomato plants. The water evidently contained potash or other fertilizing salts as well as common salt, otherwise it would have had a sterilizing effect. There were actually three springs at different levels on the hill with the lowest one being the largest. Alongside this main spring was a large hut with about twenty clay fireplaces where the brine was boiled down to dryness in large iron pans to make salt.

The path from Mein to Bario ran north over the watershed of the Apad Dari range. The last few miles, we walked through secondary jungle growing on flat land, and then came out into the irrigated rice fields of the open *bah*. Ahead we could see Bario, the highest of the Kelabit villages — and the highest settled community on the entire island — right up against the rugged Tamabo Mountains which form the northwestern border of the Kelabit highlands.

Upon my arrival at the village of Bario, I was given a great reception. I recognized quite a number of people from my visit with Frank Davidson just over seven years earlier, although they now had a very different appearance. I also noticed a big change in the longhouse. How much of this was due to their ceasing to follow their old omens and taboos and accepting as much as they had of Christianity, and how much was due to the influence of the "Z" Special commandos who had been largely based at Bario, was difficult to say.

The Kelabits of the central highlands had provided the initial backbone of support for the "Z" Special Unit Allied forces. The "Z" Special forces had a major impact on the war in Borneo, contributing some 1,700 Japanese casualties and large territorial advances. Major Tom Harrisson attributed much of this wartime success to the unreserved support of the Bornean people and to their resourcefulness, bravery, and toughness:

> To a curious extent, the attitude of the best Australian soldiers was very similar to the attitude of the average Kelabit men, so lately forced out of head-hunting.
>
> Indeed the readiness of the Kelabits and others to learn from the Australian officers and NCOs was something to startle anyone. Their capacity for mastering the handling of a Bren gun would put almost any white soldier to shame. They were even able to carry out difficult repairs, and learned to make replacements for broken parts on Bren guns, carbines, Sten guns, entirely by observation, experiment and experience. This came both from the innate qualities of the people themselves and also from their intense interest in the operations of aggression and lethal achievement — an interest so closely parallel to that in the minds of these Aussie paratroopers themselves.[1]

Lawai Bisarai was still the Headman at the Bario longhouse. He had been decorated by the British Government, and most deservedly so, for the risks he took in support of the Allied forces. Lawai was a fine gentleman and a natural leader. He listened intently at each of

1. Tom Harrisson, *World Within* (Singapore: Oxford University Press, 1990), 278, 279.

the meetings I held, particularly as I spoke about the need to leave the old ways of superstition and drunkenness and to follow the teaching of God's word, the Bible.

Alcoholism was still a significant problem among many of the Kelabits, although not as serious as it had been among the Muruts. As with the Muruts, these drinking habits were a perversion of their admirable custom of hospitality. It occurred to me that we should be suggesting an appropriate cultural substitute for *borak* which these people could use for entertaining visitors and for general hospitality. Coffee seemed the most likely and suitable one, as they could grow it themselves and could also grow sugarcane as a sweetener.

In addition to being lavish in their entertainment, both with food and drink, the Kelabits formerly practiced many extreme customs. In earlier days, for instance, their initiation ceremonies involved dousing adolescent boys with blood which spurted from the arteries of a pig, tied to a trestle and beheaded by one mighty stroke of a sword! Their death feasts, too, were extravagant affairs held at great expense to glorify the departed spirits of the wealthy. Contrary to reports I had heard, death feasts were no longer common — most houses had not held them since the introduction of Christianity before the war.

Before setting off for the next longhouse, I gave the people at Bario whatever medical attention I could. The Kelabits appeared to be in generally better health than the Muruts had been, possibly because the climate in the highlands was cool and healthy, and there did not seem to be much malaria. Of all those I examined, I rarely encountered people with enlarged spleens, indicating that malaria was not widespread.

In order to make our way from the Kelabit highlands to the Baram River, we decided on a route that would first take us through one of the two western passes over the Tamabos and then down into the headwaters of the Akah River; from there we planned to travel by long canoe down the Akah to its confluence with the Baram.

We left Bario with twelve carriers, including four women, who were almost as strong as the men. For over an hour we climbed the dividing range, reaching an elevation of about 5,300 feet at the prominent Punga Pawang ridge, where we could look back over the whole of the Kelabit highlands. I remembered this breathtaking view from my first entry to the highlands in December 1939.

Once we were over the pass, we entered a strange forest of stunted trees, so frequently enveloped by clouds that everything was overgrown with a spongy moss and dripping with water. Natural flowers are less common in Borneo than one might imagine, but here exotic pitcher plants and bright tiny orchids protruded everywhere through the moss. We had to walk warily as the path was on top of a tangled blanket of intertwined, moss-covered roots, three or four feet above the ground.

After emerging from this fairyland forest, we commenced a continuous descent of about 2,500 feet to the Kuba'an River whose source rises near the famous needlelike peak of Mt. Batu Lawi. From there we walked more than three hours at a fast pace down the Kuba'an valley to the Kelabit longhouse, arriving just before sunset. It was a tiring day.

Kuba'an was the longhouse of Pun Abi, the first Kelabit to boldly take a stand of faith when Frank Davidson and I were making our return trip to the Medihit in January 1940. I recognized him immediately and was delighted to see him. His fellow Kelabits said that he had stood true to his confession throughout the years of the war and up to the present.

Although the others in this house had given up most of the pagan taboos, they still drank heavily and appeared to have only a superficial interest in Christianity. Nevertheless, we had a good meeting and a good discussion afterwards.

The next day, we made the easy three-hour trek to the longhouse on the Tik stream, a tributary of the Anggela River. I had an altimeter and a compass with me, and all along the way I made a tracing of the journey, plotting the travelling time in any one direction as shown by the compass, while at the same time taking altitude readings. After a steep climb from the Kuba'an, I estimated that from a certain high point on the ridge we should be able to see the top of Batu Lawi in a north-northeast direction. And sure enough, when we reached this point, the peak of Batu Lawi stood sharp and clear, just beyond the range that rises behind the Kuba'an valley. It was an awesome sight.

Needle of Stone – Aerial Photograph

From the house on the Tik, the path leading from the Kelabit highlands passed through wild, mountainous country, uninhabited except for the nomadic Penans. We spent the first full day travelling up the valley of the Anggela River to its source, camped in the jungle, and then crossed the watershed into the valley of the Tutoh River.

Shortly after lunch, the man who was carrying my rifle shot a fine fat wild pig. Then, suddenly, it started to rain heavily. We trekked on, but when we came to a small flat mound with huge palms growing nearby, we decided to make camp. In the downpour the small streams were quickly becoming raging torrents, and we knew that the streams further down the mountainside would be impassable. In an hour-and-a-half, we had a camp made, a fire going, and had changed into dry clothing. Before long, everyone was roasting ribs and skewers of pork over the fire, and when some travellers came along from the opposite direction, we invited them to join us. It was my usual practice to read and explain a section of the Bible to my carriers after supper, and that night our meeting in the jungle was larger than usual.

Next morning we continued our journey down the mountainside, a rough track with broken rocks and tangled roots of trees. We crossed and recrossed a stream sixteen times before reaching our camp site at Long Labid. This point, where the Labid River joined with the Tutoh, was the obscure junction that had given a name to the entire Kelabit people.

From here on the river was navigable, so the next morning two of our men set off through some very difficult jungle to get a boat while the rest of us waited in a substantial hut that had been built specially for this purpose. We waited all that day and half of the next before the men returned with the boat and we could begin the long, hard pull up the Tutoh River, including a 200-yard portage around some huge rocks. We arrived in rain at the Salam pass where we spent the last of five nights camping in the forest.

In the morning, we climbed to a ridge about 100 feet above the bank of the Tutoh where we had camped. This ridge forms one of the most remarkable watersheds I have ever seen with one side dropping sharply about 800 feet into the broad Salam valley. The Tutoh River rises on the north side of the Tamabo mountains bordering the Kelabit highlands; from the Salam pass, where our camp was situated, the Tutoh flows north alongside the edge of an escarpment and then down the opposite side of the watershed which is much less steep. I was immediately struck by the extreme simplicity with which this remote spot could be developed into a source for generating electric power. Few details had been published on maps of this remote part of the country, and I observed that some of the details which did exist were quite wrong.

When I wrote in my journal that morning, I noted that I had been travelling in the interior for six full weeks. I missed Winsome and often wondered how things were progressing with the mission station and the school; yet the opportunities and experiences I was being afforded kept me pushing forward. The Kelabit house at Long Lellang provided one of those opportunities.

The house at Long Lellang was one of several solitary Kelabit outposts on the outskirts of the highlands; it was people from Long Lellang who had been farming at Long Labid when Charles Hose asked the question which gave the Kelabits their ethnic name. Everywhere we went we had been told that the Long Lellang people were anxious to hear the gospel, and that was certainly the case. In fact, when one of our men trekked ahead to the house to announce our arrival, several of the people came immediately to meet us.

One of those who came was a fine upstanding young man named Raja Maran. "I'm so glad you have come," he said in greeting, partly to me and partly to himself. It was his emphasis and sincerity rather than the words themselves that impressed me.

The house at Long Lellang was not large as Kelabit houses go, for there were only about 120 people. We had been told by the people who came to meet us that there was an epidemic of measles at the longhouse, and it was all too true. The Headman and several other adults had been afflicted, and some had had the fever or rash for seven or eight days. Any attempt at isolation or preventing contagion was absolutely hopeless, but I told them they could observe two precautions: they should not bathe in cold water in an attempt to allay the fever and irritation of the rash; and they should not go into the sunlight while their eyes were still sensitive.

Despite the measles epidemic, we had excellent meetings, and the people listened with rapt attention. Afterwards, Raja Maran said that he would like to accompany me on the next leg of our journey to translate for me. His father was Kayan and his mother Kelabit, so he spoke both of those languages fluently. In addition, he could speak Malay, Kenyah and even Penan.

I told Raja Maran and the others of my special interest in meeting some of the Penan people; it was Penans travelling further downriver near the junction of the Akah and Baram Rivers who (along with the Kenyahs at Lio Matu) had originally petitioned the District Officer, Mr. Jacks, to inform me that they wanted to become Christians.

Upon learning of this, Raja Maran immediately offered to go into the jungle to make contact with these nomadic people and arrange for them to meet me at Long Benali on the Akah River, about a day's journey from Long Lellang.

The very day that Raja Maran set off into the jungle, a small group of Penans suddenly arrived at the Kelabit longhouse — three young men, three children, one girl and an older woman. They came in and shook hands with me in a shy, awkward manner with expressions of wonderment and awe, their sharp, clear eyes moving rapidly, taking in everything. The children were specially attractive, with bright, clear skin and pretty, well-shaped features, more oriental in appearance than most Borneo tribes. I noticed one Penan boy embracing a Kelabit lad and I remembered hearing that Penans would learn to know and trust one individual and follow him everywhere until they returned to their forest.

I spoke to these newcomers through one of the Kelabits who knew the Penan language, and they watched me with absolute intentness, drinking in every word. They said they wanted to become Christians and give up all their old taboos. They stayed on and ate with the Kelabits at midday, and then remained for the afternoon meeting, when I showed some rolls of pictures I had brought depicting the life of Christ.

While I was happy about meeting these Penans, I felt distressed that they had come into contact with the measles. Unfortunately, they had entered the house before I knew it, mixing freely with the people and eating with them. The best I could do was instruct them in the simple precautions they should observe, if and when measles did develop.

The next day we were packed and ready to travel downstream when suddenly a man came to me with an urgent plea for help. His wife, who had measles, had gone to the stream to bathe and while there had had a miscarriage. When I got to her, she was weak and hemorrhaging. I gave her a warm drink and quinine, and had the people carry her back to the house, using a board as a stretcher. Her husband stayed with her throughout, and I was struck by the tender affection he showed for her. I prayed for them both, and the people begged me to stay and help. So I sent messengers to Rajah Maran and the Penans at Long Benali explaining my delay.

The woman was getting weaker. Her pulse was feeble and rapid, and she had all but lost consciousness. I continued praying for her and giving her sips of tea with sugar. Gradually the hemorrhaging slowed. Later in the afternoon the placenta came away and the bleeding stopped completely. By the next morning she was feeling considerably stronger, and together we thanked God for sparing her life. As we packed up to leave, the people implored me to come again — no easy thing to do, as they were so isolated.

Following a great send-off, we negotiated our way for an hour down the rapids of the Potok tributary, and then bumped along down the upper reaches of the Akah River until we came upon a temporary

Kelabit farm hut. Countless numbers of large fruit-eating bats were flying overhead — these were similar to, but slightly smaller than, the large "flying foxes" that we often saw nearer the coast, flying overhead in the evening and hanging from certain trees along the river during the day. As we approached, we learned that the Kelabits had felled one of these trees and killed some hundreds of the bats, which they were now busy skinning and smoking over a fire. The remainder of the bat colony were so disturbed that they were still flying about, forming a black cloud in the sky, a full day later.

From there we continued down the Akah through a gap in the Murud Kecil mountains. We had seen the main Murud peak from the Salam ridge when we left the Tutoh and descended the Salam valley to the Potok. Now we passed through a gap in this range to reach a small tributary, the Benali, beside which was a large farm-hut belonging to Raja Maran's father and mother. There a large number of Penans had gathered, full of wonder and expectation.

The Penans truly were a childlike people. Their expressions, manner and attitude revealed their lack of sophistication, which gave me a feeling of extra responsibility for them. They were keen to believe in Jesus and to abandon their taboos, and I felt sure they understood the elements of the gospel. I taught them how to pray. Then we managed to translate the song *Jesus Loves Me* into Penan, and they soon learned the words and the tune. *Guru* Riong also taught them another song he had translated.

After the meeting some of the Penans returned to the forest, but most stayed and slept in the hut with us. My camp bed was tight against the wall, and I had Penans asleep on the floor all around me, packed tightly together.

They were anxious for us to come again, and assured me that the next time there would be hundreds more from the forest to meet us. I hoped at some future date that I would have the opportunity to spend several days with them in their forest haunts to see how they lived.

It appeared that the Penans were sometimes exploited by their Kelabit, Kayan and Kenyah neighbors. Although the Penans made beautiful mats and other woven objects from the best rattan, they often exchanged these for a handful of tobacco and a few matches.

They wore the scantiest clothing, even according to native standards, and most of what they did wear was old and tattered. I made a mental note to bring some cloth next time to give in fair exchange for their rattan work.

In the forests, the Penans were expert at hunting with blow-pipes. During the war, a number of them had joined the "Z" Special Unit forces as irregular operatives, bringing their blow-pipes with them:

> The dreadful advantage of blow-pipe attack is its silence. If you miss with your first, just flip in a second dart from the bamboo quiver, press lips against the pith base and with sibilant puff, barely audible, whirl the next point at a target a hundred feet, or further, away.
>
> Death by blow pipe is agony. I am not in a position to say whether it is worse to die from the needle stab of a dart dipped in glucoside or in the strychnine types of poison, both of which are obtained from tree sap in the interior. The glucoside kills by shocking the heart, the strychnine by shattering the nervous system.[2]

After leaving Long Benali the next morning we passed through several sets of rapids. Like all people living on the great rivers of Borneo, our crew showed wonderful skill in managing the boats. Once we were in the rapids, it was almost as though their bodies and minds became part of the boat. Our man in the stern was particularly adept. Half the time he was in the water, swimming with his canoe, pulling it, dragging it, jumping onto water-buried rocks to swing it aside, and then leaping back into it and paddling, poling and guiding it.

At one point we came to a gorge where we plunged down a drop of several feet and our boat was swamped. But the man in the stern was already in the water, and almost before I knew what was happening, he swung his end of the boat over and supported it on a rock. We soon bailed out the boat and plunged on again. A hundred yards or so further, however, we had to get out and make our way along the bank, while the boatmen handled and guided their crafts

2. Tom Harrisson, *World Within* (Singapore: Oxford University Press, 1990), 266.

through seemingly impossible places. After that stretch, we continued down through more difficult rapids till we reached the head of the Merigong Gorge. It was absolutely impassable — a seemingly endless cataract dropping several hundreds of feet over a distance of a mile-and-a-half.

Navigating Major River Rapids

At the top of the gorge was a substantial slab hut, built above the upper ledge of a huge rock face which sloped down to the river's edge, and we set up camp there for the night. I thought the loud roar of the river plunging down the chasm would keep me awake all night, but I was so tired that I fell into a deep sleep almost the moment I laid down.

CHAPTER 16

Early the next morning the Kelabits went back upstream to their home at Long Lellang, while Raja Maran and two Penans started overland to the Kayan house at Long Siniei to ask them to bring boats to transport us.

With virgin forest above, and a roaring gorge below, I had just settled down in the hut for a morning of writing when I saw four men approaching. *Guru* Riong and Kading, who were with me, said these visitors were Kayans; as they came up to the hut, they were astonished to hear me talking to my companions in Murut-Kelabit. They asked what I was doing and who was conveying me. When I told them that my Kelabit helpers had gone back home to Long Lellang and that we were waiting for Kayans, they were aghast.

"The Kayans downriver are all under *pantang* (taboo)," they told us. "They will not be able to come for another ten days!"

Our visitors felt certain that the Kayans at the next longhouses would not break this taboo and, believing that we were stranded, they offered to help us carry our travelling gear to the foot of the gorge, where there was another hut we could stay in. There were seven of us, and we had nine loads which we had to carry about one-and-a-half miles over very rough country.

It was heavy going, but we had almost reached the foot of the gorge when we met Raja Maran and the two Penans, along with a big party of Kayans coming for us. Raja Maran had evidently been a very effective advocate, for the Kayans had actually broken the *pantang* to fetch us — a thing they would not do even for the Government! They were a merry lot, fourteen of them in all, and they had two boats. After all the loads had been collected, we set off in the middle of the afternoon and again bumped and plunged down dozens of big rapids, far worse than the rapids on the upper parts of the Akah. One of the boats was swamped, and my reserve clothes tin filled with water. Everything got wet. Unfortunately, the water even penetrated a metal container and spoiled the film I had made of the Kelabits.

After three hours of these rough rapids, our boatmen guided the boats into the sheltered riverbank at their village of Long Siniei. A large number of boats were tethered at the bank, and there were crowds of people. The village had about three hundred people in all, living in two longhouses. The Headman received me with quiet dignity and courtesy, and showed me into a large, simple, guest room.

This was my first experience with Kayans, a people whom I came to know well. Some years later, Tom Harrisson asked me to contribute a chapter describing the Kayans, and their Kenyah neighbors, for a book he was compiling on behalf of the Sarawak Museum. Following are some extracts from this publication:

> The Kayan and Kenyah people, though quite distinct, are often found in association or living in related areas, and may therefore be considered together. They inhabit the middle and upper reaches of most of the main rivers of both Sarawak and Indonesian Borneo.
>
> Although much has been said of the warlike headhunting of the Kayan and Kenyah, his main outlook on life is essentially that of the farmer. Religion, customs (including headhunting), social structure, and much folklore was directly related to the rice-farming cycle. Although a river people, they had never developed irrigated rice culture; and in climate with a rainfall as heavy as Borneo the success of the crop depended largely on the right choice of land, a good burn-off, and the timing of planting and harvest. In these matters the chief held the prerogative, but decisions were always made after consulting the omen birds and animals, the most important omen being the flight of the Brahminy Kite, an eagle.
>
> Both Kayans and Kenyahs have an implicit belief in the supernatural; only rarely did one formerly meet a skeptic. Spirit beings were roughly divided into two classes. One class, the *toh*, were usually unnamed, except the specially malignant ones. They inhabited the jungle or rivers, or hovered at night, and warning of their activities was given by omen birds or animals. Hence these omens were strictly observed. Trouble could be averted by heeding the warning or by propitiatory sacrifices. The other class were anthropomorphic gods, vaguely regarded as their ancestral

> heroes, and each had a specific name and was the subject of folklore and legend. They were considered to be the guardians or patrons of the main activities of the people, such as farming, hunting, war. Over all these was belief in a supreme spirit being, known in Kayan as *Lake' Tenangan*, and in Kenyah as *Bali Peselong*. He was considered as omniscient and as a supreme arbitrator. It was a high conception, but he was completely anthropomorphic, with a wife and family.[1]

Raja Maran, whose father came from this house, was anxious for the Kayans to become Christian. Since he spoke Kayan fluently, he translated for me as I told them about the basic elements of Christianity.

The Kayans were interested in this faith that was so new to them, but their response was quite different from that of the Kelabits and the Muruts. They said they wanted to become Christians, but not yet. Having commenced their long series of taboos and omens for the season's farming, they feared to break them until harvest. The old shaman would not meet with me or even look at me, but seven younger shamans, known as *dayongs*, spoke with me. They claimed to have direct contact with the spirit world, which they greatly feared.

At one of our meetings I paraphrased two stories from the Bible about Jesus casting out spirits. Later I had some good talks with several of the leading men and women. The wife of the old Headman, Balu Aran, was a charming person and was very keen for my wife to visit them. She was one of the *dayongs*, and when I first entered her apartment she asked if I wanted her to call down one of the spirits.

"No," I said. "But I would like to tell you about Jesus, who came to deliver all of us out of the power of the spirits."

That night it rained heavily, and next morning the river was raging. The treacherous rapids of the Akah made travel impossible, so I spent the day mixing with the people and getting to know them better.

During the afternoon I had an attack of malaria, so I promptly took some quinine and atebrin and a little calomel, and after an uncomfortable evening my temperature went down. There was quite

---

1. *The Peoples of Sarawak*, edited by Tom Harrisson (Kuching, Sarawak: Government Printing Office, 1959), 39, 42, 43.

a lot of malaria around, but with so many people and my dwindling supply of medicines, I could treat only the worst cases, most of them children.

The river was down the next day, though still higher than normal, but the people said we could travel. I was sorry to leave them, but they made me promise to return and assured me that they sincerely intended to give up their *pantangs*, destroy their charms and fetishes, and become Christian.

We left Long Siniei in two boats, with fourteen men, and went down even worse rapids than before, a journey of three hours to the Kayan village at Long Tebangan. Here again, two Kayan longhouses were situated in a commanding position on a high bank with a full view of the roaring river below.

My arrival took them by surprise, but they were all interested to hear the gospel story, and that afternoon I showed some rolls of pictures and preached to the people in one of the longhouses. The Headman, Aban Jok Ngau, was a progressive man of strong personality, and the sub-Headman, in whose house I stayed, was also quite outspoken.

After the evening meeting in his house, the sub-Headman said that he and his people wished to become Christians immediately, but that the people in the other, larger house were still under *pantang* and feared to break the taboo. Next morning, I went to this larger house and spoke again to the people. All the men were keen to believe, but the women were afraid. After some discussion, it was decided that I would go down to Long Akah to visit the Kenyah chief, *Penghulu* Tama Weng Ajeng, and return in about three or four days time, when they all intended to renounce their old pagan worship.

Although I had hoped to travel straight to Long Akah without overnighting at any villages along the way, my plans were changed when we stopped in at Long Tap, a Kenyah village halfway to Long Akah. The custom in the Baram area was to escort a traveller from one village to the next; however, at the time we arrived at Long Tap, most of the people were out on their farms, and no one was available to accompany us, so we had to spend the night there.

Many in this village could read and speak Malay, and after I had spoken to them that evening, they copied out several hymns in

Malay and a hymn in Kayan, which I managed to translate with their help. I felt they wanted to jettison their old pagan religion straight away, but their Headman was not there, and it would have been unthinkable for members of a longhouse to take a decision of this magnitude without at least discussing it first with the Headman.

The following day, these people prepared a large boat in grand style with a wooden canopy over the middle section; since the rapids were not as bad from here down to the mouth of the Akah, this larger, more cumbersome — and also more comfortable — boat was manageable. As we cruised downstream, I noticed that a lot of rubber trees had been planted in this lower section of the Akah which had been settled by the Kayans and Kenyahs for many generations.

Upon approaching the village of Long Akah, we could see the old government fort on a commanding site, and the tempestuous Akah River pouring into the broad sweeping rapids of the Baram, all set against a backdrop of majestic mountains.

At the junction we started up the Baram, past the bazaar, and after about half-an-hour reached the *Penghulu's* house at Long San. Information about my visit had been sent to him, but the messenger had not arrived, so my coming was a complete surprise.

As I entered the huge communal area, the *Penghulu* welcomed me and conducted me to his section of the long, open veranda-hall which is characteristic of every traditional longhouse. I sat next to him on a low stool, while the people sat respectfully at a distance.

I had heard of *Penghulu* Tama Weng Ajeng from people all along the Akah and even in the Kelabit country, but I was hardly prepared for meeting such an impressive personality. I guessed he was in his early forties, and though he stood less than five-and-a-half feet tall, he appeared massive, for he was broadly and powerfully built. His hair was cropped in Kenyah style, his face was round and chubby, and his earlobes had been stretched from childhood.These features, coupled with his serene expression, gave him a Buddha-like appearance. He spoke in a measured and thoughtful manner.

After a suitable interval, the *Penghulu* showed me to his own quarters where I could bathe and change. His section of the longhouse was made up of a set of apartments covering an area bigger than our whole house at Budok Ngeri. An entrance passage led around a corner to a huge hall, while off to one side were the servants' quarters and the cooking area. Along the other side was an inner room and two separate alcoves. There was also a storeroom and a bathroom. The roof was high, and several hurricane lamps and a pressure lamp hung from the ceiling. Hanging on the walls were guns and numerous framed photographs.

As I entered his apartments, his wife received me graciously and with great dignity. Her name was Tijan Anyi; she was the daughter of the ruling chief of the Kayan village at Long Laput, further downriver. She wore simply a black sarong from the waist down and had quiet, gentle movements and the unmistakable stamp of good breeding.

Both Kayans and Kenyahs valued and respected the ruling class. The social structure was largely hereditary, and marriages were usually arranged between families of similar status.

Kayan and Kenyah women were small-boned and shapely, and generally had light-colored skin, even lighter than some Europeans. In those early postwar years, they still wore heavy earrings on extended earlobes. Their earlobes were pierced in infancy and the lobes were then greatly extended by adding heavier and heavier rings until they hung far below the neck to the top of the breast. Also, they often wore a little tassel of fine beads from a small hole pierced in the top of the ear.

The ordinary working dress was a small length of cloth wrapped around the body and overlapping at one hip, and tied by tapes or cords, leaving a gap down the thigh on that side. When working, they gathered this cloth up, drew the front section between the legs and tucked it in at the back, giving them freedom of movement. In addition, the women had their legs tattooed from mid-calf up to and covering the whole thigh. The tattooing consisted of fine triangles and circles and straight lines, all close together and in a pleasing pattern, thus giving the appearance from a distance of long dark stockings. Tattooing involved many long painful hours spaced over several years as needles were used to punch in ink made from a mixture of soot and tree resin.

Both Kayans and Kenyahs had a refined sense of decorum, respectful behavior and social etiquette. For instance, when I ate, the

Penghulu's wife came to sit on a stool at my side to talk and see that I was provided for. She began by deprecating the quality of the food; even though it was very nice, she was observing the correct etiquette by inferring that I deserved something better. She sat there while I ate, then brought me a cup of coffee afterwards.

When we moved to his room, the *Penghulu* and I talked more freely.

"For a long time I have felt that the old taboos were meaningless and I have wanted to forsake them," he told me.

On one of his trips to Marudi, he had asked a Roman Catholic priest to come up and teach them, and he also had told the District Officer that he wanted to change from the old customs. Then, about four or five weeks before my arrival, the *Penghulu* went downstream to meet the Governor, who was visiting Marudi. After the Governor's visit was over, the *Penghulu* brought the Catholic priest, Father Jansen, back to his house at Long San. Father Jansen was there about three weeks and had returned to Marudi only about a week before I arrived. He told the *Penghulu* he intended to bring back two younger priests and would build a house and church at Long San.

The *Penghulu* had a neat notice-board set up in his house saying that on May 9, 1947, he had forsaken his old *adat*, or animism, and become Christian.

Eventually we got around to the question of what my plans were for further visits in the Baram area, in view of the fact that Father Jansen had arrived there first.

"Perhaps a division of territory could be arranged," the *Penghulu* suggested.

I did not think that his idea was very workable, nor did I feel it was right to define peoples' beliefs by establishing artificial boundaries, and we discussed this openly.

"In addition," I told him, "we both know that the Government supports freedom of choice in matters of religion."

He acknowledged this and agreed that everyone should be able to make his or her own choices with complete freedom. But, as a temporary resolution, I offered to focus my efforts on the longhouses outside his sphere of authority until after I had spoken with Father Jansen, and he seemed relieved with this compromise.

Upon leaving the *Penghulu's* house, we started back up the Akah River and once again confronted the Batu Murik rapids, the most dangerous section of the river, named after two Murik people who had drowned there. We scrambled through the bush and over huge rocks for a distance of about 300 yards while the boatmen dragged and poled and pulled the boats up through the rapids. Enormous rocks remained where the river had broken through a mountain barrier, and the water tumbled and boiled between these huge boulders. There was a great deal of shouting and excitement among the crews, but after an hour of supreme effort they came through safely and we all got into the boats again. The journey back to Long Tebangan took three times as long as it had to come downriver three days earlier.

When we arrived, I went to stay in the same longhouse as before, where the people still wanted to turn away from spirit worship. However, those in Headman Jok Ngau's longhouse were less favourably inclined so I arranged for *Guru* Riong to hold a meeting in the sub-Headman's house, while I went to Jok Ngau's house.

"Let the Kenyahs adopt new customs if they wish," some of the Kayans said. "But we Kayans, not yet. Let's wait and see."

That evening I sat and waited a long time for people to gather. At first only children came, so I taught them the one Kayan hymn I had translated. Then a few women gathered.

One woman, Awan Usung, spoke up apologetically for all of them. "It's not that we don't believe you," she said, "but we are afraid to forsake our old spirit customs."

I had asked Jok Ngau to come and interpret for me, but I waited and waited, half-an-hour, one hour, and longer. In a matter of such importance, no one other than the Headman was willing to interpret, so I just sat and waited.

I prayed inwardly about the situation, for I knew that a spiritual battle was being fought. Finally Jok Ngau appeared and we agreed, since the hour was late, that it would be best to meet the next day. The Headman was a fine man with a rational, strong character. I felt sure that he himself was in favor of a change, but he knew there was some hostile opposition and apparently he did not want to bring the matter to a head there and then. It was a tactical wait on his part.

By then it was almost midnight and I was utterly weary in mind and body. I could hardly concentrate on what I was saying and caught myself making many slips in language, so I was glad that I could finally lie down and rest. I fell immediately into a deep sleep, oblivious to the nighttime interruptions of life in a longhouse. A pack of dogs erupting in frenzied barking at intruders, real or imagined, moving in the jungle; a baby crying; a water buffalo rubbing his mud-caked hide on the timber posts supporting the longhouse — I was awakened by none of these.

The next morning I returned to Headman Jok Ngau's longhouse, and again I sat and waited; but this time the Headman came and sat with me. He shouted orders for the women and others to come and assemble. He told me that the men were ready and willing for change, but the women feared to break with the spirit world. So I took a picture roll and went from family to family, showing the women some of the pictures and inviting them to come to the meeting.

The woman named Awan Usung was the most reluctant. She was one of the nine *dayongs* in the longhouse and was their spokesperson. When she finally agreed to come, it was the turning point, and others followed her lead.

Jok Ngau translated for me as I spoke simply, concentrating on the essentials. I stressed the power of Christ over the spirit world, and I spoke about Satan, who became the enemy of God and the enemy of mankind whom God had created.

Attitudes were starting to change. People who had been opposed or merely neutral now listened favorably to the gospel story — except for Awan Usung.

"Let others forsake the old way," she said firmly. "I will not."

The Headman said to me quietly, "You leave it to us to decide." So I left the big gathering and returned to the other longhouse.

After lunch the Headman came to me and affirmed that the matter had been settled. Awan Usung had relented, and there was no further opposition to our teaching.

The people wanted *Guru* Riong, Kading and I to carry away their fetishes and charms associated with spirit worship and cast them into the jungle, but not to burn them, as they feared to breathe the smoke. It was arranged that we would do this the next day. They also asked me to teach them how to pray; they wanted to pray for protection against the spirit world. So that afternoon, with their assistance, I translated the Lord's Prayer into Kayan, along with another prayer they could use in the morning and evening. We also translated a prayer they could use before meals. I emphasized that these prayers were only models, and that they should feel free to pray using their own words.

That evening we had a good meeting with everyone eager to listen and learn. But the next day, Thursday, June 5th, was a day I shall never forget.

It was the day that the first Kayan longhouse in Sarawak formally turned away from the spirit worship and taboos which they had followed for hundreds of years. This was nothing short of a miracle, because these people had lived in dread of the spirits and were always trying to appease or outwit them.

Yet in spite of all the costly sacrifices of pigs and fowls, the Long Tebangan Kayans were frequently hungry and their farms were neglected through obedience to adverse omens. Restrictions imposed by taboos as a result of hostile omens or dreams often meant that they would accomplish only one week of work on a farm in a month. Sometimes contrary omens or bad dreams dictated the abandonment of a farm, or a canoe under construction, or even compelled a newly married couple to separate.

Against that background, the morning was filled with an air of expectancy, with everyone wondering just what would happen. The *dayongs* had been busy from early dawn performing the final rites or ceremonies for the spirits. Each *dayong* first performed a ceremony with loud incantations near the longhouse, and then at the river's edge. I could not interfere, nor did I think it right to attempt to do so, as the village had still not actually abandoned their taboos. The ceremonies were carried out with great solemnity. The spirit world was very real to them, and they genuinely wanted to be free from their bondage to these malevolent spirits which had dominated their lives.

After breakfast all the people, about 300 or more, assembled in the open hall of the longhouse and I addressed them, explaining what we would do. Then I prayed in the Malay language for God's power and protection, and I taught them the Lord's Prayer in Kayan.

Realizing that the spirit priests, the *dayongs*, were the key people, I asked all nine of them to sit in front. Then I asked each one individually if they were willing to renounce their submission to the spirits, and trust in Jesus Christ alone. As each one openly assented, I took their hands in mine and prayed with them individually that God would cast out the evil spirits and give them his Holy Spirit. I wanted it to be perfectly clear to all the people that their spirit priests had rejected everything to do with the former spirit worship. Then I asked *Guru* Riong to pray for the whole village.

The next step was to get rid of all the fetishes and charms upon which they had relied for protection. Many of these were tied under the rafters of the longhouses. They asked me to start cutting them down.

"No," I said. "If you are really trusting in the power of Jesus, then one of you cut down the first."

The men had their war *parangs* at their waists. Suddenly one of them — a man who had lost six children despite frequent offerings to appease the spirits — sprang up and, with a wild cry, cut down a fetish smeared with the blood of a sacrifice. After that, all the men went through both longhouses, cutting down their own charms and fetishes with their long knives. At first they slashed at the charms with fierce yells, but after a while the procedure quietened down. They continued until not a vestige of spirit worship remained.

It was more difficult to deal with the charms and fetishes which the women possessed. These were mostly concerned with their rice farming activities and with the protection of their children, and the people really feared contact with these items. In each family apartment they made a hole in the floor and lowered the fetishes and charms to us, beneath the house. There were old musty boxes filled with bones, bundles of rags smeared with the blood of sacrifices, bamboo cylinders filled with moldy cooked rice, and an assortment of roots, leaves, spiders, cockroaches and even some rats' nests. As I received one of the bundles, a young python, about three feet long, slithered out! Apparently, it had been preying on rats.

Guru Riong, Kading and I, along with the men and some of the women, carried these things out to a place in the forest not far downriver, where we cut them all open and scattered the contents, to the accompaniment of some frightened shrieks from the women. On our return to the longhouses, the people, especially the women, spontaneously held up their arms to heaven and exclaimed, "Oh, Lord Jesus, we are trusting you now. Please protect us."

As they went up the steps into the longhouse, the women broke into a dance of celebration, an uninhibited display of joy and gratitude — the kind of dance which in the past would have celebrated the return from a successful war expedition. And as I entered the longhouse I felt as though a fog had lifted; the oppression of the evil spirits was gone, replaced by an indescribable sense of relief, freedom and release. The mist of darkness had been dispelled.

After the initial, spontaneous celebration, the people killed a pig in each longhouse and had a feast, at midday in one house and in the evening in the other. After the evening feast I prayed with the assembled village, giving thanks to God and asking for his blessing and protective power over all the people. We sang, and I taught them more about what it means to be a Christian. What a tremendous difference there was in the peoples' attitudes. The atmosphere had completely changed. It was a genuine spiritual awakening.

A test of their new faith came the very next morning. The men decided not to work in their fields on this first day of their new way of life, but to go hunting instead. So they took their spears and hunting dogs and set out downstream. The first animal the dogs chased up was a large sambhur deer, an animal which under their old beliefs had been strictly taboo to the Kayans.

"What shall we do?" they wondered.

"Well, now that we are Christians we should not fear the taboos. Let's chase it."

So they gave chase.

Incredibly, the deer ran into a Kayan cemetery — a place they had greatly feared because of the spirits of the dead!

This certainly gave them pause, but again they determined to trust God to protect them and continued their chase. To their amazement, the deer's antlers became caught in some branches; they speared and killed it and brought it back to the village.

That evening the venison was shared by all the people, and they gave thanks to God not only for the food, but for the evidence of his power and favor. No one got ill or suffered any kind of misfortune. God rewarded their trust in him and strengthened their faith.

Chapter 17

We left Long Tebangan in a flotilla of long canoes. The Headman, Aban Jok Ngau, and crowds of others accompanied us downriver to the longhouse at Long Senayau where we arrived to a huge welcome that had the atmosphere of a homecoming. It actually was a homecoming in reverse, as the people at Long Senayau had formerly lived in a third longhouse in the Long Tebangan village. Two years earlier they had decided to move to land that was more fertile and downstream from the dangerous rapids.

Their Headman, Aban Anyi, was a fine old gentleman. He was greatly respected and had some special charms which no one but himself dared touch. His wife was also very influential; she was not only a *dayong*, but also a *nyiho*, which meant she was responsible for determining the omens controlling the farming cycle.

It was wonderful having the Kayans from Long Tebangan with me — they could not stop talking about how the power of God protected them from the spirits.

That afternoon I did some medical work, treating a number of adults and several children for various ailments. The women, especially, expressed fear about what might happen to their children if they gave up the old spirit customs. As I spoke about God's offer of salvation and answered their questions, I tried to make the issues clear. Once again, as I had done at Long Tebangan, I stressed that the *dayongs* should express their individual commitment first. Then I asked the whole assembly to affirm that they also would turn away from following the spirits, and they all solemnly did so. Later they threw out their demonic tokens. The old Headman had one magic charm which he greatly revered, but he resolutely cast it away.

"I inherited that charm from my father," he told me afterwards. It had a value of more than three hundred dollars, a large amount of money for him.

After all the evidences of satanic worship had gone, there was a feeling of intense relief and celebration, expressed by spontaneous dancing. In a later discussion with the Headman, I discovered something of real significance.

"When the people started to dance," he told me, "I held back and watched them closely to see what would happen. On former occasions whenever the *dayongs* danced, evil spirits would come into them and possess them. They would fall into a trance and utter sayings beyond their control. This time when the *dayongs* danced, nothing of this sort happened."

It was convincing proof to him that the spirits had really gone.

In the midst of all this, some Kayans arrived from Long Laput, the largest longhouse in the Baram area, and they listened intently as I spoke. Next morning, the Kenyah *Penghulu*, Tama Weng Ajeng, came with seven others from Long Akah. I was glad these visitors could see for themselves the joy of the people and the changes that had taken place in their lives.

Later that day we all witnessed a definitive change from one of the old pagan practices — the ritual of naming a child. One of the important taboos for a newborn child was that it must be kept in a dark inner room for some weeks and bathed only in rain water. The mother had to sit with her back to the fire for a fortnight to make her perspire profusely, and the only food she was allowed was plain cooked rice. On no account could the mother take the child to the river for several months, and then only after it had been given a name at a ceremony involving sacrifices of blood offered by a *dayong*.

The people asked me if I would pray for this ten-day-old baby and give him a name. I consented gladly and arranged for a service later that day. I also drew up a prayer of dedication in Kayan, which they could use as a model after I was gone.

That afternoon we went down to the river and, as I prayed for their protection, the mother gently bathed the child in the river water. It was an act of great courage and faith for this woman to break an ancient taboo with this her firstborn child. When we returned to the house, we dedicated the baby to God and named him Ibau Wan.

In the evening, we had another service at which I again taught and answered questions from these people who were facing such radical changes in their lives. I was amazed at how open and teachable they were.

I had intended leaving the next day, but word came that the District Officer would arrive from upriver after passing through the Kelabit country, so I decided to wait for him. This gave me time to rest and also to study more of the Kayan language. I was pleased with the progress I was making in learning this new language as I had already been able to translate three hymns and five prayers into Kayan.

After the District Officer, Mr. Morgan, arrived, I travelled with him down to Long Akah. He said that while he was upriver, he had become seriously ill with malaria, or something similar.

"I thought I was going to die," he told me. "And then when I started to recover, I was so weak I had to be carried on a stretcher for several days."

He also expressed his amazement that the Kayans of Long Tebangan had become Christians since he knew how resistant they had been to change. I had an excellent opportunity to describe the events of the past few days to him before we reached our destination late in the afternoon.

Strategically located at a juncture of several trade routes, the village of Long Akah included a small Chinese bazaar, and an old government fort built during headhunting days. We spent the night at the fort which now served as the headquarters for the government upriver agent and, while there, I drafted a telegram for Winsome, which I asked Mr. Morgan to carry downriver and send on to Lawas.

"Expect to be back in Lawas about mid-July," I wrote to her. "Hope we can both return to the Baram shortly thereafter. Opportunities here at present are great."

The following day I said farewell to most of the Kayans. I was genuinely sorry to leave them, but they gave me a team of six expert boatmen and a longboat to take me on my journey.

One of them, Anyi Jau, was a noted singer of chants, the traditional way in which the Kayans recorded and passed on to posterity the great events in their history. This young man was famous for his ability to improvise and sing these chants, and he provided entertainment on demand. The chants, songs and stories of Borneo would fill many books. In a land without writing, these had been passed on from generation to generation in outstanding feats of memory and marathon imitation.

An hour after leaving Long Akah we passed a Penan house. These Penans, like those I had met at the headwaters of the Akah, roamed habitually in the jungle but had recently been persuaded to build a house and try farming. About seventy or eighty people were supposed to live in this house which was large enough for only about twenty. It probably served its purpose, however, since they still spent much time in the jungle so were seldom all together at one time. Only seven Penans were there during our visit, and all were ill with fever. They were nominally attached to the Kenyahs of Long Akah for trading purposes, but they seemed rather neglected and appeared very dejected.

The next five Kenyah villages were all under the control of *Penghulu* Tama Weng Ajeng so we did not stop. We continued generally south, but our progress was slow and tiring as there were many difficult rapids. The fifth village was situated at Long Paku, the most southerly point of the Baram River; from there, the river took a huge bend to the east and northeast.

We were now deep in the interior of Borneo. The elevation was still only a few hundred feet above sea level, and oftentimes the air was motionless, the clouds low, and mists hung about the hills until late in the morning, sometimes till midday. The equatorial sun was relentless during the day and even the nights were sultry.

The virgin jungle contained massive trees, some close to 200 feet high, yet with root systems amazingly close to the surface. In order to counteract their top-heaviness, some of the largest specimens developed root buttresses at the base of the trunk — huge woody flanges assisting to prop up the towering giants above, and forming one of the most striking features of the Bornean rain forest.

A short distance beyond Long Paku, as we were ascending some rapids, a drove of wild pigs crossed the river. The Kayans in one of the boats ahead of us succeeded in diverting the animals and managed to capture a small one. Then a huge boar swam near our boat, and I fired my rifle and wounded him. He got to the gravel wash at the edge of the river and tried to climb the bank, but it was too steep. By then I was out of the boat and on the gravel edge myself. He turned to attack me, but I stepped back on the rocks and fired again. This time I hit him in the head and he rolled over, dead. He was an enormous boar with huge tusks and very fat. Everyone was jubilant over this kill as we were running rather low on food.

Later in the afternoon we arrived at Long Ta'an, the site of the largest Kenyah village we had seen, with five longhouses under one Headman. These Kenyahs were of the Lepu Aga clan and lived in territory under the control of a *Penghulu* named Mapei Arang, who I had not yet met.

Nearly all the people were sick or recovering from measles, so the boar I had shot was a welcome addition to their food supply. Sadly, by this time, my supply of medicines was badly depleted, and I could treat only the most urgent cases, including two children with pneumonia to whom I gave an antibiotic.

I tried to get to know the people and help them medically, and also collect a number of Kenyah words and phrases. After three meetings, some of the people said they wanted to follow God and not the spirits; others said it depended on the *Penghulu* and the lead he gave. They were openly friendly, but the old *nyiho*, the shaman in charge of the farming cycle, seemed a rather shrewd man who opposed our message.

After leaving Long Ta'an, we pressed on up the Baram. Most of the journey took us through stretches of calm water, interspersed with a few rapids, but in two places the river passed between high walls of rock — hazardous passageways when the river was swollen, though not difficult at low water levels. We paddled continuously for six-and-a-half hours, alternating paddlers, until late in the afternoon when we turned into the mouth of the Moh River, a big tributary sourced near the Indonesian border. *Penghulu* Mapei Arang's home village of Long Moh, comprising four longhouses and about three hundred people of the Lepu Tau clan of Kenyahs, was another fifteen minutes upstream.

Upon arrival, we discovered a sad situation. The whole village had been infected with measles — hardly a well person anywhere. Everyone looked miserable, with sore eyes, high fever, diarrhea, blotched skin and incessant coughing. And just as we arrived, a child died. He was about three years old, and the only child of his parents.

The people told us that the *Penghulu* was away hunting wild pigs. They expected him to return that evening, but he was delayed by a heavy rain. However, his family entertained us graciously in his big apartments, and a sub-Headman of one of the four longhouses came to visit with me. He spoke Malay well, and I had a long talk with him. He was a thoughtful man and asked many penetrating questions.

The next day *Penghulu* Mapei Arang returned. He was an old man, but had an active, supple body and a sharp, intelligent and strong face, deeply lined and with sunken eyes. He looked every bit the warrior. He wore a tiger tooth through a hole punched in the upper shell of each ear, in his day the unmistakable mark of any Kenyah or Kayan man who had successfully taken a head. He spoke Malay fluently, and had travelled to Java, Singapore and all parts of Sarawak. He was defensive at first, concerned that I might want to pressure him into change.

"My people and I have followed our old customs for centuries," he said. "Even if you teach them, well, perhaps in four or five years they still might not understand it."

I assured him that I had no intention of trying to hustle him into abandoning his old customs.

"I would like to get to know you and your people," I told him. "And I would like to tell you about what I believe. But everyone must choose for himself entirely."

His attitude softened after that, and he began to tell me about some of the Kenyah beliefs. We discussed his concept of God and talked about the unreliability of spoken traditions handed down from our forefathers. In that regard, I told him that God has given us an unchanging revelation in his word, the Bible. He then shifted to the subject of alcohol and asked why I did not drink. I gave him simple and cogent reasons.

"You are straight and true," he said, "different from other white men I have met."

I took this as an invitation to explain more about my faith.

"Yes, I want the truth," he said in Malay. "No half-measures."

During the afternoon I did some medical work, but with my medicines in such short supply, I had to pass over dozens who needed treatment.

In the evening I had another meeting with most of the older men, followed by a good and thoughtful discussion. They knew about a Kenyah clan across the border in Indonesia who had become Christian through the work of the Christian and Missionary Alliance, and they viewed this favorably. In addition, the *Penghulu* was keen to have a school. He had apparently asked the Government several times to open a school and was rather disgusted that so far they had not done so.

The next day I inspected several possible sites for a school and house for a teacher, and possibly a mission station. The people had great hopes that we would be able to help them. *Penghulu* Mapei Arang gave us a good send-off with a big boat and a large crew, and I felt we had won his confidence.

The next village upriver was a group of three longhouses at Long Sebatu, about two hours up the Baram from Long Moh. This village and the neighboring one at Long Semiang were both under the control of *Penghulu* Tama Weng Ajeng and, in keeping with the understanding we had reached when I met with Tama Weng three weeks earlier, I did not plan to spend any time there. However, these people had heard of my arrival in the area, and although they knew about Tama Weng's attitude, they invited us to visit and said that they wanted to hear my message and become Christian.

They insisted that I stay overnight and asked me to visit one of the houses where there were many sick people. They were in a sorry state. One young man had died the day before and had not yet been buried. Most of the others had succumbed to the measles epidemic. At least two seemed to have pneumonia, including one young man, a son of the Headman, who died an hour later. His older brother was also seriously ill.

The situation was indeed pitiful. Most of the ill were unwashed and neglected, so I showed them how to wash a sick person with soap and warm water. I proceeded to wash two people myself and insisted that they wash the others before I would give them any more medicines.

These people literally yearned to turn from the worship of the spirits and to trust in God. It seemed that the Holy Spirit had prepared their hearts. The Headman and others wanted me to stay and help them cast off their old religious customs in two days time. They said the death of the Headman's son prevented them from doing so immediately. I felt, however, that it would be wiser to wait for a few days, until after I had returned from Lio Matu. By that time they would be calmer and also would have had an opportunity to inform *Penghulu* Tama Weng Ajeng of their intention. The Headman of the nearby village of Long Semiang was planning to go downriver and it was decided that he would advise the *Penghulu* of the Long Sebatu people's desires. He said that his village also wanted to become Christian.

The next morning I did two more rounds of visiting the sick before making the short two-hour trip to Long Semiang where there were two big longhouses. The people there were known by the ethnic name Murik, with affinities in language and culture to both Kenyah and Kayan. We had a midday meal with them, treated a few sick folk, and then went on to Long Tungan, about two-and-a-half hours further upriver.

These people were also a distinct ethnic group known as Nyamuk Kenyahs and were under the control of *Penghulu* Mapei Arang. During the time we spent with them, they showed little desire to hear the gospel message. They were in the grip of the measles epidemic, so I treated about forty people with solution for sore eyes. As usual, I advised those with measles to keep out of the sun and not to bathe in cold water. Some heeded, but some did not, trying to cool their fevered bodies regardless of the consequences.

Given the wide exposure we had, it was a miracle that neither *Guru* Riong nor Kading contracted measles.

Less than an hour further upriver, I reached the first Badang Kenyah house in the Lio Matu area — an auspicious moment, for it meant I was at last able to fulfill the invitation from these people sent through the District Officer eight months earlier!

The Badang Kenyahs lived in two areas, separated by less than an hour's journey. The Headman of the whole group was Lian Bilong, and he lived in this first village at Long Salupa.

That evening I had a long talk with the Headman and a few others. Lian Bilong was a man of strong personality and was unusually outspoken. He had advanced ideas and said he had not followed omens in making his farms for over two years. However, he still feared the evil powers of the demon world, made sacrifices and followed the complex rituals associated with the Kenyah taboos. In our discussion he spoke with vigor and courage in denouncing the old customs and sacrifices to the demon spirits.

In one season's farming cycle, he estimated the community would sacrifice forty fowls and several pigs to the spirits, as well as much rice and *borak*. None of this would be eaten, but would be put on poles as offerings to the spirits. In addition, each family had its own individual sacrifices to make, and if any illness or calamity occurred, many more sacrifices were required.

Like the Kayans, these people had a complex system of rituals and taboos, but the Kenyahs used more images and shrines. Each Kenyah community had a system of images, shrines and sacrifices, some with local variations.

All around the longhouse, images crudely carved on logs stood upright in the ground. There were also some very tall poles with a grinning effigy roughly carved at the top of each. These were surrounded by scores of short poles on which offerings were made to the spirits. In addition, there were special shrines, sacred stones and bones. And then there were the skulls hanging in the longhouse.

Each family apartment had its little conical wicker receptacle for votive offerings, and each rice storehouse was equipped with its own shrine and a set of miniature articles symbolic of farming operations. The Kenyahs also had special war shrines, including those they had set up when they went to fight the Japanese with the "Z" Special commandos who had parachuted into the Baram area under Major Toby Carter.

Their experiences with the commandos had brought them into contact with the Muruts and Kelabits, many of whom had already been freed from the fear of the spirit world. And now a spiritual confrontation was about to take place among these Kenyahs.

The Headman, Lian Bilung, and some other leaders were ready to leave their old customs and spirit worship, but others resisted out of fear. Like the Kayans, these people wanted to be free from the intolerable burden of it all, but they feared that the spirits would be angry and return to harm or kill them. So after speaking to them on Sunday morning, I left them to think and talk about it till after lunch, when we all assembled again.

This time I could sense there was a real battle — not just a wordy dispute — and I could feel the powers of evil strongly resisting any decision for action. So I read to them again from the gospel story about how Jesus cast out demons and how the demons feared him. At last there was a unity of assent, although some who agreed were still fearful. The people of the main longhouse had decided to become Christian, which was about half the Badang Kenyah community in the Lio Matu area.

That same afternoon all the occupants of this main longhouse held a service of prayer at which they affirmed their renunciation of the old life of serving the spirits and their acceptance of the new life, following Jesus Christ.

As before, I prayed individually with the *dayongs* and those who invoked the spirits. After that the people removed all the charms and fetishes from the longhouse and rice storehouses and burned them on a large fire. Then they knocked down the carved images outside the house or cut them down with axes. One very tall pole, which they particularly feared, came down with a resounding crash. All of this was a tremendous step of faith for them to take.

An expectant mother, who had had great difficulty in giving birth to her previous child, asked me to pray with her specially, which I did. Then she bravely took off her protective charms and gave them to me.

In the evening we had a meeting of prayer and celebration. The Kenyahs were naturally musical and learned new songs and hymns quickly; they even improvised some beautiful harmonies. And through it all I could feel their sense of freedom and relief from the influences of evil.

The next morning we arranged to go with a large party to the other section of the Badang Kenyah community, about an hour's journey upriver. This was the last section of the Baram River that was navigable by any kind of craft. Beyond this point, walls of rock formed impassable gorges.

At Lio Matu the river level is about 700 feet above sea level, and within a few miles it rises to around 1,500 feet in an area occupied by the Saban people. From there the river passes through more gorges until it is about 3,000 feet above sea level at the southern end of the Kelabit highlands, at Ramudu. The name Lio Matu means "hundred islands," referring to the many islands in the Baram River as it emerges from the lower end of its tempestuous course out of the Kelabit highlands.

Soon after arriving at the upper village at Lio Matu, I held a meeting with the people and encountered strong resistance from some of them. I had heard this village had an old and influential *dayong* who was said to have great occult powers. The people told me he was ill and asked if I would go to see him.

I found this old man suffering from advanced tuberculosis. I explained that this illness was not due to demons but to contagion, and that good food and proper care would help him. I also told him that each person in the family should have their own eating utensils.

Later, at midday, a deputation from one of the three longhouses came to see me. They assured me that they believed the message of the gospel to be true, but rather than accept it now, they said there were many reasons why they should wait until some future time.

I told them that if they sincerely wanted to follow God, they had to earnestly seek him.

"If we acknowledge God to be the creator," I said, "then we should not expect to dictate the terms in our dealings with him."

Recognizing that there was still opposition, I asked for the main Headman of all the Badang Kenyah people, Lian Bilung, and the local leaders to assemble everyone. I said it was better for me to talk to all the people rather than to a deputation, as each person must answer to God individually. When the people gathered, I could sense the atmosphere of strong conflict. I outlined the gospel message again and the people started to gravitate into two groups — those who wanted to become Christian and those who wanted to wait. The tension was tremendous.

"The old *dayong* wants to speak to you," someone said to me suddenly.

I noticed that this influential old man had entered the house unobtrusively some time before, so I went over to where he was sitting.

"I want to follow Jesus," he told me firmly.

Immediately there was a great commotion, and one of the strongest objectors leapt to his feet. "Then we will all follow," he shouted.

"The Lord Jesus has triumphed and Satan has lost," others cried out.

Everyone was rejoicing — a dramatic moment.

We gathered everyone together, and all the people affirmed their commitment to abandon spirit worship and trust in Jesus Christ alone. I prayed for all of them, and especially for the old *dayong*, that God would deliver him from the demon powers that had possessed him.

It took them two hours or more to destroy all the shrines, hew down all the images, and cast out all the charms and hundreds of sticks upon which votive offerings had been impaled.

One fetish in the form of a crocodile, outlined in stones, had been invoked as a protection against the Japanese during the war. They were very frightened of this and other major fetishes, and as they removed them they prayed, "O Lord Jesus, help us, and do not let the spirits return. You are responsible for us now."

That evening we returned downriver to Headman Lian Bilung's house at Long Selupa, and the next day Lian held a huge feast. The Badang Kenyahs from the whole Lio Matu district came to share in this celebration. Afterwards, we had another meeting and I taught the people more about various aspects of Christianity.

The following day, I had packed up to start back downriver to Long Sebatu. The boat was already partly loaded when people came to tell me that the expectant mother for whom I had prayed had begun to feel birth pains. She was rather apprehensive in view of her last experience and because of bad omens at her marriage. Since these people had just been set free from the powers of Satan, I knew I should stay and pray with this woman.

Next morning, the baby was born — a beautiful little girl. But the midwives soon became worried about the next stage and started shaking the women. I tried to get them to stop but had limited success. However, I did manage to help get things tidied up.

By that time it had started to rain, and it teemed all morning, but at midday there was a lull, so once again I prepared to leave. However more trouble came, and the people asked me to stay. The woman had become extremely exhausted and could not urinate. To remedy this condition, the midwives were making her drink so much water that she began vomiting it up again. I tried giving her some sips of hot tea, but this did not seem to help. Her pulse was becoming weaker. Her husband wanted to perform a pagan rite, and her brother demanded that she be given more water, but I was able to divert them on both counts.

I stayed on with her and I prayed as she slept. Suddenly I felt the oppression lift, though she did not appear to be any better.

The midwives brought hot stones wrapped in cloth to place on her abdomen, and I thought this might do some good. However they also wanted to pound up hot chili and use this to stimulate urine by placing the chili paste in the birth canal. I was horrified, and was able to stop them. Next they brought green ginger and made her swallow some. They took more raw ginger and pounded it and were going to put it into the birth canal. It had not even been cleaned, and I pointed out that there was earth mixed with it. So they washed some more ginger tubers, and pounded them, and placed that inside the woman. Not long after that the urine came. I was greatly relieved, but wished I had had a catheter instead!

She was still dazed and weak, but the crisis was over. She needed food, so we cooked two eggs and mixed them with rice and got her to eat it slowly. In a short time she started to revive.

All in all, that afternoon had been a tremendous strain — much harder than a full day of preaching!

Some hours later, the woman told me that while she was sleeping she had a vision of someone who said to her in her own language, "All will be well."

Using the events of the afternoon as a reference, we determined that this dream must have occurred during the time that I was praying to God for her recovery! My prayers had been answered. In a remarkable way God was teaching her — and me — to trust him more completely.

CHAPTER 18

Upon arriving back at Long Sebatu, I found that three more people had died during the six days I was away, and several were still seriously ill. That evening I had a long talk with the Headman and the senior men of the village until well after midnight. They told me they were truly weary of serving the demons and longed for freedom.

By the time I went to my room that night, I had a throbbing headache. Hours of discussion and answering questions had left me absolutely drained, both in mind and spirit. Also, I had been wrestling with myself over plans and strategies that daunted me. Even though God had been doing amazing things on a day-by-day basis, my mind had become preoccupied with trying to orchestrate the future. Feeling doubt and discouragement, I collapsed, exhausted, into bed.

The next day, June 28th, was my 47th birthday, and what a notable day it turned out to be.

After an all-too-short sleep I woke to the crying of a two-year-old with a bad pain somewhere, and soon after his parents came to ask for medicine. When they left, I prayed for special strength for the day; and my Scripture reading brought to mind that God was ready and able to give his "grace to help us in our time of need."[1]

I also prayed that God would preserve a witness to himself among the peoples of the Baram. Little did I know that just two years later we would have an experience with the Kenyahs of this very house that would revolutionize our personal lives.

At about six-thirty the old Headman came in to talk. He could see that I was still reading, so he turned to Kading who was cooking breakfast. Kading had a knack for diverting people when I was preoccupied, and he replied to the Headman's questions in monosyllables at widely spaced intervals. Soon two other men came in and sat down patiently. Then, when I started shaving, they began questioning me about the day's program.

---

1. Hebrews 4:16

After breakfast I visited some more sick cases in two of the longhouses, and then hurried back to the larger of these houses where we were to have the first big meeting. With these Long Sebatu people there was no protracted struggle before the decision was made to turn from the old pagan customs, but the courage of the decision and the reality of freedom from the powers of evil were no less real. When all the materials associated with spirit worship were gone, the people from the two houses gathered for a period of celebration and singing.

Then, feeling very positive, I proceeded to the third longhouse which, although in the same village, was some distance away and housed people from another Kenyah clan with slightly different customs and language. As I approached this third longhouse, I could hear the people wailing — another young man had just died.

I entered the house and found the parents and sister weeping over the body of the older brother of the young man who had died just eight days before. I had met this man on my first visit upriver, and even then knew he was very ill. At that time he had told me he trusted in God, so I suggested that we give him a Christian burial.

In view of this recent death, I did not think they would want to go on with destroying the pagan fetishes and charms — but they did! So we held a community service of dedication and commitment to God and then proceeded to burn several loads of the demonic tokens. We also buried about twenty-five human skulls.

Having lived all their lives in fear of the demonic powers they had seen manifested through using these charms, some still doubted that such powers could be overcome. I heard later that one of the old *dayongs*, seeing me disposing of some of their most feared charms said to those around him, "He will be dead by this evening!"

It was nearly dark by the time we held the burial service for the young man. I remember reading out the magnificent promise of life after death: "The trumpet will sound, the dead will be raised imperishable, and we will be changed."[2]

It had been a strange birthday for me, mingling joy and sorrow; yet through it all rang a note of triumph. And despite the old *dayong's*

2. 1 Corinthians 15:52

forecast, I was still decidedly earthbound the next day. We had a good Sunday service with the entire village; as was the case at the other villages, the people made great progress in their spiritual understanding once the evil influences were gone.

Earlier in the day, the Headman of Long Semiang had arrived from Long Akah, bringing the news that the Catholic priest, Father Jansen, was coming upriver from Marudi. I had spoken with this Headman before he went down to Long Akah and told him that *Penghulu* Tama Weng himself had agreed that all people should be free to follow the teaching they believed to be right. The people of Long Sebatu had clearly indicated that they desired the simple message of the gospel. They also appreciated the counsel, the teaching and the medical help I had been able to give them.

The next day, the Headman from Long Semiang asked me if I would go upriver to his village when Father Jansen arrived that afternoon, and I agreed to do that.

Father Jansen was an old man of about seventy, short and slight, seemingly shrunken by years of exposure to the tropical sun. He was bald with a gray tuft of beard. His thin face was deeply lined, and steel-rimmed spectacles rested on a nose that looked to have been broken. When he opened his mouth to speak, he revealed a collection of crooked teeth in lamentable condition, the result of a lifetime spent in places that offered no dental care. His blue eyes appeared gentle and disarming so I was taken aback when he addressed me.

"I'm sorry to see you here," he said bluntly with a strong Dutch accent.

"Well in that case I'm rather sorry to see you," I responded. "And furthermore, you've had access to the Baram for forty years. Why all this sudden concern?"

This initial exchange certainly dampened further conversation. Shortly thereafter, we proceeded upriver in separate boats. The *Tuan* Padre and I were not off to a very good start.

After we arrived at Long Semiang, I told Father Jansen that I would like to make a fair and equitable arrangement with him. I suggested that each of us should speak for an hour that evening, as many of the people wished to hear from us both. He refused, saying that he was not allowed to enter public controversy. Then I suggested that he take the evening and I take the morning, but he refused this also, saying that he wanted to go his own way entirely.

After dinner that evening I taught the people some hymns, but I could see that the atmosphere was disturbed so I did not attempt to hold a service or do any teaching, and at about nine o'clock I returned to my room. Later on, the priest came out from his room and commenced teaching, but very few listened to him, only one or two who had known him years before.

Later that evening, however, the Headman told me that he had consulted with his people and they felt obliged to follow the priest as the *Penghulu* had sent him upriver. Under the circumstances it would have taken exceptional moral courage for the people to resist pressure from both the *Penghulu* and the priest.

The next morning some of the people asked me to show them my rolls of pictures, and quite a good crowd gathered. In order to avoid needless trouble, I did not speak for any great length of time, but I did want to establish my right to preach when I was asked to do so. Later, after I had packed up, many people came asking me to pray with the sick and to give them medicine. As I did so, I reminded myself of the need to be faithful and to persevere.

I left before midday and returned to Long Sebatu where I received a really touching welcome.

"Even if the *Penghulu* is angry with us," the Headman said, "we will continue to believe what you have taught us."

Upon leaving Long Sebatu, I met up again with Father Jansen who had set off from Long Semiang that morning, and for awhile our boats were side by side on the river. Neither of us could call at Long Moh as their whole village was under a taboo, so I stopped and spent the night at Long Ta'an and the priest went on downriver. The next day when I got to Long Paku, I learned that Father Jansen had stayed the night there but was already gone.

Most of the people were away, so I could not get a boat to go on further and had to stay overnight. After the evening meal the people who were there asked to see the picture rolls and sing the hymns I had translated into Kenyah. I was careful to wait until the Headman himself asked me to speak, and we had a good meeting together.

Many people needed medical treatment, so I told them that if they could take me down to Long Akah, I would send medicines back for them. Eight people had died here recently. I estimated that fifty or more people in the area had died within the last six weeks from the measles epidemic, mostly children and young people — a heavy loss for the people of the upper Baram.

Three men took me down to Long Akah, a full day's journey. There I stayed with *Penghulu* Tama Weng Ajeng. He was friendly, and I had a long talk with him, telling him frankly about events upriver — the positive developments among the people at Long Sebatu, and the unfortunate confrontation with Father Jansen. His wife, Tijan, and the people of the longhouse were also open and friendly, and that evening the *Penghulu* invited me to speak to them. They listened well, especially some of the young men.

Next morning I reminded the *Penghulu* that the Roman Catholics had been established in Marudi for nearly forty years, with a mission and a primary school there, but had made little impression on the people upriver. But when the gospel had been given to the Muruts and Kelabits in Sarawak, and to the Batang Kayans in Indonesia, the people of the Baram had seen the changes it had brought and had realized that God's message was for them also. The *Penghulu* admitted that this was true.

"If only you had come earlier," he said.

Penghulu Tama Weng Ajeng was a man of character, courage and vision who, in his small world, had attained the stature of a statesman. When the "Z" Special commandos under Major Toby Carter parachuted into the Baram area in 1945, the whole force was dependent on the goodwill of Tama Weng, the most influential chief in the remote interior where they started their adventure. They told him their purpose for being there and threw themselves completely on his mercy. He had several alternatives. He could betray them to the Japanese; he could arrange to have his own warriors remove their heads; or he could simply evade the issue, refusing to have anything to do with these latest intruders, claiming that it was not his fight. Alternatively, he could hide them and actively aid and abet them in organizing a revolt against the occupying army.

He did not hesitate. Calling the Kenyah and Kayan *Penghulus* and Headmen into conference in his house near Long Akah, he announced that he favored rebellion. For three days the discussion continued, and after many arguments and counter-arguments, the chieftains resolved unanimously to offer their help to the handful of Allied invaders. Undoubtedly their decision was weighted by the relationship they had had with Rajah Vyner Brooke and his Government before war broke out in the Pacific. And once they had made this decision, they never wavered, but worked and fought with unremitting zeal for the cause.

It would be naive to suggest, however, that Tama Weng's motives were always wholly altruistic. He also had a political agenda and a desire for material gain. Lalang, the wealthy chief of the Kayans, known as "the Queen of the Kayans," was growing old, and she had no son. Tama Weng was already Lalang's son-in-law, his marriage to the lovely Tijan having been arranged years earlier by his own famous father. His next step was to increase his influence in that important Kayan house at Long Laput, so that his authority might gradually extend among the Kayans as well as his own Kenyah people. For that reason he married his son Kalang to Lalang's adopted daughter, Ubong:

> The union of Kalang with Ubong was an act of high politics, a shrewd stroke of statecraft, like one of the dynastic marriages between children of royal houses in medieval Europe. It united two important governing families in two neighboring societies. For long Tama Weng had planned it, and in achieving it he gained a diplomatic triumph.[3]

After my visit with Tama Weng, he arranged transport for me to go back up the Akah River. Before I left, however, I asked for two things: I asked him to keep an open mind himself and to not hinder others from making their own free choice.

The Kayan house at Long Senayau was a short distance up the Akah. The people seemed to be doing well after their first three weeks of being Christian, and they asked me to stay the weekend with them.

---

3. Malcolm MacDonald, *Borneo People* (London: Jonathan Cape, 1956), 264.

They were happy in their newfound liberty, and it was a joy to hear them praying. But a number of them had also experienced Satan's counter-attack. Some, especially the women, had dreams of spirits trying to attack them. One woman said that even in daytime they troubled her, but she said they ceased when I came. Many people, both men and women, asked me to pray for them individually.

They also asked about baptism, so I read them some related verses from the Bible and explained that their sins were removed from their hearts by faith and not from their bodies by water. I also explained that baptism was important as an expression of their faith. That evening I taught them more fully, and next morning I spoke about baptism at the morning service. As a result, twelve asked to be baptized, including the old Headman, Aban Anyi. Several times he raised his right arm to heaven asserting that he would follow Christ to the very end.

"Our father and mother [meaning the old pagan religious customs] are dead," he said. "I have thrown away my valuable charms inherited from my father and now I trust God wholly. I also place my utmost confidence in you, so I look to you for teaching and guidance."

Aban Anyi was the grandfather of the Seling family, several of whom later had a prominent part in the church in Sarawak.

During that weekend at Long Senayau we discussed the issue of drinking at great length. Drinking was a difficult question for them, as it was an essential part of their traditional hospitality. Among the Muruts and Kelabits the issue was more clear-cut, as it was directly associated with sinful practices such as drunkenness and sexual promiscuity. But not so in Kenyah culture or with most of the Kayans. Indeed, they said that my major fault was that I would not drink with them! Only evilly disposed or surly people with something to hide refused to drink! Several of them had been really hurt because I refused to drink even a little. I hoped they would accept and understand that if I were to drink with them, it would greatly offend the Muruts and Kelabits who had turned away from drunkenness and become Christian. More than that, the Muruts and Kelabits would have felt I was sinning and leading others into sin, thereby undermining the credibility of my ministry.

I left Long Senayau on Monday morning for downriver, and called in to see Tama Weng once more. I wanted to find out his attitude to our Mission building a house at Long Akah. As we discussed the matter, I definitely felt that he would like to have us there. He was concerned about offending Father Jansen, however, so we left the matter of building a house suspended until our next visit.

We continued downriver to Batu Talang where a Kayan village of the Uma Pu clan were busy building a new longhouse for sixty families. The place was a beehive of activity, with dozens and dozens of boats bringing timber and other building materials. Although everyone was busily involved in the construction, they erected a tiny temporary hut where I could stay. I was able to have a meeting with them and did a lot of medical work the next morning before we went on to Long Pilah where *Penghulu* Kebeng lived.

Kebeng held authority over the many villages of the Uma Peliau Kayan clan, including Long Tebangan, where there had been such a notable Christian breakthrough. *Penghulu* Kebeng had heard of the people at Long Tebangan becoming Christian, and even though his village was under taboo, he arranged for me to stay nearby in the government primary school building. Later that evening he also arranged for me to have a meeting in the huge open hall of the longhouse, where I showed and explained the picture rolls. A good number attended and seemed to understand.

Next morning *Penghulu* Kebeng organized transport for me with a Chinese trader who was going downriver to Long Laput. On the way we passed two more Kayan villages, Long Miri and Uma Bawang, each with about forty family units and both under taboo.

Near the village of Long Laput were many limestone caves inhabited by countless numbers of small swifts. These birds would fly at high speed into the complete darkness of the inner caverns, guided solely by sonar reflections from their own tiny and frequent squeaks. Partially digested insects were ejected from the swifts' beaks to form their nests, which were then selectively removed by the villagers and sold to Chinese traders. Bird's-nest soup was a highly priced Chinese delicacy, and these sales provided the people at Long Laput with a continuous source of revenue.

The main house at Long Laput was huge, the longest in Sarawak, with ninety-eight apartments extending for just short of half-a-mile along the river bank. Among those living at Long Laput was Lalang, the Queen of the Kayans. Since she was away, I held only one night of meetings.

Next morning I continued downriver. We called at the Long Lama bazaar, stopped briefly at two Kenyah longhouses at Long Banyo, and finally reached Long Ikang about dusk. The people here were closely related to the Kenyahs at Long Sebatu, who had received the gospel so gladly. The longhouse was solidly built, and the Headman's apartments were huge — a great open hall with five smaller adjoining rooms used as the private quarters of different members of the family.

That evening Headman Aban Gau entertained us with an excellent meal, and after dinner we discussed some of the issues involved in leaving traditional spirit worship to become Christian.

Aban Gau was about ten years younger than *Penghulu* Tama Weng Ajeng and considerably slimmer. Whereas Tama Weng displayed monumental calm, Aban Gau readily expressed his sentiments.

Politically, their association was close with both serving as representatives of the Kenyahs on the recently created District Council. On public questions they planned and co-operated together in promoting progressive policies. In later years, Aban Gau himself became a *Penghulu,* and Tama Weng was elevated to the position of *Temenggong,* meaning paramount chief. Both leaders were gentlemen of strong character, highly regarded by the Government officers, and I was to enjoy a cordial relationship with them throughout the coming years.

I had packed up early the next morning to be ready for a Chinese launch going downriver, but it was delayed. When we finally got underway, we made only about four knots per hour, and with several stops in between we did not arrive in Marudi until about five o'clock. I went up to the Catholic Mission and met Father O'Brien, who we had known before and during the war, and he invited me to stay the night. We had a good talk that evening, including a frank discussion about my differences with Father Jansen who had accused me of exerting undue pressure on the Long Sebatu people. As I had been careful to avoid doing this very thing, I felt it was important that Father O'Brien hear about my interaction with the people from me personally.

The next day I continued on to Miri, where I called on the Resident, Mr. Gilbert. He was openly critical of my entering the Fourth Division territory without his knowledge and said he had written a strong letter to the Resident of the Fifth Division, Jim Anderson, about my presence in the Baram. Needless to say, I was astounded.

I explained to him that last October I had received a letter from Mr. Jacks, the District Officer at Marudi, reporting to me that the Kenyahs at Lio Matu and the Penans at Long Akah wished to become Christian and inviting me to visit them. Mr. Gilbert said that he had not known of Mr. Jack's letter to me nor of my official reply to him that I intended to accept this invitation. He also had not received the message from Mr. Meikle, the District Officer in Lawas, that I was proceeding to the Kelabit country and then on to the Baram after we had investigated the longhouse murders on the Luping River.

In light of these facts, Mr. Gilbert's attitude changed dramatically and he withdrew his censure. He also told me that Father Jansen had been vigorously protesting my presence in what he regarded to be his territory. However, after a strenuous half-hour discussion, I was able to present my perspective of the situation, and I promised to send in a written report about my visit.

I had a bad stomach upset that night and was up several times vomiting. I had not been sick the whole time I was in the interior, and I was grateful that God had kept me free from such attacks. I was also glad for some rest the next day and I started work on my report for the Resident.

The following day I stopped in to meet and visit with Major Toby Carter, who was now working with Shell. He seemed a very fine gentleman, and I was particularly interested to hear first-hand about his interaction with the Kayans and Kenyahs as he led the commando forces in the Baram during the final year of the war. Then

I made one more visit to the Resident, Mr. Gilbert. He assured me that he had no objection to our visiting the Baram again, provided we gave him advance notice of our coming, but the matter of any permanent settlement in the Baram area would require approval from Kuching.

Later I boarded the S.S. *Marudu*, and we steamed overnight for Labuan, arriving just after ten the next morning. I made hurried enquiries at the office of the shipping agent, Harrissons and Crosfield, about onward transport. To my dismay, I learned that the next vessel to Lawas was due to sail in two days and would take a week to arrive. Anxious now to be on my way back to Winsome, I fretted and fumed, but also prayed that God would open a way for me to get home sooner. Then I noticed a vessel leaving immediately for Brunei and was able to board it. We arrived in Brunei at three o'clock, just in time to catch the government launch to Limbang. I was in Limbang by five and met Jim and Dood Anderson, who invited me to stay with them at the Residency.

I was there for a day, completing my report for Mr. Gilbert and visiting old friends, and the next day, July 19th, I took a government launch to Lawas.

What a joy it was to see Winsome again — and even sooner than I'd anticipated, for she happened to be in Lawas town when I arrived, and I met up with her in the bazaar where she was surrounded by a group of students from our new school. She had a warm, easygoing personality and everywhere she went people were attracted to her. I certainly was.

Although my journey was long and oftentimes difficult, it had been a wonderful experience, and being with Winsome again was the perfect ending. We walked home together through the rubber estate to Budok Ngeri.

Chapter 19

During the three months and ten days I had been in the interior, a mountain of correspondence had piled up at our headquarters at Budok Ngeri. We had no secretarial or clerical assistance during those early postwar years, so although I had never been trained to type properly, out of sheer necessity I developed a passable proficiency using two fingers.

Correspondence was not our greatest concern, however. Brian and Irene Morcombe's health was not good, and within three weeks of my return, they and their little baby went to see the government doctor at Brunei for medical assistance. His report indicated that their food was not sufficiently nourishing and their workload was too great. Neither of these came as a great surprise to us, particularly the latter. We had been praying earnestly about our need for new workers however, and help started to arrive.

Our longtime friend, Enid Davidson, along with her six-year-old daughter, Margaret, came at the end of August 1947, accompanied by the recently married Alan Belcher and his wife, Madge. As Enid had been required to go back to Australia in mid-1941 on account of her pregnancy, her husband Frank, who died in the Japanese prison camp, never had the joy of knowing his daughter.

It was good to have Enid back at Lawas. She was a university graduate and a trained teacher, and with her knowledge of both Malay and Murut-Kelabit languages, she was well able to teach in the Bible school. Our greatest need at the school was to prepare pastors for the rapidly increasing number of churches in both Sarawak and North Borneo, and Enid was the ideal candidate to do this.

With so many opportunities available to us, I thought and prayed much about which field of service Alan and Madge Belcher should occupy. Initially it seemed that North Borneo may be the logical choice, as Alan had been there before, but the need in the Baram seemed even greater, so I suggested that they visit the Baram area to assess this for themselves.

At the same time, we received reports that the Muruts and Kelabits of the interior were still greatly disturbed by the violent murders on the Luping River, so Winsome and I felt we should once again visit both the middle and upper Trusan as well as the central highlands.

Before she left Australia to rejoin me, Winsome had been given a special gift by an elderly woman in New South Wales — it was a portable organ donated expressly to be taken to Borneo. Winsome was absolutely thrilled and, under her musical touch, the instrument was a delight to all of us at Budok Ngeri. It was not the concert hall Winsome had once dreamed about, but her audience was certainly no less appreciative, and her musical reputation spread rapidly.

The organ was about three feet wide, three feet tall, one-and-a-half feet deep and weighed just over forty pounds. It was designed so that the legs and foot-pedal bellows could be folded for moving, and as we prepared for our next journey into the interior, the people begged us to take the organ with us. We reminded them of how awkward it would be to carry, but they would not be deterred. Our carriers, both Muruts and Kelabits, who were all volunteers and refused to take any payment, said they could carry it on their backs! The organ certainly added a new sparkle to the Murut and Kelabit hymns the people had learned to sing, and everywhere we went these joyful songs inspired their worship.

Long Lapukan, on the tributary of the Luping River where the killings had taken place, was full of sad memories so the people were gradually moving to Long Luping, the confluence of the Luping and Kelalan Rivers. The Headman, Sia Tagko, was a man of strong character, and he encouraged the people to look forward.

We stayed only one night at each village and pressed on up the Beluyu valley until we reached the source, where we then descended gently into the picturesque irrigated rice fields of Ba Kelalan at the lower end of this hidden valley.

The people at the central village urged us to stay on for Christmas, so we visited various villages in the area and then returned on Christmas Eve to stay with my old travelling companion, pastor *Guru* Riong, and his wife and family.

Christmas Day, 1947, was a memorable one for us. People from all over the valley kept coming to the village all morning. I had a meeting with the church leaders to discuss various problems, and then we held a crowded service in the church. This was followed by a huge feast, and then games and sports. In the evening we had another service in the church, followed by the Lord's Supper, at which there were 112 communicants.

By this time, these people had been Christians for over thirteen years, and their lives were completely different from what they had once been. The old orgies of drunkenness and degradation were now completely gone. The population, which in 1934 was about 275 for the whole valley, was growing rapidly — there were dozens of children, and they were all so happy!

The day after Christmas we crossed the border into Indonesian territory and went on to Belawit where we stayed with pastor Aris Doemat for two days. Then we crossed back to Sarawak territory and started our circuit of the Kelabit highlands, and the little organ accompanied us everywhere.

At Bario we met Tom Harrisson, who was back visiting the village where he had set up his wartime commando base. Since his return to Borneo after the war, he had been awaiting confirmation of his appointment as Government Ethnologist and Curator of the Sarawak Museum at Kuching.

One of Tom's many positive contributions after the war was to help establish a primary school at the Mein longhouse, with *Guru* Paul Kahoun as the headmaster. *Guru* Paul was an Indonesian from the island of Roti, near Timor, which had long had a strong Christian influence through the work of the Dutch Reformed Church. Paul, desiring to be a Christian worker, had been admitted to the Christian and Missionary Alliance Bible School at Makassar in the Celebes. Subsequently, he and other teachers had been brought to Borneo by John Willfinger, and some time after John's execution at the hands of the Japanese, Paul had gone to live in the remote Kelabit highlands. In addition to his teaching skills, Paul was an effective preacher, and it was largely through his work that the Kelabits turned away from practices involving spirit mediums.

Guru Paul's firm adherence to biblical standards did not always line up with Tom Harrisson's views of what was in the best interests of the Kelabit people. While I admired Tom's commitment toward helping the people, it seemed to me that he wanted the Kelabits to retain all of their cultural practices as a living study in anthropology, even though he recognized that change was inevitable, and sometimes even desirable. As he would later write:

> I suppose I was one of the last people in the western world who wished to upset and alter other people's beliefs as such. But it would have been impossible to have conducted any operation had we followed local observances and determined the movements of our runners — or our aeroplanes — by the position of the first barking deer to sound off on the track in the morning, or the direction in which an eagle was last seen to be soaring over the mountains at sunset.[1]

In any event, the major changes among the Kelabits came from within, after they had seen for themselves what God had done in freeing the Muruts from the powers of darkness. Experiences like these caused the Kelabits to see the reality of the message of the gospel, and they came to realize that this did not mean a change of culture, or the learning of a new religious ritual, or following a new human teacher, or a new national allegiance, but a living faith in God who had created all mankind.

The changes taking place among these people were of such magnitude that they attracted considerable attention and debate. The December 1947 edition of the *Sarawak Gazette* featured a comprehensive report on the Muruts written by the Resident, Fifth Division, along with an editorial insertion of some comments by Tom Harrisson which I believed created an incorrect impression.

I felt compelled to respond to the issues raised in this publication, so while we were still at Bario, I wrote a rather long letter to the editor of the *Sarawak Gazette* in Kuching. Following are extracts

---

1. Tom Harrisson, *World Within* (Singapore: Oxford University Press, 1990), 236.

from this letter, which was published in full in the April 1, 1948, edition of the *Gazette*:

> On this present journey I have again verified that neither songs nor dances nor any ancient arts and crafts have been lost or discouraged through the conversion of the Muruts to Christianity. It is a fact, acknowledged by the Muruts themselves, that within living memory the only songs and dances known to them were those associated with head-taking, and these ceased to be practiced under government control; although I understand that until their conversion occasional murders were celebrated by a head feast held secretly a year or so later. Other songs and dances, still common among neighboring tribes, and much of their truly ancient tribal culture had before this become submerged in a morass of drunken degradation.
>
> It was under such depressing circumstances, well-known to all who knew the Muruts in the old days, that certain arts and crafts deteriorated, and their conversion to Christianity has in fact encouraged these very desirable parts of native life. All through the vast Murut hinterland (and in speaking of Muruts we must ignore international boundaries) certain arts and crafts are specialized in different localities. For instance the Muruts at Brayong still have a thriving rotan *lampit* mat industry, and they also make the excellent *kelapit* rotan baskets which are their specialty. Again, the Murut women's sun hat is something which is unrivalled by the sun hats of either Tagals or Kelabits. They still make *parangs*, padi baskets, mats, and during the cloth shortage, their bark coats, and in certain Murut localities they have vigorously revived the art of weaving. Under the pressure of modern influences the pattern of native life and culture is bound to change, whether as a result of Christian teaching or of increasing contact with coastal influences. Indeed the change to wearing shorts and cutting the hair had begun among the Muruts long before the advent of the mission.
>
> We are very conscious of the dangers incidental to the abandonment of pagan superstitions and practices, and the need for intimate knowledge of the customs and culture of the people who look to us for spiritual guidance, and we are glad of all constructive suggestions that may help to this end. It is in this spirit that we approach the profound changes that have already taken place on the Kelabit plateau

and those now being initiated among the Kayans and Kenyahs on the Akah and Baram.

This is being written at Bario in the heart of the Kelabit country where with my wife we have had most helpful and constructive discussions with Mr. Tom Harrisson concerning these vital problems.

Yours faithfully,
C.H. Southwell

That same edition of the *Gazette* carried a short letter of response by Tom Harrisson:

Mr. Southwell has shown me his letter, with which I am in sympathy. I had a mind to issue a caveat about rapid changes in *adat* [animistic customs], mainly with reference to the Kelabits, about whom I know a certain amount. Now that I have had the pleasure of a talk on the spot, I believe constructive results may indeed follow. And I have been impressed by the sincere work and devotion of this Mission here.

Tom Harrisson

After leaving Bario, Winsome and I, along with our carriers and the baby organ, continued our circuit of all the villages on the highlands, and then returned through Belawit and Ba Kelalan where the rice harvest was now in full swing.

When we came to the upper reaches of the Trusan, we stayed four days with our dear friends at Rumah Marong with whom we had spent those memorable months in 1942 while hiding from the Japanese. Although I had been here eight months earlier, Winsome had not seen these people for more than five years, and it was a great joy for both of us to reminisce with them about our times together — some of the happiest and most fruitful of our lives — and also to catch up on subsequent events. From there we went over the border into an enclave of North Borneo territory through which the Matang River flows — the place where we had received the written orders from the Japanese to surrender in September 1942.

When it came time to return to the coast, we decided to explore new territory. We followed a path which made a shortcut through wild country and then travelled along the Matang River down to

Long Sia and Long Mio, where each village had built new churches. From the valley of the Matang, the rocky west bank sloped upward in a sierra type of terrain until it reached about 5,000 feet above sea level, then abruptly broke off and fell away steeply. This upward sloping country was covered by dense, stunted, rattan forest which until the late 1920s was home to a fairly large number of the small, black Borneo rhinoceros. When these rhinos, with their thick hides, would force their way through the dense jungle, they left readily visible trails. The Muruts dug pits along these trails and covered them with strips of bark upon which they spread a camouflage of moss. When the rhinos fell into these pits, the Muruts killed them with spears.

As long as the only weapons available to the Muruts of the interior were spears and ancient muzzle-loading guns, the rhinoceros population had been able to hold its own. By the time we came to Sungei Pranga in 1928, however, people near the coast were able to get modern breech-loading shotguns, and they would trek into the upper Trusan to hunt the rhinos. As a result, these magnificent animals had been hunted almost to extinction.

During the latter part of World War II, many Japanese who were retreating from Limbang and Brunei attempted to escape to the big Japanese camp at the Sapong rubber estate at Tenom in North Borneo, above the Padas Gorge. These fleeing Japanese climbed the steep and rugged western edge of this rhinoceros country and, not knowing the paths, many of them lost their way and never reached Tenom. Years later, their skeletons were still being found in the tangled, thorny jungle.

Winsome and I passed through this country, spending four nights in Murut villages and five nights in jungle camps where the relaxed banter of our carriers was punctuated by the magical calls of gibbons, argus pheasants and hornbills. We reached Budok Ngeri on February 25, 1948, ending a journey that had taken two months and ten days.

When we went on these extended trips, we had to carry all our supplies with us — clothing, medicines, bedding, tenting, cooking equipment, foodstuffs. We packed these in lightweight metal containers which we fabricated from four-gallon kerosene tins. By cutting the tops off two containers and dressing the cut edges, we could telescope one container onto the other, thereby making a relatively waterproof carrying case. We then had special backpacks made locally out of rattan to fit these containers, and the loads were distributed so that each person's pack would weigh no more than about thirty pounds.

Trekking through the jungle is hard work. Energy drains rapidly in the heat and humidity of the tropics, while roots and vines seem strategically placed to trip the unwary. Moss grows in the most inconvenient places — on rocks forming the path and on trees felled across streams — and the footing can be treacherous even when it does not rain.

Equal-Opportunity Carriers

The people of Borneo, while generally not as large as Europeans, exhibited amazing toughness, stamina and agility packing through the rain forests and over the mountains. I developed reasonable skills in this kind of travel myself, but I usually tired before our carriers did. And my footing was never as good. And even when I was younger, I could not have walked into the central highlands with a pipe organ on my back!

Part V
Unforeseen Changes

Everything difficult indicates something more than our theory of life yet embraces.
– George MacDonald

Unless there is an element of risk
in your exploits for God,
there is no need for faith.
– J. Hudson Taylor

CHAPTER 20

Despite our years of travelling and teaching, there were still three large sections of the Baram River and its tributaries that I had not visited. One was the Tutoh River tributary which enters the Baram exactly halfway between Marudi and the Long Lama bazaar. The Tutoh in turn has its own large tributary, the Apoh, which enters the Tutoh from the south. The third major unvisited tributary was the Tinjar River which enters the Baram a few miles upriver from Marudi. The Tinjar itself is as large as the Limbang River where we first commenced work in 1928. The people in the Tinjar and Tutoh areas were mainly of Berawan origin while the Apoh area was peopled mainly by Kayans, one village of Kenyahs and a large numbers of Penans, the elusive hunter-gatherers.

When Alan and Madge Belcher returned from their visit to the Baram area in late 1947, they brought news that the people of these three large tributaries were anxious to hear the message of the gospel. Interestingly, I myself had a long-standing invitation to visit this region.

In years past, Tama Tingang Malang, the Berawan *Penghulu*, had been the paramount chief of the whole Baram area, and I had become acquainted with him in 1930 through a remarkable set of circumstances. A party of Ibans had been ordered to go to the Medihit tributary of the upper Limbang to meet up with Edward Banks, the Curator of the Sarawak Museum, and with Mr. Pollard, the District Officer of the Baram district. I had the good fortune to accompany the Ibans on this important rendezvous, and thus it was as we returned down the Limbang River I sat next to *Penghulu* Tama Tingang Malang and had the opportunity to tell him about our Mission and how Carey Tolley, Frank Davidson and myself had come from Australia to bring the gospel of Jesus Christ to the people of his land. He evidenced great interest, and he asked me to come to his village at Long Terawan in the Tutoh tributary of the Baram and open a school there. I had to tell him that since we had only recently come to Sarawak, we were not yet able to respond to his request to settle there, but I assured him that we would certainly try to come in the future.

That had been eighteen years ago. The breakthrough among the Muruts and the Second World War had intervened, and *Penghulu* Malang was no longer living, but it seemed that his invitation was still open.

Winsome and I left Lawas on April 9, 1948, going by the usual sea route to Labuan and on to Miri; from there we travelled the seventy miles by slow cargo launch up the Baram to Marudi. Here we stayed with the District Officer, Mr. Morgan, which afforded a superb opportunity to discuss our work and purpose openly and frankly with him.

After leaving Marudi, our first stop was a Kayan village at Long Apoh, the point where the Apoh River flows into the Tutoh. The village was divided, with two Headmen, one of whom was an Iban married to a Kayan woman. The Iban Headman and his people listened intently to the gospel message, but did not commit themselves.

Next day we went on up the winding Apoh River which flows through fertile, alluvial country. At low water the Apoh is a sluggish stream, and it took us a day to reach the Kenyah house at Long Watt. There, Headman Tama Wong was cordial and prepared a welcoming meal for us, but his response to our message was one of decided reservation.

Not far from Long Watt was Long Atip, a large Kayan village of the Uma Pu clan. This clan had villages in all the main Baram tributaries, and their *Penghulu*, Tama Paya Anyi, lived at Long Atip, along with several *dayongs* reputed to have great occult powers. When we told them about the power of God over all demon forces, it was obvious that the *Penghulu* and his *dayongs* were deeply disturbed.

We stayed two nights at this village and then spent a night each at several other longhouses getting to know the people. By that time everyone in the area was becoming preoccupied with preparations for the forthcoming annual Baram Regatta at Marudi, so we decided to return there for this event. We had never been present at a Regatta in full swing, and this was the first big one since the war. Thousands of people gathered from all parts of the Baram district, including many foreigners from the oilfields at Miri.

The Baram is a noble waterway. For about thirty miles upstream from the sea, its banks are lined with nipa palms growing in brackish water, and beyond the banks are seemingly endless swamps feeding streaks of cola-colored water into its powerful currents. Further upriver the nipas give way to sago and coconut palms, followed by rubber gardens. Then, seventy miles from the mouth, the true right bank rises abruptly to about sixty feet above the highest flood level. This high bank extends back from the river for more than a square mile, forming the townsite of Marudi, the only high land near the riverbank from this point to the sea. All other land is subject to flooding.

Once the longboats began to arrive for the Regatta, the riverbanks, as well as the townsite, became crowded with thousands of people and hundreds of boats ranging from about thirty feet long to eighty or a hundred feet long. Most of the boats had palm leaf coverings as protection from the rain and sun, but which could easily be removed for the actual races. During the Regatta, some of the people lived and slept in their boats, but most built temporary shelters on the riverbank.

The entire Regatta was a colorful event with a carnival atmosphere. From the time of their arrival at Marudi, the people set about to make final preparations for the long canoe races. Though the sizes of the boats varied, the basic design was a dugout hull, hewn in one piece from a large tree so as to provide a shallow curved cross-section, streamlined at bow and stern. The sides were made from one long board, likewise hewn from a tree in one piece, attached to the hull either by nailing or, traditionally, by tying with split rattan. At the bow the people always attached a figurehead carved in wood, representing a hornbill or a monkey or some other jungle creature. The largest boats accommodated around sixty paddlers, sitting two abreast on narrow seats.

The boat races were held over a period of two days, with different classes for short, medium or long boats. There was also the championship race for boats of unrestricted lengths and an unlimited number of paddlers. This race, which covered a distance of two miles, started around the bend upriver. As the boats rounded the bend, the crowds waiting at the finish line near Fort Hose broke into shouts of encouragement for the paddlers. The man at the stern steered the boat, while the man at the bow set the pace by his shouts and the speed of his strokes. It was thrilling to watch. Perhaps twenty really long boats, filled with paddlers, emerged from around the bend of the river, the water surging from the bows and splashing from the paddles, the bodies of the men gleaming with sweat. A gun was fired as the first boat crossed the finish line, and the winning crew stood up in the boat and thrust their paddles in the air with mighty shouts of victory.

In the evening, dance competitions were held on a stage set up in the open air, lit by pressure lamps. Competitions were conducted for both men and women, in individual as well as team dances.

War Dancer

The men's dances were mostly mimes of individual combat, with sword and shield and war coat. Each action displayed taut muscles and tense expressions as the dancers depicted the wary, cat-like approach, stealthy movements, and the final sudden spring and flashing sword of the warrior.

In contrast, the women's dances were graceful and dignified and attracted the most attention. Their dancing involved a slow sinuous movement of body, arms and feet. Each woman improvised her own dance movements within a certain general pattern, and this individual styling prevented the performances from becoming monotonous.

All the dancing was performed to the accompaniment of a steel-stringed instrument called a *sapi,* which resembles a guitar. The sounding-box on a *sapi* is hewn from a single piece of light wood, and this is attached to a long stem. Five steel strings of piano wire are attached to tuning keys situated at the top end of the stem and tuned to the pentatonic scale. The *sapi* is not used to play a tune, but is strummed to create different types of rhythm.

Over the years, we became quite familiar with these forms of cultural expression, and at one Regatta, I was even invited to be one of the panel of judges for the dance competitions.

Since I had travelled so extensively among the Kayan and Kenyahs in the upper Baram the previous year, I knew a great many people at the Regatta, and they were glad to finally be able to meet Winsome. By this time, a good number had become Christians, and we were able to give practical advice to hundreds of people who for the first time were free from their old pagan practices. On Sunday, during the festivities, we arranged an open-air church service in a grassy, bowl-like area that formed a natural amphitheater on the high bank. Along with the believers there were many curious onlookers, which gave us an excellent opportunity to introduce ourselves to the people from those villages.

After the Regatta was over, we started back upstream. We had brought an outboard engine with us for use in travelling on the

Baram, so we spent three days at Long Lama putting a transom in the stern of our longboat. Then with engine in place, we travelled a half-hour upstream to the large Kayan village at Long Laput, where Lalang, the hereditary Chief of the Kayans, received us and entertained us with a chicken dinner. We held several meetings there and found some of the people interested and others resistant. Lalang herself was intensely interested but tried to cover it by making funny remarks. She certainly lived up to her reputation as a character.

Three days later, however, as we made preparations to leave, Lalang asked to speak to us alone.

"Some say that the Kayans of Long Laput will never become Christian," she told us. And then, using a double negative as is often done in polite speech in Asia, she added, "But Lalang doesn't say she won't become a Christian."

Lalong asked Winsome over and over not to forget her and told us to be sure to visit her again. We never did get the chance. Less than two months later, while we were still upriver, we heard that Lalang had died.

After leaving Long Laput we went straight upriver to Long Akah and then on to Long Tebangan. We had originally thought of returning directly from Marudi to the new territory on the Apoh River but, while we were at the Regatta, a number of our friends from Long Tebangan persuaded us to visit their village first. Almost exactly twelve months had passed since the spiritual breakthrough among the Kayans at Long Tebangan, and they were still experiencing a great sense of liberation. We spent ten enjoyable days with them, teaching them more about God.

Having gone as far up the Akah as Long Tebangan, we decided to continue on to Long Siniei, the first Kayan village I had visited on my initial trip to the Baram the previous year. The people here belonged to the Uma Pu clan — a different clan of Kayans than the people at Long Tebangan, and were ruled by a different chief, *Penghulu* Tama Paya Anyi. We had met this chief when we visited his home at Long Atip on the Apoh River just before the Regatta; being a *dayong* himself, he had opposed our message.

Now, as we moved about among the people at Long Siniei and spoke with them, we became aware that many welcomed the good news of deliverance from the powers of the demon world. But others, either from fear of the occult powers or fear of a loss of their own status and prestige, were resistant to change. This was especially true of the members of the hereditary upper social class, and some of these leading people sent messengers to *Penghulu* Tama Paya Anyi asking for his help to prevent any change from spirit worship.

The journey to Long Atip would take the messengers about ten days, there and back, so Winsome and I decided that while waiting for their return we would go further upriver to Long Lellang to visit Raja Maran and the Christian Kelabits. This meant a difficult journey through some of the wildest parts of the Akah River and up the Merigong Gorge, but we got there safely and spent seven days visiting and teaching.

On returning to Long Siniei we found that *Penghulu* Tama Paya Anyi had still not arrived, so we continued our teaching among the people. When at last he did come, most of the people indicated that they desired to leave the old satanic beliefs. The *Penghulu* was puzzled and did not know what to do, so I was glad to have the opportunity for some direct talks with him.

"*Penghulu*, when the tide of the seas rises and falls, you cannot stop it," I told him. "So it is with the gospel. When the power of the Holy Spirit is working in the hearts of people, you cannot stop him."

The *Penghulu* listened, but said nothing.

About midday, I noticed a flurry of activity in the longhouse with many women going into one of the larger family apartments. Some time later one of the men came to me. "We are all going to become Christians," he said. "Balu Paya Deng has called all the *dayongs* and other leading women into her apartment and told them that she believes the gospel message is true, and she is going to follow Jesus Christ and his teaching."

Balu Paya Deng was the chief *dayong* and a most influential woman. Even the *Penghulu* could not withstand her.

When he heard that the whole village had decided to become Christian, the *Penghulu* said in alarm, "Don't do it while I am here. Wait till I have gone!"

At one point the *Penghulu* tried to stop the people from throwing out one of their sacred charms; as a result, a woman became demon possessed. The people called me to come and help. They were holding a Bible over the head of the raging woman, thinking this would drive out the demon. I told them that the Bible is not a magic charm. Rather, the message of the Bible instructs us to call upon God for his power. So Winsome and I laid our hands on the woman and prayed that God by his mighty power, and in the name of Jesus, would cast out this demon and deliver her. The woman calmed down and stopped raving. She described the pain of the demon as "worse than malaria." We saw this woman many times in later years, and she was never demon possessed again.

The next morning the *Penghulu* left with his followers for the long walk through the jungle back to Long Atip. Following his departure, we had a big gathering of all the people of the village, and everyone took part in casting out everything to do with spirit worship. As it was the women who had special responsibility for the rituals and charms concerning rice, Winsome went around all the rice stores with the women, and helped them pray and remove the pagan protective charms and fetishes.

A real spiritual battle had been waged at Long Siniei, but it ended triumphantly.

Our plan now was to visit the Badang Kenyahs at Lio Matu in their isolated position in the upper Baram. Following a fast trip down the Akah, we stopped at six other Kenyah villages on the way up the Baram, including a new village at Long Sela'an. There had been much sickness and death among these people when I had visited their temporary site at Long Sebatu a year earlier, so it was a great joy to see how much better they looked now. All of the people at this village had become Christian — in spite of the pressures from their *Penghulu.*

When we at last reached Lio Matu we stayed five days. Along with our teaching we did a great deal of medical work, for in those days government medical services did not reach this remote area.

Winsome and I then commenced the long journey downriver, stopping at only a few village longhouses. The Mission field conference was due to be held at Lawas at the end of August, and we needed to get back. We arrived on August 13th, having been away for four months.

Two full years had passed since I had returned to Borneo to reopen the postwar work of the Mission. Now, our Mission constitution required the convening of a field conference for the election of officers and for general administration. The conference commenced on August 30th and lasted until September 6th.

This was the first field conference since 1939. Only three of us, Winsome, myself and Enid Davidson, were official members of the Mission. Trevor White and Alan Belcher had come to Sarawak after the war began and had not yet been received into membership, while Madge Belcher had been in Sarawak a little less than a year. Since the founding of the Borneo Evangelical Mission in 1928 I had served as the field leader and, under the circumstances, I felt that all should be welcomed as full members and given voting rights.

While we all realized that these were days of tremendous opportunities, both in Sarawak and North Borneo, opinions differed as to how we should respond with our limited resources. During the time Winsome and I were making the month-long journey back to Lawas, I had pondered and prayed about future plans for the operation of the Mission, and I presented my thoughts to the others concerning the potential and the challenges that lay before us. I suggested that Winsome and I should continue itinerant work among the Kayans, Kenyahs and Kelabits in the Baram areas for at least the next two years, perhaps longer.

Then came the discussion on the election of officers. To my complete surprise, it was suggested that Alan Belcher should stand for election as chairman with full administrative responsibility, and it was clear that Alan himself wanted this position.

I could hardly believe this was happening. Since returning to Borneo in August, 1946, I had been going flat out to respond to the urgency of the situation and it had not occurred to me that changes were even being contemplated.

My initial reaction was to fight this decision. But I knew that was not the right answer. Such conflict could well destroy the Mission, and it would certainly undermine our credibility with the people of Borneo with whom we had invested the last twenty years of our lives.

I felt then, and still believe, that a change in leadership of the Mission was, at best, premature. I was devastated, but in the end I knew I had only one viable choice. I had to accept it. Accept it and depend on the One who promised that "in all things God works for the good of those who love Him."[1]

1. Romans 8:28

Chapter 21

Ancient beads were the most important measure of wealth among many of the peoples of the interior when we first came to Borneo. Beads were a means of saving and investment, and a medium of exchange in trade. In addition, antique beads had a major impact on Bornean culture as they were important indicators of social status among some of the ethnic groups. These rare and ancient beads were passed from generation to generation as family heirlooms and formed an integral part of the marriage dowry among the upper classes.

The rarest and most valuable of these beads are very old. On one occasion I showed some samples to Italian antique dealers in Genoa, who pronounced them to be of Venetian origin.[1] Others came from the Middle East. Some of the deep blue Kelabit beads match those I have seen in the British Museum which were found in Mesopotamia and are believed to have been brought there by Phoenician traders.

Beads were held in particularly high esteem by the peoples of the great Baram River area. More than silver or gold or any other possessions, antique beads were the hallmark of standing and prestige. Among the Kayans and the Kenyahs, the most valued of these beads, the *Lukut Sekala*, was considered the equivalent of a human life. Each separate group of peoples in the Baram and in the central highlands had beads of different broad classes indicating that they probably had been obtained through diverse sources in antiquity.

Beads are more durable than most other artifacts of Bornean culture. Most are made of glass with composite colored patterns fused into them by skilled craftsmen, and even after centuries of wear they retain their beauty. Unfortunately beads are not fire resistant, as was tragically demonstrated by the great Kelabit longhouse fire of September 1948.

---

1. Some years ago I was provided with funds and commissioned to make a collection of beads for the Sarawak Museum. I obtained a wide range, including the most rare specimens, some of which are still on display in Kuching.

While we were still in Lawas for the conference, three young men — Sam Gollan, Ken Cooper and Horrie Hamer — joined us as new missionaries from Australia. It was decided that Sam would work with Trevor White at Ranau in North Borneo, while Ken and Horrie would join Winsome and me at Long Tebangan.

Transportation from Lawas to the Baram was difficult to arrange, and the resulting delay was providential. While we were waiting, we received word that a disastrous fire had destroyed the Mein longhouse in the Kelabit highlands, and one old woman had died as the result of burns. The Sarawak Government decided to send a large quantity of relief goods, mainly rolls of cloth and supplies of hardware to assist in rebuilding, and asked me to accompany these goods and oversee their distribution. Thankfully, the message arrived before we had left.

We decided that Winsome would accompany Ken and Horrie through Miri to Marudi and then up the Baram River to Long Tebangan, while I would go with the carriers who would transport the relief supplies to the Kelabit country.

I left Lawas on October 9th, travelling up the main mountain trail to the source of the Trusan at Ba Kelalan and then around through Belawit to the Kelabit highlands, arriving at the Mein village fourteen days later.

It was a pathetic sight — the longest Kelabit house burnt to the ground. The site was littered with shards of valuable Chinese jars which had been shattered by the heat. Even more lamentable were the masses of ancient beads melted and fused together. These were irreplaceable, many of them hundreds of years old, and some of Babylonian and Egyptian origin which were possibly over two thousand years old. A few ancient beads of carnelian stone and some made of agate, a form of quartz, did not melt but had lost their color.

The people usually wore their strings of beads on their bodies for safekeeping, but as they were sowing rice among the charred branches of their burnt-off fields, they had left their beads at home the day the fire struck.

The people were very grateful for the assistance the Sarawak Government had sent. I stayed three days with them in the temporary longhouse they had built and, in spite of the tragedy, they tried to press on positively with their lives. While there I was even able to perform a wedding!

Guru Paul Kahoun had become engaged to a Kelabit woman and they wished to be married. I was decidedly underdressed for the occasion as I had only my travelling clothes with me, but *Guru* Paul wore a proper dark suit with a white shirt and black bow tie, all of which had been preserved in this remote area right through the war years. It was delightful, and the Christian ceremony was a portent of the great changes in Kelabit society which were yet to come.

While in Kelabit country, I completed a pastoral visit to all the longhouses in the highlands, staying two nights in each house, and then left for Long Lellang. From there I went down the Akah River through Long Siniei, arriving at Long Tebangan on December 1st where I met up with Winsome, Ken and Horrie who had arrived from Lawas more than a week earlier. I had covered the most difficult terrain in a relatively short period of time, and God gave me strength for that.

"I was pleased to see that Hudson looks well on arriving from his arduous journey," Winsome wrote in a letter to my mother a few days later. "I can't help noticing how blissfully contented and happy he looks in this kind of work. It is the work that has always been on his heart — to go out and tell the gospel to all who are longing to hear it, and to encourage young Christians — that is why he looks so restful."

In actual fact, both Winsome and I felt joy and fulfillment in this travelling ministry, for in the same letter she described her own experience visiting the people in a longhouse. "During a lull in talking, sometimes I drop asleep amidst the amazing noise," she wrote, "and then wake up refreshed."

Winsome and our two new recruits had had a remarkable experience of their own on the journey upriver. After reaching Marudi, they had proceeded to make their way up the Baram in a longboat with a small outboard engine and a Kayan crew. Winsome had forgotten to buy additional supplies of food in Marudi, and it was not until they were well underway that she realized they only had some rice left, and nothing to eat with it. About midday they were rounding a bend in the river in smooth water shaded by overhanging trees when, suddenly, a big fish leapt into the air and landed in the boat!

While certain big fish do leap into the air to catch insects, the probability of one jumping into a motorboat is low indeed. Particularly just at lunchtime. And for a party without provisions. That grateful party accepted it for what it surely was — an amazing gift from God.

We intended making Long Tebangan a centre for assisting local churches and a base from which to reach out to the whole of the upper Baram and its tributaries. Our first building was a school which doubled as temporary living quarters, so for a few weeks we lived a primitive pioneering existence. The floor consisted of rough, hand-hewn boards, and the walls were made of bark sheets; these reached only halfway to the eaves, so when rain came with a driving wind we had to move into the centre of the building to avoid being soaked!

We started construction on a house, and the outer shell and roof went up quickly. While it was being finished under Ken and Horrie's direction, I went downriver to Marudi to bring up the balance of the goods they had shipped from Australia. During this time Winsome lived in the Headman's apartments in the longhouse on the other side of the swiftly flowing Akah River.

The village consisted of three truly long houses, with crowds of hunting dogs both underneath and within the house by day. The house could be entered from either end by climbing a notched log with handrails on both sides. At night the dogs were driven outside and the notched log was rolled over with the smooth side uppermost, which the dogs could not climb.

The design of Kayan and Kenyah longhouses was ingenious and was intended as a protection against being stormed by enemy raiders. The structure was supported by a clever use of cantilever construction. Under the centre of the house were two rows of very large hardwood posts known as the *seniung*. These two rows of posts were six feet apart, but running lengthwise the space between each post could be much greater. Long, heavy beams of wood spanning the full width of the house were balanced across the tops of the huge *seniung*. Longitudinal top plates then supported the walls and roof.

Longhouse Entrance

This style of construction virtually precluded an enemy from causing the house to collapse by hewing down the main building supports. In order to attempt to do so, the enemy would have to venture right under the centre of the house where they would be vulnerable to spears thrust at them from above. And even if they were successful in cutting down one row of the *seniung*, they would be in danger of the house collapsing around them before they could retreat.

In the longhouse of a powerful chief, the *seniung* would sometimes be eighteen inches in diameter and would last for generations. The Kayans and Kenyahs were essentially riverine people, and if the village moved to a new site, these *seniung* posts would be rafted with them to the new location.

We started a school for the children as soon as possible after arriving at Long Tebangan. Ken and Horrie were learning Malay themselves, so teaching these Kayan young people the rudiments of reading and spelling simple words helped their own language study.

The Kayan language had not yet been reduced to writing, but by listening to their conversation and using the Malay language as a medium, we were able to collect a fairly extensive vocabulary. We also studied the structure of the language, which was quite distinct from the other languages we had encountered. In Kayan, for instance, there is no truly passive form of the verb as there is in Malay, Iban or Murut-Kelabit.

We had built both the school and our house on the opposite side of the river from the Kayan village. To come to school some fortunate children crossed the river in canoes. Others would strip off their loincloths and hold them, along with their schoolbooks, in one hand high above their heads; then they would enter the swiftly flowing river upstream, and the current would carry them, swimming and kicking, across the river and land them on the opposite bank some distance further down. I still have photographs of those children bobbing through the water as they crossed the river on their way to school.

The children loved attending school. We taught them the usual three R's and instructed them in hygiene and general knowledge, as well as singing and Bible stories.

Just after the beginning of the new year, 1949, people from Long Siniei arrived on their way back from downriver and wanted to take us with them. We packed up that same evening and left the next day with a good supply of medicines, the baby organ and our portable sewing machine, which Winsome used to help the women do sewing work. This trip lasted just eleven days, but it was full of activities: medical help, domestic problems, sewing jobs and teaching. We also told the people about our new school and I interviewed prospective students.

Upon returning to Long Tebangan we worked on making basic furniture and cupboards for our house. Later that same week we received notice that the new District Officer, Mr. Griffin, was to visit the Akah area, and the people immediately began preparations to welcome and entertain him. During the pre-Christian days this always meant brewing large quantities of *borak*. But this time the Headman, Jok Ngau, asked me to explain to the District Officer that the people had decided to give up the use of *borak* and this was not meant as a discourtesy. I was glad they had the conviction and moral courage to take this stand.

Mr. Griffin was delayed by a high and raging river, and when he did arrive we were surprised to see *Penghulu* Tama Paya Anyi travelling with him. This Chief of the Uma Pu clan from Long Atip on the Apoh River, had strongly resisted the Christian message in our earlier encounters — first at his village the previous year, and again after the Baram Regatta, when he came to Long Siniei to oppose those who wished to leave the old spirit worship and become Christians. But now, amazingly, his attitude was entirely changed.

"The last time I met you it was in opposition to the message you brought," he said to me openly. "Now I have seen what it has done for other Kayan people. Please, will you come to my people in the Apoh and bring the message from God."

Winsome and I left Long Tebangan on March 1st and arrived at Long Atip five days later, having visited several places along the way. *Penghulu* Tama Paya Anyi (literally, the father of Paya the daughter of Anyi) welcomed us warmly to his spacious apartment in the longhouse, but told us he had many concerns. Although he was a *dayong* himself, there were others more deeply involved in the powers of the spirit world than he was, and they were reluctant — or fearful — to lose their occult powers and prestige. So Winsome and I went from one family group to another, and the *Penghulu* also called several meetings of the people where we could tell them of God's good news of deliverance from the powers of evil.

Our fluency in Kayan was still rather limited, so the Kayans who had travelled with us from Long Tebangan were able to explain the gospel message more clearly than we could. They could also bear witness to the fact that God did in truth protect them from the omens and dreams and fears that had dominated their lives from infancy.

After three days, the *Penghulu* again gathered the people together — about five hundred in all — and they affirmed their desire to follow Jesus Christ and to cease worshiping the spirits. As with the other Kayan longhouses that had become Christian, we emphasized the necessity of full commitment, with no half-measures. This meant going through the whole longhouse and the rice storage huts, ridding them of their protective charms and fetishes.

The most suspenseful moment came when *Penghulu* Tama Paya Anyi asked us to accompany him to his little spirit sanctuary where he took down his *kawit*, a set of charms used by every *dayong*. He then opened this shrine up for all to see and, one by one, removed the nine successive coverings that protected the central charms. These included a hooked stick, a token notched log ladder, a rope (piece of string) and a special kind of bead for the spirit to sit upon. This *kawit* had been prepared by other *dayongs*, with sacrifices, at his initiation and was considered most sacred. No stranger was ever permitted to see the contents of the nine successive coverings.

Before opening the *kawit*, the *Penghulu* solemnly spoke to the spirits and informed them that he was no longer serving them or looking to them for their magic powers. Forthwith, he said, he was serving the Almighty God alone. Until he actually and openly claimed the power and protection of Jesus Christ, he would not have dared to desecrate this spirit shrine. This ceremony by the man who was both *Penghulu* and *dayong* was highly significant and a true triumph of faith.

And the evidences of God's protection were real. All the villages who had turned away from their charms and fetishes said that injuries during their work or farming were far less numerous and serious after they became Christians than before when they lived in servitude to the pagan spirits.

After six days at Long Atip, we went on to Long Bedian, less than two hours' journey upriver, and were received warmly. The Headman, Tama Sang, had discussed the matter of conversion beforehand with his people, and they had all agreed to renounce their pagan spirit worship and follow Jesus Christ. The next day, the people told us they wished to dispose of their fetishes and sacred charms. The Long Tebangan people who were with us were now familiar with that process and rendered splendid assistance.

The following day, five young couples told me they wished to be married according to Christian customs. I explained God's teaching on marriage and told them that the purpose of marriage was not only to produce children, but so that a man and a woman might have the closest union of heart and mind. I also explained that they must love each other unselfishly. Four other young couples who had married under pagan customs also requested to be married in a Christian ceremony. This meant nine weddings that day, and each couple wanted to have their own wedding feast. So Winsome and I went from one family to another, eating a little at each of the nine feasts.

We stayed an extra day to hold discussions on practical matters of Christian life. Then we packed up again and left with a large number of boats going upriver. This time we were on our way to the Patah tributary of the Baram.

We paddled up the Apoh all day until we reached a suitable camping place near the point where the upper Apoh was closest to the Patah River. It was late afternoon and the people were in a festive mood as they made a big camp on the riverbank. Next morning we went upriver for another two hours, then beached our boats high on the riverbank and climbed a hill through the forest to a watershed between the two rivers.

One party had gone ahead and arranged with the Patah Kayans to meet us with boats, for which we were grateful after the long walk. Half-an-hour later, we reached the village.

We spent the first full day doing medical work, as this was the most isolated of the Kayan villages. For two evenings we taught from the Bible, and on the third day we held a meeting of the whole village in the Headman's longhouse at which the people pledged their full commitment to follow Jesus Christ.

After three more days of teaching, we returned the way we had come, stopping two days each at Long Bedian and Long Atip, where we gave further teaching and answered questions.

As we continued on down the Apoh, we were taken aback to find that we received no invitation to stop at the Kayan house at Long Watt. It was not until much later that we learned the real reason — which extended back to the time of the war.

After the Allied forces landed at Miri towards the end of the war, they proceeded to occupy the vast Baram River system. Several armed clashes ensued, and as the Japanese retreated upriver, they burned longhouses and killed the son of Aban Deng, the Headman of the Uma Beluvuh clan of Kayans at Long Apoh.

Somehow these calamities at the hands of the Japanese crystallized into resentment against all those involved in the war, including the Australians, and when we returned to the Baram in 1946, this resentment was turned upon us and the Christian message as well. This led three Headmen, Tama Wong of Long Watt, Tama Uding of Long Terawan and Aban Deng of Long Apoh, to vow under solemn oath that they would never become Christians. Each of them displayed a carefully polite attitude toward us, but firmly resisted the gospel message.

But God's Spirit was working in the hearts of the Baram people and many were ready to receive him. So even though these three Headmen had vowed to refuse the gospel, they could not deter the great mass of people from responding.

When the three Headmen saw that their resistance was ineffective, they became outwardly friendly. Sadly, though, their solemn oath was so binding that they never did accept the gospel for themselves. On the other hand, some of our best and most faithful

Christian leaders eventually came from the villages over which those three Headmen held sway.

This vow by the three Headmen was the basic reason that the Uma Beluvuh Kayan village at the junction of the Tutuh and Apoh Rivers had split into two sections. The smaller group, consisting mainly of Headman Aban Deng and his relatives, remained at Long Apoh, while the majority moved to a new site at Long Panai. It was at Long Panai that Winsome and I stopped, and for seven fruitful days presented the message of salvation and deliverance.

When it came time to return back up the Baram to our base at Long Tebangan, we were hindered again and again by high flood water. When we finally arrived, we immediately planned to commence another journey upriver as far as Lio Matu. Ken and Horrie were managing well with the school, and the church at Long Tebangan fully supported our plan of reaching out to other villages. So four days later, having selected and packed all our stores and medicines, Winsome and I were ready to set off again.

We did not get as far as we had hoped, however. While returning from Long Panai the previous week, the river had, on several occasions, risen to flood level, then retreated slightly, and then rose again. After such repeated flooding during the rainy season, it was usual to have a period of moderately low water. But not so this time.

As soon as we started up the Baram again, we were held up at the first longhouse for two days, at the next house at Long Selatong for six days, then for four days at Long Anap — all Kenyah villages at which we were able to preach the gospel. Finally we reached the Lepu Aga Kenyahs at Long Ta'an where we were again delayed by flooding. The people here wanted to perform some pagan rites, so we decided to continue upriver, but were unable to do so for four days because of high water.

When we finally set off, the river was still very high, and it was with great difficulty that we made any progress at all. Eventually we reached the mouth of the Buang, a tributary rising in seven limestone peaks known as Batu Tujoh, and found it impossible to go any further. We were just below Ong Kamut, a particularly turbulent stretch of water where the great Baram narrows to flow between two cliffs of rock.

We gladly entered the calm Buang tributary and camped in an empty farm hut, well above the raging river. There we waited as, day after day, it rained intermittently. Then on the fifth day it rained continuously, and I felt sure we would have a big flood that night.

Winsome and I had set up our camp beds under the farm hut, while our boat crew slept in the hut above us. Our boat was tethered to a tree, and I left a storm lantern alight in the boat so I could gauge the rising waters. As the hours passed, I saw the lighted lantern moving higher and higher as the river rose. By eleven o'clock it had reached the top of the bank.

Winsome was asleep under her mosquito net, so I woke her. "Get up, Winsome, we have to get out of here."

"Oh no," she moaned, "I'm too tired."

"All right, please yourself," I said, "but there's going to be a flood."

So she put her feet out, and they were in water. This time she needed no urging! I pulled the boat up and hastily loaded our camp beds inside. At the same time I told the men in the hut to cook up some rice, and rather unwillingly they did so before we all climbed into the boat.

The water rose steadily, up to and over the roof of the hut. All night long we could hear the awesome roar of the river crashing through the narrow walls of Ong Kamut. As dawn broke, the only dry land visible around us anywhere was the top of a nearby hill. Our boat was floating well up among the branches of the trees!

That morning it finally stopped raining, and we were glad we had cooked some rice. By late afternoon the river was falling. By evening we could walk on the muddy bank, and we all crowded into the hut.

The next morning, with the river rapidly falling, we felt it wise to return downriver on the swiftly flowing stream. What sights of devastation met our eyes as we sped downstream. The village at Long Ta'an had escaped lightly, as their longhouses were on a high bank. But the next longhouse downriver had collapsed under the force of the stream, even though it was built with huge posts.

We passed through some turbulent stretches of river, but safely reached Long Selatong, the village we had left twenty days before. Three days later we arrived back at Long Tebangan with vivid memories of the most dramatic flooding we had ever experienced.

Chapter 22

Perhaps the highest achievement of craftsmanship among the peoples of the Baram was their steel work. The Badang Kenyahs at Lio Matu were particularly skilled at iron and steel making, having perfected their own manufacturing process many years ago when imported steel was difficult for them to obtain. A good deal of ingenuity and resourcefulness is required to smelt iron ore into mild steel and then craft it into tools and weapons, all in a jungle setting.

Small deposits of hematite, a high grade iron ore, are fairly commonly found throughout the Baram area in pebbly river beds at low water. Hematite is quite easily recognized by its deep reddish-brown color, and once a deposit was identified and excavated, it was cleaned to separate out the other sedimentary rock, and then broken into pieces about the size of small walnuts.

The other material requirement is a supply of clean charcoal. This was produced by cutting and stacking hardwood into a large pile, covering it with clay to control the admission of air, and then burning the wood under conditions of slow combustion.

The jungle blast furnace consisted of a pit about four feet in diameter and three feet deep with an array of bamboo pipes laid out to form tuyeres. The pit was filled with a mixture of iron ore and charcoal, and during the smelting operation, air was forced into this furnace through the bamboo tuyeres by a number of cleverly designed bellows.

These native bellows were twin air pumps comprised of two cylinders made from giant bamboo, about four inches in diameter and cut to a length of about three feet. Each bamboo cylinder was open at the top and fitted with a wooden piston lined with feathers to make it as airtight as possible. At the bottom of each cylinder, an outlet valve consisting of a flap of tinplate opened on the piston upstroke to admit air, and closed on the downstroke, thereby forcing a blast of air through the tuyere into the furnace. With the bamboo cylinders in an upright position, a person could work the pistons up and down rapidly for several minutes before trading off with a relief worker. Twin cylinder pumps supplied a continuous blast of air, and by using a battery of pumps connected to separate bamboo tuyere pipes, a sufficiently high temperature could be maintained at the centre of the furnace to produce mild steel. This native steel was then forged into swords and knives which were often decorated with scroll work on the blades. Baram tools and weapons were highly regarded for their appearance and for their tough edge which would not chip easily.

I obtained several pieces of smelted iron from the Kenyahs at Lio Matu over the years and, in 1990, I donated a large piece weighing about ten kilograms to the Museum of the University of Western Australia. While I was in the Japanese internment camp, I constructed a set of twin pump bellows using the native design, and these bellows formed a key part of our forge which we used to shape scrap spring steel into tools. I still have most of these tools with me today.

I arrived back at Lio Matu in late July of 1949. Winsome did not accompany me this time as our travel plans involved new routes I had not tried before. My carriers and I had made our way up the Akah, fighting fast flowing rapids right up to Long Lellang. From there we went overland through territory that was new to me, heading southeast over two successive watersheds in the Murid Kecil mountains, an isolated but magnificent group of peaks. After more rugged travelling, we came to Long Sait, where we found some of the Penans I had met nearly two years before. We spent the weekend with these nomads of the forest and then continued by boat down the gentle, pebbly rapids of the Selungoh River to the Baram, and then upstream to Lio Matu where the Badang Kenyahs had recently built a new longhouse.

From Lio Matu, I set out to reach the remote settlements of Saban people, three days' journey along a steep mountainous trail up the Baram valley to Long Banga and Long Puak, as well as the lone outlying Kelabit community at Long Peluan. No one in our Mission had ever visited this area which slopes up from the Baram valley in an easterly direction to the watershed between Sarawak and Indonesian territory. In recent years, several Saban villages had migrated over the watershed into a fertile section of the valley located about halfway down the long, rugged gorges between the Kelabit highlands and Lio Matu.

The Saban language is aspirated to an unusually high degree, but its vocabulary has affinities with Murut-Kelabit, and also with some Kenyah dialects. Even so, the Sabans are clearly a distinct ethnic group with their own unique culture. The Saban people have their own special metal work and weapons, and distinct varieties of ancient beads and decorative beadwork.

Despite their remote location, the Sabans were keen traders as they lived on the trade route between the far inland part of Indonesian Borneo and the coastal areas of Sarawak. I found them not very responsive to the gospel. A few were receptive but most of them were more interested in trading goods than in spiritual issues.

On my way back down the Baram, I was able to spend several days at Long Moh with *Penghulu* Mapei Arang. The Lepu Tau Kenyahs at Long Moh had some shamans who were heavily involved in occult practices. On one occasion I arrived at their village just as they were preparing to commence a big festival which they held only once in several years for the initiation of their children into adulthood. The ceremonies also involved fertility rites. Once the festival started, the whole village was placed under taboo. No one was allowed to enter or leave the village until the ceremonies had been completed, so I was there for the entire proceedings.

The people had set up a tall pole about thirty feet high with a head carved at the top. In the middle was a big slot, like a mortise, about fifteen inches high and six inches wide, and into this was loosely fitted a huge tenon, about twelve inches by five inches. This tenon was cut on one end of a long horizontal pole, around sixty feet long, which was balanced at its centre point on top of a post about ten feet high. On the opposite end of this horizontal pole was a small frame upon which young people could stand and make it spring up and down, thus causing the tenon end to clatter up and down in the mortise slot. Resonators had been carved into the tall vertical pole to amplify the sound, so as the tenon pounded up and down, it produced huge booming sounds.

In addition to making noise, this apparatus also served a utilitarian purpose. A beam of hardwood projected from the central post and was connected to the frame on which the people stood; this beam hammered on a hardwood anvil which was set up directly below. This beam and anvil combination was used to crush sugar cane packed in rattan bags, thereby producing sugar juice which was used in the initiation ceremonies.

For several nights during these ceremonies there was constant entertainment with graceful Kenyah dances in which both men and women took part. There were also the "long" dances in which about thirty or forty people formed a ring and followed one another, all doing the same movements and at the same time chanting poetic phrases sung in lovely improvised harmonies. I was amazed that they had the stamina to continue both day and night.

Sacrifices formed a prominent element of these initiation festivals. At the festival I attended, a sacrifice was required for every one of the seventy-six children present, and this meant selecting seventy-six pigs. These pigs were bound up with rattan, and a prayer was whispered into the ear of each pig, and then a few hairs were plucked out and burned. Next the pig's throat was cut, and the blood was collected in a basin and then daubed on the child's head and arms. Finally the pig's carcass was cut open, and the liver was taken out and put on a platter and examined by the "expert" *dayongs* to see if the omens were good. The large number of sacrificed pigs meant there would be a big feast with an abundance of meat and cooked rice.

I did not see all the ceremonies, nor was I told everything concerning their significance. I heard afterwards that the *dayongs* at Long Moh considered that the initiation ceremonies had been unsuccessful, and they accounted for this failure by my presence as a Christian. For that reason they held another initiation ceremony in strict secrecy a few months later.

Although I know from my own contacts with *Penghulu* Mapei Arang that he was deeply moved by the gospel, he was not willing at that time to make a personal commitment. But God had begun to work in his heart. About three years later, while I was in Australia, *Penghulu* Mapei Arang became ill with pneumonia. I was told that as he lay on his deathbed, he persistently called out for "*Tuan Sapu*", the shortened name by which I was often known in Borneo. He also urged his people to accept the gospel. Only God knows what was truly in his heart in those final months.

During the time I was upriver, the Kayans at Long Tebangan finished cutting down an area of secondary jungle for their seasonal rice farms, but instead of the usual period of dry weather they had rain every day, and hence could not burn off what they had cut in order to begin planting rice.

"What should we do when we need dry weather, but it rains every day?" the Headman asked Winsome.

"We should pray to God about it."

"We will do just that," he responded. "We will ask God to hold back the rain so that we can burn off our farms." So they prayed in faith and God honoured their faith by giving them several days of dry weather, just enough to allow them to get a good burn.

The amazing thing was that all the other villages, both in the Akah and in the main Baram River areas, had continued rainy days, and the people there had to laboriously gather up the felled jungle into piles and try to burn them up. All around the district people asked, "How did you manage to burn off?"

"We prayed in faith, and God answered our prayer, and we thanked him for it," the Long Tebangan Kayans responded. And God answered many of their other prayers too, preserving them from danger and healing their illnesses.

The lives of the Kayans at Long Tebangan were not without problems, but through these problems we saw them mature. We also continued to teach them from the Bible, and in this the second year since their conversion, their faith grew in strength and conviction.

On our next visit to the upper Baram, our plan was to eliminate the long journey up the Baram River by going a short distance up the Akah to a tributary called the Makuti. Then we could cut across country by going up the Makuti to its source, and from there to the source of the Sela'an River, which we could follow down to its confluence with the upper Baram. Apart from saving time, this routing was intended to avoid the most dangerous rapids in the Akah and the Baram. We little knew what major consequences that simple change in plans would bring. As it turned out, this journey was God-directed and his timing was to the very day.

Winsome and I left Long Tebangan with eleven men on October 24th following this new route. We lost our way in the jungle in the watershed area between the Makuti and the Sela'an. After spending an extra night camping in the forest, four of the Kayans made their way down the Sela'an on a raft, and they returned with six Kenyahs and two boats to transport us.

The first few rapids were quite big but after that we had no difficulty in reaching Long Siman, where a community of several families of Kenyahs from the main village of Long Sela'an were making their farms that year. It was a remote spot where a lone rhinoceros, probably the last of its herd, had been shot close to the rugged mountains forming the watershed.

The people were anxious to have us stay with them in this isolated area for the weekend. I remembered with what joy these same people had accepted the message of the gospel two years before, in June 1947, when they were living at Long Sebatu, and we were glad to have the opportunity of encouraging them.

On October 31st, we set out again and about midday arrived at Long Sela'an where we stopped briefly. While there, Winsome attended to a woman who had given birth to a baby girl the day previously. The mother was in a weak and anaemic condition.

"Mem, I want two things, prayer and medicine," she said to Winsome. She had suffered from malaria during most of her pregnancy and was very weak, so Winsome gave her anti-malaria medicine and prayed for her.

We then had to go on to the next village at Long Semiang and two days later we went further upriver to the Badang Kenyahs at Lio Matu. We stayed there for five days as Winsome had a very heavy cold. During this time I was able to hold several teaching sessions and ninety-six people asked to be baptized at a special service on the Sunday afternoon.

The next day, we packed up and left Lio Matu for downriver, arriving at Long Sela'an shortly after midday. It was a sad arrival. The woman to whom Winsome had given medicine, had died just ten minutes earlier. People were gathered around the mother, weeping. The little baby, born eight days before, was lying on the mat beside her, and a woman was squeezing water into her mouth from a piece of cloth.

"Mem, see this little baby, could you please try to save her life? We don't like our leading people to die out, and this baby is one of those."

Owing to her anaemic condition the mother had not been able to feed the baby since birth, and she had been kept alive by water alone. She was crying and was very weak. Winsome's heart melted as she looked at the little baby. "I will try," she said.

So we unloaded our boat and moved into the longhouse. The father, Aban Bilong, had already lost his first wife, and he had one baby daughter, about two years old, surviving from his second wife who had just died. Now this second baby seemed doomed to die also.

Winsome's training in midwifery and nursing had been in high demand ever since she came to Borneo. We had no feeding bottle with us, but we did have some powdered milk which we used for our tea and we also had a small medicine dropper. Winsome immediately made some warm milk, and it was most rewarding to see the baby revive as she eagerly drank the milk being fed drop by drop from the tiny pipette. Feeding her from this medicine dropper was a slow process, as she was apt to choke on the drops without the natural action of sucking. After some time, Winsome suddenly thought of piercing the rubber top of the medicine dropper to make a rubber teat, so I heated a needle to prevent the hole from closing up again, and pierced the rubber. We then drew up milk into this small pipette and quickly turned it upside down, and put the rubber top into the baby's mouth. We watched the milk go down the pipette and when it was empty, she gave a little squeak of wanting more.

"She will be intelligent," I said. "She already knows what she wants!" By the next day she was crying more vigorously. Indeed, in my diary I recorded that, "she yelled for food!"

I asked if anyone else had recently had a baby. Could such a mother take this newborn baby as well? There was no one available, so her father, Aban Bilong, asked if we would look after her.

Late that day we had a Christian burial service for the mother and we sadly committed her body to the grave. Thankfully, however, the baby had survived and was gaining strength. Following the burial service, we held a short service of dedication committing the little baby to God's care. We wanted to give her a name that the people liked and we settled on Mina, after one of Winsome's aunts who had been a missionary in Africa.

On the third day we set out to return to our base, and the people sent a Kenyah woman with us to assist in carrying the baby while we went up the Sela'an River. That night we slept at a camp in the forest with the baby on a pillow at our heads.

Next day we made a raft and two men went down the Makuti to get boats. News that we were bringing a baby with us went ahead, and when we arrived at the river bank at Long Tebangan, there was much excitement. "We did not know you were expecting a baby!" someone said, and the gathered crowd erupted in laughter.

At the first service in the church at Long Tebangan after our return, we rededicated Mina to God, and several Kayans prayed for her also. Winsome had always loved children. We both felt that God had really given this baby to us as a gift, and we were thrilled to have her.

Chapter 23

The Merigong Gorge formed a natural boundary between the Kayans and Kelabits in the Akah. The Kelabit people are believed to have lived on the upriver side of the Gorge for centuries, and on my next journey I encountered some fascinating evidence of this, a colorful description of which was provided by Tom Harrisson in later years:

> A great wonder happened in the headwaters of the Akah, on the border of Kelabit country, recently. The river changed course on its own. In the middle of the new river bed was an enormous boulder, the top of it carved with a spread-eagled human figure complete with head-dress, extended ear lobes, loin cloth and leg bangles. This rock carving is not unlike other ancient ones; but instead of being executed in high relief is incised into the stone surface. It differs also in having feet which swirl into fin shapes; the hands show ordinary fingers, though only four.[1]

This rock carving has distinct similarities to other Kelabit monuments, most notably the rock carvings near Ramudu, the most southerly point of the Kelabit highlands, and many days' travel from Long Lellang. Interestingly, when we arrived at Long Lellang in early December 1949, the people there knew nothing of the existence of this carving, so the change in the course of the river must have occurred within weeks of our journey.

While I was travelling this time, Winsome remained at Long Tebangan with Mina where she could give her careful nursing and attention. The mission house was not yet finished, so they stayed in the Headman's family apartments in the longhouse, where they had the company of the Kayan women, and where Winsome's methods of caring for Mina were daily object lessons for the women to see.

From Long Lellang, my carriers and I set off on the long, difficult trek through Penan country and over the Tamabos. Upon reaching

1. Tom Harrisson, *World Within* (Singapore: Oxford University Press, 1990), 113.

the Kelabit highlands, I made a complete circuit of the highland longhouses, teaching at each stop, and was greatly encouraged by the response of the people. It was New Year's Eve, 1949, by the time we reached the southern end of the highlands.

I spent the first week in the new year walking due south along the high mountain ridge leading from Ramudu to the lone Kelabit outpost village at Long Peluan, and then down to the Saban country. After a week with the Saban people, I continued on down to Lio Matu. From there we started the long boat trip down through the Kenyah villages on the Baram River and then back up the Akah. I reached Long Tebangan near the end of January 1950, after two months of continuous travelling.

It had been three-and-a-half years since I had come back to Borneo from Australia, and almost three years since Winsome had come, and neither of us had taken a break.

From the time of my arrival back in Borneo, one great objective was always before me — to present the gospel while the doors of opportunity were open. People had been so shaken by the war that their hearts and minds were receptive, and they were ready for change. I felt that nothing had a higher priority and that was the reason why I had worked so hard to establish a base at Lawas — and then to keep on travelling. But the time had now come when we needed some rest.

Nearly eighteen months had passed since we had been at Lawas. During this time several new missionaries had arrived, as well as our first mission aircraft.

One of our earliest members, Stafford Young, had enlisted in the RAAF during the war and had been impressed with the value of using light aircraft to reach places in the interior of Borneo. In prewar years, while still a missionary himself, Stafford had walked to such distant places as Ba Kelalan and Ranau. Though now settled in Australia with a wife and family, it was his vision and generosity that had made possible the purchase of a light Aeronca airplane. This small two-seater plane with its hand-started engine was shipped from Australia to Labuan through the courtesy of Shell on one of its oil tankers.

The other gift that made the flying program possible was provided by the Lawas Rubber Estates. Mr. McLaren, the manager of the estates, had retreated from the Japanese into the interior with Frank Davidson and Brian Morcombe, and was later interned with us at Batu Lintang. Based on his recommendation to his directors, an area of unused land on the opposite bank of the river from Lawas town was given to the Mission for use as an airstrip. This was ideal, and there was sufficient land not only for an airstrip, but also for the headquarters of the Mission and for the bible school students as well.

While we were at Lawas, Winsome and I discussed future opportunities in the Baram with Alan Belcher and Enid Davidson. We now had two main territories of focus: the Akah and upper Baram area centred around Long Tebangan; and the Apoh and lower Baram area centred at Long Atip up the Apoh River. We all agreed that Winsome and I should open up this big, new and populous area on the Apoh River. Horrie Hamer was to be married soon to Joyce Ritchie, and it was decided that he and his new wife would go to Long Tebangan. Ken Cooper was engaged to Joan Davis and they were to work at Lawas.

After about three weeks in Lawas, Dr. John and Kitty MacArthur, our friends from prewar and internment camp days, invited Winsome and me to stay with them on Labuan Island. Dr. MacArthur was the government malariologist who identified the *Anopheles Leucosphyrus* mosquito as the main carrier of the plasmodium parasite that was responsible for most of the incidence of malaria in the forest-covered interior of Borneo. He found that this type of mosquito bred only in clear water and in shaded areas, and he advocated malaria control by ecological methods, in this case by felling the jungle at the source of the stream, which would prevent the breeding of this particular species of mosquito.

The MacArthur's island home provided a wonderful respite for us, and it was not long before I felt rejuvenated and anxious to get back to the Baram. We had planned that I would initially go alone to get the new base started at Long Atip, during which time Winsome and Mina would stay at the Mission base near Lawas. The MacArthurs would not hear of this, however, and insisted that they stay on with them. So, my reluctance to be separated again was at least somewhat offset by knowing that Winsome would be in the resort-like setting on Labuan.

Following our goodbyes, the outgoing trip from Labuan along the coast and up the Baram seemed to take forever. I did not arrive until eleven that night, but the new District Officer, Mr. Griffin, was still up and talking, and he kindly invited me to stay with him.

Next morning I told him of our plans to open a new mission station at Long Atip in response to the request of the people of the Apoh, expressed through their chief, *Penghulu* Tama Paya Anyi.

Upon my arrival at Long Atip, I held a consultation with the *Penghulu* and the leading men. I had made some plans and estimates of what was required for a new mission station, and told them of my proposals. After discussing these ideas and estimates among themselves, the *Penghulu* responded on behalf of them all.

"We want to build the house and school without any cost to you," he told me. "If you pay for the building, our money will be spent on things which we will soon consume, but you have come to give us teaching and medical help which will last us all our lives."

On this visit to Long Atip, Long Panai and Long Bedian, I noticed a big change in the people. Fear had changed to confidence, with a sense of freedom and trust in God. They had had trials, including some sickness, and from over 500 people, around ten had died during the last year. Also, about a month earlier, lightning had struck a wild sago palm between the houses. This would have been a most serious happening under pagan custom, requiring major ceremonies to appease the spirits, but none of these things had caused them to lose trust in God.

Leaving Long Atip, I went up the Apoh and over the watershed to the Kayan village on the Patah River, Long Daloh, and spent three days there. At that time, it was one of the most isolated of the Kayan villages. Earlier in the century the upper Patah area had a large and influential Kenyah population; with the cessation of headhunting these Kenyahs migrated to their present location in the upper Baram. Halfway down the Patah from Long Daloh, we passed through a dangerous gorge which had made the upper Patah a haven from marauding headhunters.

After reaching the main Baram stream I went upriver to Long Akah and finally to Long Tebangan to tell them about our new plans. It was not easy to bring them the news that Winsome and I would be moving to the Apoh. As with the Muruts in the upper Trusan, they had become very dear to us, and they regarded little Mina as a gift from God to their community.

I stayed a full week at Long Tebangan. As we had been based there for two years, we felt that we really knew the people well. Best of all, many of the people had not only learned about Jesus Christ, but by the grace of God they had come to know him personally, and they showed a real spiritual sensitivity.

I gathered together as much as I could of our personal belongings and took them with me down the Baram, and then up the Tutoh River to the Kayan longhouse at Long Panai; I left most of our goods with the Headman, and then returned downriver again to Marudi for the Baram Regatta scheduled to start in early May.

As at the Regatta in 1948, people from all over the Baram River system came downriver to Marudi by the thousands, camping on the riverbank or in their longboats. The whole of Marudi — river and land — was a most colorful sight.

During the previous two years we had done so much travelling that we were now well known among the people. I wished Winsome could have been with me to enjoy the festivities and renew acquaintances.

At this second Regatta since the war, the people knew what to expect and were better prepared. The boat racing was keenly contested and the atmosphere was filled with excitement. In the evening, native dance competitions were held; as always, these competitions were dignified and graceful, a true expression of their culture.

On the Sunday, we had a large open air service with people seated in crowds around the grass-covered natural amphitheater we had used two years earlier.

When the Regatta was over I made my way downriver and proceeded on to Labuan. I arrived on June 12th just as one of the new recruits, Bruce Morton, completed assembling the Aeronca, and next day he was ready for the first test flight. The little plane performed beautifully. It was a real joy to see it in the sky, flying so effortlessly, foreshadowing the tremendous benefits it would bring in providing transport to the far interior.

I did not stay many days in Labuan. Winsome was keen to return, along with our little eight-month-old Mina, to the Borneo mainland. Transport was still rather rugged — a converted military landing ship to Kuala Belait, and then a land rover along the beach to the mouth of the Baram River, followed by a slow journey on a cargo launch to Marudi, where we again enjoyed the kind hospitality of Mr. Griffin.

Using our outboard engine and a newly purchased longboat, we went upriver to our new location at Long Atip on the Apoh River. As before at Long Tebangan, our temporary residence was in the spacious school building, where we walled off a room for our own use.

A week later, on June 28, 1950, I celebrated my fiftieth birthday. I had often wondered where I would be when I reached fifty! I was thankful to God to be right there, opening up a new centre among people who just a year before had received Jesus Christ's liberating gospel, and now were hungry for teaching on how to follow this new way of life.

I spent my birthday making tables, sharpening a new axe and my carpentry handsaws, talking with visitors and also doing medical work in the longhouse, which was about 1500 feet long.

We selected a site for our house on the opposite side of the river from the Kayan longhouse. Unlike the Akah, the Apoh was a placid little river running through a fertile alluvial stretch of country. Not far away were lovely blue hills and Mt. Mulu was only fifteen miles distant.

Mt. Mulu has the distinction of being Sarawak's second highest mountain but is better known for the enormous caves winding through its heart. In places, naturally acidic water dripping into these caverns has sculpted fantastic shapes out of the limestone, forming a channel for a clear, green underground river. When we first moved to Long Atip, I spent hours exploring the impenetrable darkness of the Mulu caves. In more recent years, I have heard that over 150 miles of caves and passages have been explored in the Mulu range, and one of the caverns is reputed to be the world's largest enclosed space.

Many more Kayan people lived in the Long Atip area than at Long Tebangan, so teams took turns working on the new mission house. We longed to get on with this new building but other obligations loomed before us. The first was the visit of the Governor from Kuching.

The District Officer, Mr. Griffin, had told us when we came through Marudi that the Governor had heard of the conversions in the upper Baram and he intended to visit the area to see the situation for himself. This would include a visit to Long Tebangan in late July and we felt that we should be there to receive him.

Winsome and I, with baby Mina, set out for Long Tebangan on July 12th, down the Apoh and Tutoh, and then up the Baram, spending a night each at several villages. At the village of Long Kaseh, several families became Christian.

We then went on to the Kayans at Batu Talang where the Headman was Akam Ajeng. Eight *dayongs*, including some powerful women *dayongs* lived there, but I was told that the whole village of five longhouses wanted to hear the gospel. After spending two nights talking with the people and answering questions, all were united in their decision to forsake the old animism — spirit worship and belief in omens — and to trust Jesus Christ. As in other places, we gathered all the people together in a big assembly and held a solemn dedication service, and I prayed that God would cast out all the demonic powers and give the people his Holy Spirit. In the evening I spoke to a big gathering and next morning we had a busy time answering questions and giving practical advice on matters ranging from the birth of babies to Christian practices at burials.

We went on to Long Akah later that same day and were grateful to make it through the rapids before it was too dark to see. It was two more days up the Akah River before we reached Long Tebangan, where we had a great welcome. Many visitors had already arrived from Long Siniei, and more were expected. Baby Mina was bewildered by the exuberant crowds, but she kept her poise wonderfully.

The river had fallen, so the rapids were steep, and it was not until five o'clock in the evening of July 26th that the Governor, Sir Anthony Abell, arrived to cheering and the firing of guns. The people had prepared a big entertainment program of dancing and speeches for the official party which included six government dignitaries and five local chiefs. The Governor attended the festivities until midnight, and then returned across the river to stay with us in the mission house, while the people continued the celebrations till nearly morning.

The Governor and his party left the next morning and Winsome and I followed after lunch to Long San, the Kenyah village of Tama Weng Ajeng who by then had been elevated to *Temonggong,* or Paramount Chief.

Once the festive events were over, we made our way back downriver, responding to a request to visit Long Terawan, the village of Tama Uding, one of the three Headmen who had taken a solemn vow never to become a Christian. From there we continued downstream to Miri, and around the coast to Lawas where we arrived on August 13th, just in time for the second postwar Mission field conference.

At this conference it was a great joy to have one of the new missionaries, Win Burrow, a trained nurse, designated to assist us at Long Atip. The following extract is quoted from a report that Winsome and I wrote around that time for the Mission newsletter:

> At the present, we are opening up a new station among the Kayans of the Apoh tributary of the lower Baram. How different from the first station at Sungai Pranga twenty-two years ago! Then it was among a pagan people — now among a people who have turned to Christ and invited us to come to them. The task is even more urgent than ever, for in no other part of our Borneo field have over a thousand new Christians waited over a year for teaching . . .

Around that same time, we were joined by another especially capable new worker, Ray Cunningham, who had earlier served in Borneo during the war as an engineer in the Australian army. His first project with our Mission was to construct an airstrip and hanger on the new land that had been granted to us near Lawas.

Now, with Ray's assistance at Long Atip, and with the voluntary help of the Kayan people, we soon had the mission house ready for occupation, and this enabled us to commence the school. The absence of rapids in the quiet Apoh River allowed us to respond quickly to calls for medical help, and to make pastoral visits to the many villages in this area. For most of the balance of the year I travelled extensively in both the Apoh area and in the lower Baram.

In November, one of our students, Uring Ibau, a daughter of *Penghulu* Kebeng, told us that the wife of one of her relatives had given birth to twin boys — one had died and the mother was not able to breast-feed the other baby properly. During my next journey I called at the village of Uma Bawang. I gave the mother some tins of condensed milk and told her how to feed the baby, but the next time I stopped at their village not much milk had been used.

The following month, I visited Lawas for discussions with Alan Belcher about the problem of locations for new missionaries. I spent Christmas Day there and then returned to Long Atip on January 6th of the new year, 1951. I had been at home for only eight days when I left again, this time with Ray Cunningham to visit Long Tebangan. While we were away, Winsome and Win Burrow carried on with the work at Long Atip.

On the way upriver, Ray and I called in at Uma Bawang, and again on our way downriver a month later. On each occasion the baby boy was still suffering from malnutrition, even though tins of milk were still available. I urged them to use the milk more frequently.

I had been home at Long Atip only a few days when the little mission plane flew overhead. It was exciting for all the Kayans, and for us too, as it dropped a bundle of mail with letters for all of us.

As we finalized plans for our next journey, a new worker, Leah Cubit, arrived from Lawas where she had been doing language study. She was very versatile and could share the responsibilities of the new mission station with Winsome and Win Burrow while Ray and I were travelling. We set off again in late February and in four days' time we reached Long Akah. After waiting five days for a boat from Long Tebangan, Ray went up the Akah River, and I proceeded up the Baram all the way to Lio Matu.

I spent the next three weeks visiting the four largest villages in the area. At Lio Matu, I encountered many medical and spiritual concerns, and I attempted to address both. Immediately after one evening meeting, a young married man to whom I had previously given some cod liver oil for his tuberculosis suddenly had a severe hemorrhage. Blood literally poured from his mouth, and he fell down on the bamboo floor. In a few minutes he was gone. Tuberculosis was widespread all over the Baram, but it was especially prevalent in Lio Matu.

After a week there, I went to Long Sela'an for two days, and then to Long Moh where again I did a lot of medical work before continuing downstream. I arrived back at Long Atip on April 15th. Upon my return, I found that another new development had unfolded, and this proved to be one that would profoundly impact our lives.

Ten days after I had set off on my trip along with Ray Cunningham, a visitor suddenly appeared at Long Atip. It was the mother of the little surviving twin boy from the Uma Bawang village. She felt unable to care for the baby, so she left her village along with some other women and paddled three days down the Baram and up the Tutoh and Apoh Rivers, arriving at Long Atip. Her baby boy was looking very weak and thin, but God had surely guided her to the place where she could receive compassion and help. With the baby in her arms she came to Winsome and said, "Mem, this is your baby, you are his mother." It was March 5, 1951. By counting back from the time we heard of his birth, we believe that the boy was born on November 5, 1950, making him exactly four months old when he came to us.

At last this little baby received good regular food and Winsome noted in her diary, "He's a nice little fellow. He slept and ate all day, and was a very good boy."

Winsome's diary contains many references about him, but we had not yet given him a name. Someone remarked that I had made a hobby of collecting Kayan beads, and this time I had collected a baby!

"Why not call him by the name of the most precious bead, the *Lukut?*"

So at first this boy's name was Lukut Southwell, but as he grew up, he became known as Luke Southwell.

Chapter 24

It was good to be back at Long Atip with Winsome and the two children. We both enjoyed being parents, despite the sleepless nights. In addition, our little school was thriving and, with the new airstrip, it was easier for friends to visit us.

We were scheduled to go on furlough to Australia soon, but we felt that first we should make one more journey through the whole upper Baram area in which we had been working. So on May 11, 1951, we set out, taking Mina and Lukut with us, and in two days we reached Uma Bawang. It was just two months and ten days since Lukut's mother had given him to us, and she just looked at him in amazement.

"*Mahalu*," she exclaimed, which means "excellent" or "splendid" or "how fortunate." Lukut's mother and father were so delighted with his healthy appearance that they were keen to have him stay with them while we were travelling upriver.

Our third stop after leaving Uma Bawang was the Lepu Aga Kenyah village at Long Ta'an, where the people were somewhat divided. Some had made a Christian profession; others had not. But all were very active and hard-working individualists. The village had six longhouses, and we stayed with Tama Jalong, a brother of the Headman.

Winsome and I had hoped to stay several days so that we could give more teaching to the Christians, but a well-known old *dayong* wanted us to continue on upriver so that he could perform some pagan rituals for the whole village.

We had just packed our boat and were prepared to go when Tama Jalong asked me to give medicine to a sick woman in one of the longhouses. He took me in a small canoe to see her. After the treatment we started paddling back, when suddenly a frenzied panic broke out. We could hear people shouting and could see them throwing firewood out of the houses and emptying bamboo water containers. Men were running along the fronts of the houses and climbing up into the storage spaces among the rafters. Then there was utter silence.

"Pray, *Tuan*," Tama Jalong implored me. "Pray!"

"What has happened?" I asked him.

"A woman has just died in childbirth. Her spirit will be seeking to grab and devour any man she can find."

Tama Jalong kept his composure, but he must have been terrified. There we were in an open canoe in the middle of the stream, and he believed that the spirit of the dead woman was looking for victims!

"You cannot leave now," he told me. "The whole village is taboo. You must stay here. Get your boat unpacked. I'll show you where to go."

Tama Jalong took us to another set of apartments and told us we could stay there. Later we learned that it was the family apartment of the chief *dayong*!

We did not see the old *dayong* again until about two years later when we stayed with him once more. By that time he was no longer a *dayong*, but a humble-minded Christian. His life had been changed 180 degrees.

Our next stop was Long Sela'an, where we stayed with Aban Bilong, Mina's natural father, who saw her now for the first time since she was a week old. She was one year and seven months old and had been walking about five months. As we all sat on the floor, Mina stood facing Aban Bilong, and before long she just naturally toddled across to him, and he took her in his arms.

It was evident that he would have been happy to take her back as his daughter, though he said he was quite willing to accept our decision as to her future. He told us he would like us all to consult his cousin *Penghulu* Aban Gau, who lived downriver at Long Ikang, before a final decision was made. It was heartrending, but we agreed that after we had completed our visits to the upper Baram, we would meet with the *Penghulu* to discuss Mina's future.

From Long Sela'an we went on to Lio Matu, where we were immediately faced with a lot of medical work. There we met up with Ray Cunningham, and I left Winsome and Mina at Lio Matu while Ray and I travelled up the mountainous path to the Saban country. On our return journey down the Baram, we stopped for three days at

Long Moh. Ray and I joined with *Penghulu* Mapei Arang to meet the Penans up the Moh River, and after that Ray left us to return by a northerly route overland to Long Tebangan.

Winsome and I continued down the Baram with Mina and our Kenyah boatmen, making many calls at longhouses and smaller settlements to provide teaching and medical assistance. The river was low and consequently the rapids were steep. It was only through God's care of us that our boat was not swamped on two occasions, and I was relieved to get my little family safely up the Akah to Long Tebangan.

The great rivers of Sarawak form vital arteries coursing outward from the mountainous heart of the country, providing a ready means of transportation. As a result, people who farmed near the navigable sections of these river systems developed amazing skills in handling their long canoes, and none were more skillful than the Kayans and Kenyahs of the Baram area. For propulsion they used paddles or, in shallow water, poles made from strong, supple saplings about ten feet long. Their skill in both propelling and steering their boats against the stream in turbulent rapids was a delight to see. The ability they had to balance their bodies while steering their boats always thrilled me. These were skills they had learned from childhood — during all the years I lived in Sarawak, I could never emulate them.

While Winsome and Mina visited with our friends at Long Tebangan, I made a quick trip down the Akah with some of the Kayans. The river was raging that day as we approached the treacherous Batu Murik rapids where the water divided into two streams around a mass of large boulders as well as one huge rock about thirty feet wide and twenty feet high. Because the state of the river constantly varied, we always had to decide on the spot whether to shoot the boat down the small waterfall on the right or to try going down the cascade on the left side of the main rock. If neither side was suitable, we had to drag the boat over the rocks. It was always a matter of swift judgement, depending on the height of the river and whether it was rising or falling.

On this particular day, the smaller boat ahead of us seemed to favor shooting down the small waterfall on the right-hand side. One of their paddlers was standing up in the bow of the boat to scan the condition of the river. Suddenly, seeing that the waterfall was too high, he frantically waved to us to go to the left side. He could not turn back, but his boat was light, and though it plunged over the fall it did not get swamped.

For us the warning was too late. We were too heavy and had too much momentum. As our boat plunged over the top of the small waterfall, we were instantly swamped.

"Save the old man," someone in our boat shouted in Kayan — meaning me!

Fortunately we did not capsize and our boat became jammed between two rocks in a pool in mid-stream; this prevented us from going over the main waterfall, which might have proved fatal. As the river rushed by, I clambered onto one of the big rocks.

All my goods were either in the boat full of water or floating in the pool, so the men swam about and collected the floating bundles and travelling tins, and piled them on the rocks. Then they bailed out the boat and manhandled it, little by little, down the main waterfall and dragged it to a sheltered spot.

We opened up all the bundles and tried to dry everything in the hot sun. My camera was soaked, and the carrying case disintegrated. Some days later, however, I was able to dismantle the camera and clean it properly, and it still worked.

When I arrived back upriver, Winsome and I made a visit to Long Siniei. Then, the day we returned to Long Tebangan, suddenly, to our great surprise, Ray Cunningham arrived from Uma Bawang with our baby Lukut! About six weeks after we had left him with his father and mother, Lukut had become ill. But, as with the time he was first brought to us, God knew his need, and he led Ray to call in at Uma Bawang at just the right time. Ray had a boat and engine and he brought Lukut up to Long Tebangan along with a few Uma Bawang people. Joyce Hamer diagnosed Lukut's trouble as pneumonia and gave him an antibiotic, which saved his life.

As soon as Lukut's condition was under control, we went downriver to Long Akah and met up with Aban Bilong and his relatives from Long Sela'an, as had been arranged. Then we all continued down to Long Ikang to discuss Mina's future with the Kenyah leader, *Penghulu* Aban Gau.

Apart from our natural love for her, we felt that the circumstances of Mina's survival were an indication that God had a purpose for her life involving us. We told the *Penghulu* that our aims and desires were to have full charge of Mina until she was able to choose for herself, provided it was with the goodwill of her natural father. We requested that these provisions be included in a letter to the *Temonggong,* Tama Weng Ajeng, and his assent secured. After a lengthy discussion, both *Penghulu* Gau and Aban Bilong agreed to these conditions.

Winsome and I had prayed that if we were to keep Mina as our child, the father would say, "I have decided to give her to you." And that is exactly what he did!

Later at Marudi we had this agreement typed out and signed by Aban Bilong and ourselves. Eventually, we officially adopted both Mina and Lukut in accordance with the laws of Sarawak.

Before leaving for Australia, we also wanted to visit the Limbang area where we had first commenced work in 1928, and we were able to travel as far as Lawas on the Mission plane.

While there we met two visitors, Mr. Wood and Mr. Harris, who were on a fact-finding trip to Borneo. Both had formerly served in China under the mission originated by Hudson Taylor. Following the Communists' expulsion of all missionaries from mainland China, the China Inland Mission had adopted a new name, the Overseas Missionary Fellowship, to better reflect its service in the whole of East Asia, embracing all those areas where ethnic Chinese were a large and important element of the population. These experienced missionaries were uniquely equipped to discern the areas from which a renewed outreach could be made to the vast East Asian field, and though our contact was brief, I was very glad to meet them and to encourage them regarding the potential for extending their work to Sarawak and North Borneo.

The Overseas Missionary Fellowship eventually did establish a presence in Borneo, and effective January 1, 1975, the Borneo Evangelical Mission voted to merge with this larger organization. Thus, in a sense, things turned full-circle, for it was through Hudson Taylor's ministry that I had come to co-found our Mission in the first place.

Our visit to Lawas also coincided with the arrival of Jim and Laura Ward. Jim had a Ph.D. in electrical engineering, and Laura had studied medicine at London University. These two talented and highly trained people had responded to God's call to invest a part of their lives in pioneering outreach in the forests of Borneo. Before they met, Jim had attended Westminster Chapel and it was through his membership that Dr. Martin Lloyd-Jones' famous church in London presented the Mission with a larger airplane, fittingly named the *Westminster Chapel.*

After that short but meaningful visit at Lawas, we set off for Sungei Pranga, the site of our first mission station on the Limbang River, an area we had longed to revisit. Upon arriving at Limbang town we found an old friend, Si Kok, a Chinese shopkeeper from Ukong, who was going upriver that day and offered to take us with him. I wrote in my diary:

> It was quite emotionally moving to see the old sites and the familiar bends in the river that we had traversed so often in the 1920s and '30s. We reached Ukong and then our friend sent us on to Sungei Pranga the same day. We found that the Ibans from Gani's longhouse had moved about fifteen miles down the Limbang to the bend in the river opposite our old headquarters at Sungei Pranga. We reached there at six-thirty that evening and gave them a great surprise. They gave us a very warm welcome in return.

They were in the midst of a *gawai,* a feast to one of the pagan spirits, when we arrived. These Ibans had been some of our best friends in the prewar period. At that time their longhouse was the furthermost Iban settlement upriver, and when we retreated to the upper Limbang in December 1941, following the invasion of the Japanese, these Ibans from Headman Gani's longhouse helped us greatly. Not only did they convey us upriver, but we also left many of our personal possessions in their care.

Now, ten years later, and six years after the war, they brought out and laid before us all those things that they had kept in store for us, including a valuable old bronze Brunei gong which I had bought in 1935. This action was a true reflection of the character of these Ibans, and an excellent example of their trustworthiness and integrity.

Three Murut families, now Christians, were occupying the land which had formerly been our mission station at Sungei Pranga, and their house sat on the small hill where our school building had been. These people came to see us and took us across the river to the bigger hill which had been the site of our old headquarters. The Japanese had torn down our house, even pulling the hardwood posts out from the concrete. My diary records our impressions:

> It was almost unbelievable to see the hill so overgrown in less than ten years. We even had difficulty in finding a landing place on the river bank. Only two of the many coconut palms I had planted were left. Others had been cut down, but the durian tree I had planted was bearing fruit. Quite big trees were growing on the hillside, and high saplings were growing out of the holes in the concrete where the posts had been. The cement surface of the former ground floor was completely covered with matted roots and rotting vegetation. It came as a shock that this place we had known as our home could have reverted to the jungle in such a short time.

Next, we went on upriver to the large Iban village at Tanah Merah, which was the very first place we had met with Iban people. We had come to know these people well. Though they were friendly, hospitable, completely honest and always welcomed us to a meal, they had been warlike people in the past, as witnessed by the bunches of blackened skulls — grim reminders of past headhunting — which hung in front of every household.

Now, all these years later, they welcomed us warmly and we were soon exchanging news in their vigorous Iban language. The young people we had known as teenagers were married with children of their own, and they were delighted to see our little Mina, now nearly two years old.

That evening we steered the conversation to the Christian message. They were quite happy to listen to stories about Jesus from the Bible but, as in the past, most had little more than an academic interest. They were hardworking farmers and had prospered. And perhaps because honesty was a strong element in their culture, they felt no need for repentance, nor any urgency to enter the kingdom of God. Like materialistic people of our Western society, they illustrated Jesus' teaching, "It is hard for a rich man to enter the kingdom of heaven."[1]

From Tanah Merah, we went upriver to the Medalam tributary where a new leader, *Penghulu* Badak, lived. The former chief of this whole area, *Penghulu* Belulok, who we had known well, had died during the war. The people of Badak's village were completely bilingual, speaking both Iban and Murut.

The next morning we moved on to Kedu's Iban village at Meruyu. They had not heard we were coming, so our arrival was a complete surprise, and they gave us an uproarious reception. We had lived there for two years, from 1937 to 1938, so we knew these people better than any other Iban community. Just as the first few young people were beginning to respond to the Christian message in 1938, we were compelled to leave them as Winsome had to go to Singapore for surgery followed by a time of recovery. Then came the war, and when we returned to Borneo the response of the people in the Baram had claimed our full attention. Thus, we had not seen these people for many years.

We stayed for two nights at Kedu's village, chatting with people and doing some medical work. We told them of the dual purpose of our visit: to meet our friends and to bring them the gospel message once again. They responded politely, but later they said that during

1. Matthew 19:23

the war, when fighting the Japanese, they had invoked all their old pagan deities — and *Tuhan Isa* as well! I stressed again to them that there is only one true God, not merely one of many. I also reminded them that Jesus would surely come back to this earth again and that he required a real change of heart, not merely giving up certain habits or adopting various rituals.

When it came time to return downriver, we asked the Ibans to take us the short distance down to the three families of Murut people at Sungei Pranga who had become Christian during the war while visiting relatives in the Trusan. There, on Sunday morning, we had a time of worship and praise to God for all he had done for us. The quiet dignity and peace of these three families offered a marked contrast with the desperate drunkenness we had seen among the Muruts in the pre-Christian days.

We also met up with our old friend Undi, the first Christian believer, and his wife Sema. They had maintained their Christian stand over the years and we were delighted to see them.

Our visit among the Ibans of the upper Limbang provided a vivid retrospect of the years we had spent among them. Although we found several individuals who were committed to following God, the majority were indifferent. But looking back over the years, I realize that God has his own plans and his own timetable. Just as, "when the time had fully come, God sent his Son,"[2] so his time for the fuller response of the Ibans to the gospel message was still to come.

After leaving the Ibans, we pressed on downstream to Ranggu where there was a small group of Christians that constituted the Bisaya church. They had maintained a consistent witness during and after the war, and we spent a happy evening with them.

The next day we caught a ride to Limbang town with the recently established Sarawak Government travelling medical dispensary. It so happened that the government launch was going to Lawas the next day, and the new Resident, Mr. Fisher, arranged for our passage. We

2. Galatians 4:4

arrived in Lawas on September 22, 1951, marking the last stage of my twentieth journey during the postwar period from 1946 to 1951.

After our constant travelling by river and jungle track, it took us several days to reorient our minds and then select and pack our things for the life that lay ahead during the next few months. We spent four days with John and Kitty McArthur in Labuan and then flew directly to Darwin, Australia, arriving eight-and-a-half hours later. After overnighting there, we flew on to Sydney.

Winsome and I took the evening express train to Melbourne, arriving on the morning of October 10, 1951, whereupon we received a tremendous reception from relatives, friends and representatives of the Mission. It was a wonderful homecoming. I was particularly glad to see my dear mother again. She was eighty-nine, and although frail, she was mentally alert and active. We spent some good days with her and my brother Howard and his family.

During the final weeks of 1951 we met with our Mission council and with my home church at Williamstown in Melbourne. We also had a number of speaking engagements in the states of Victoria, New South Wales and Tasmania where we were invited to tell of our experiences in Borneo. In addition, I had the great joy of visiting one of my oldest friends, Dr. Delwyn Rees, who I had not seen for twenty-three years. He had served as a medical missionary in northwest China and had just been released from two years detention by the Communists.

Another highlight of our time in Australia was attending a course conducted by Dr. Kenneth Pike of the Summer Institute of Linguistics. We had actually been practicing, to a limited extent, some correct linguistic principles, but Dr. Pike's genius for the systematic study of languages was the key which opened to us methods for correctly reducing to writing the three Borneo languages — Murut, Kelabit and Kayan — that we had learned to use in a spoken form. Winsome and I had earlier learned Malay and Iban too, but these were already written languages. One of the great challenges we found in dealing with unwritten languages was to utilize correct systems of grammar, syntax and vocabulary from the outset — without undue influence from other local or foreign languages.

We knew it was essential that proven linguistic principles be followed rigorously if a precise translation of the Scriptures was to be made available for the thousands of people of inland Borneo who were now becoming literate. We wanted them to have the Scriptures in their own languages so that they would become a truly indigenous church, independent of expatriate control.

CHAPTER 25

We arrived back in Borneo on July 1, 1952, and as our biannual conference was scheduled to start in three weeks time, we stayed at the Mission headquarters near Lawas. During this period, I responded to a long-standing request to complete the details of streams and mountain routes on a map of north-central Borneo. On the many journeys we had made through the years, I had used the "time and compass" method to prepare numerous sketch maps, and I now compiled all these data to produce a large, composite map. This was later reproduced by the Department of Lands and Surveys in Kuching and became the official map used for many years before the first government aerial survey was undertaken.

During the weeks leading up to the conference, both Winsome and I sensed that the meetings would be important ones. The number of missionaries had greatly increased since the last conference in 1950, and several difficult matters needed to be resolved. But more important than policies, strategies and methods was the matter of attitudes, both towards God and fellow workers.

One of the guest speakers at the conference was our friend, Dr. Delwyn Rees, who we had seen earlier in the year in Melbourne. In his main address, Del quoted the Lord's declaration that, "I live in a high and holy place, but also with him who is contrite and lowly in spirit, to revive the spirit of the lowly and to revive the heart of the contrite."[1] Using this text, he emphasized the humility of heart which is needed if God, by the Holy Spirit, is to impact our lives, and he reminded us that God's requirements are quite different from the qualities we are inclined to see as important.

During discussions of mission strategy, the group concluded that Winsome and I, in view of our knowledge of the Kayan language and the linguistic training we had received from Dr. Kenneth Pike, should concentrate on translating the Bible into the Kayan language.

1. Isaiah 57:15

Unfortunately, we soon found that the suggestion to be located at Marudi for this work was unsuitable. Although the town was important as an administrative centre for government in the Baram District, it was far removed from any Kayan population. Kayan nationals were only transient visitors there and thus not available as resident language informants.

At first we tried renting a large government bungalow. Then the Government required it for their own use. Next the Mission purchased the top floor of a shop in the bazaar for our residence, to be used also as a church. This too proved unsuitable.

One positive result of our time at Marudi was that we found a number of Christians among the police. In prewar days the police had been mostly Malay or Iban, but in later years recruits also came from among the Murut, Kelabit, Kayan and Kenyah people, and many were from Christian villages. At first our little Sunday services consisted almost entirely of police, government hospital workers and others in government or civil employment, but after harvest time our numbers swelled with a steady stream of visitors from upriver.

Eventually, the upper floor of the shop was sold and the Marudi Council gave us two blocks of land in the town where we were able to construct a new church building.

In early 1953, Horrie and Joyce Hamer went on furlough, and as no one else was available for Long Tebangan, it was suggested that Winsome and I return there. This was a real joy and an answer to our prayers.

There was now an airstrip at Long Tebangan, together with a transceiver radio connection to the headquarters at Lawas, and what a difference that made to the accessibility of that lonely spot. Instead of having to make the slow and hazardous journey up the rapids, we could now go from Marudi by outboard powered longboat up the calm Apoh River to Long Atip, and from there fly by the Mission plane over the mountains to the Long Tebangan airstrip. The transport of ourselves and our two children, together with nearly one ton of goods, was accomplished in seven trips of about twenty-five minutes each way. Winsome and Lukut and all the goods went in earlier trips, and I came in on the last flight with Mina.

As we crossed the last ridge of rugged, jungle-covered mountains, the valley of the Akah River came into view below us. Until I saw it from the air, I had not realized that Long Tebangan lay in such a deep and narrow valley. As we came down in an ever tighter spiral descent, I felt like a fly caught in a circular trap trying to find its way out!

We had been back at Long Tebangan less than a month when we received word by radio that Winsome was to be awarded the Queen's Coronation Medal for her work among the people of the Baram, particularly those at Long Tebangan. This was an honour, not only for Winsome, but for the Kayan people as well. Our friend Jok Ngau, who was Headman at Long Tebangan when we first came to the Baram, had recently been named *Penghulu* of the entire Uma Peliau clan of Kayans, and crowds of Kayan people from nearby villages came for the investiture ceremony.

The new District Officer, Alastair Morrison, arrived from Marudi accompanied by his wife Hedda,[2] who was a photographer of international stature. In preparation for the official ceremony, a table draped with the British flag was set up in the long assembly hall running the full length of the longhouse. Mr. Morrison made a short speech, the citation was read out, and then on behalf of Her Majesty Queen Elizabeth II, he decorated Winsome with the Coronation Medal. Along with the medal, Winsome received a booklet with a photograph of the Queen in her regalia and a message from the Governor of Sarawak, Sir Anthony Abell.

I have no idea how many such medals were presented throughout the British Empire to commemorate the coronation of Queen Elizabeth II. It would be safe to say, however, that not many were presented in a longhouse. And it would be hard to imagine a ceremony anywhere in the world with a more appreciative audience.

2. Hedda Morrison, *Life in a Longhouse* (Kuching, Sarawak: Borneo Literature Bureau, 1962).

Our posting at Long Tebangan was a new beginning in many ways. While we were stationed there the first time, a great deal of our efforts had been committed to itinerant work. During the intervening three years, the pressure for travelling had become less urgent as missionaries had been stationed at Long Atip on the Apoh and at Lio Matu in the upper Baram. Thus, we could dedicate ourselves to Bible translation work and the preparation of a Kayan dictionary.

The study of the Kayan language was a natural and enjoyable progression for me. I had compiled an extensive Kayan vocabulary during the period of 1948–52, incorporating the two main dialects of the Uma Peliau and Uma Pu clans, and several subdialects of the Kayan language. The Uma Peliau dialect was spoken by most of the Kayan villages on the main Baram River, while the Uma Pu dialect was spoken more by communities living in the Apoh, Patah and upper Akah regions. Taken together they were completely and mutually intelligible.

I was fascinated by the study of the Kayan language structure, together with the idioms and the literary usages which would enable us to make an acceptable translation of the Bible. I also had a good helper in Tama Sing, one of the upper class leaders of the Uma Peliau clan. We immediately put our language study to use in active teaching in the school, in the Sunday services and in the young people's Bible studies. Ken Nightingale joined us and helped with all of this work.

Our situation at Long Tebangan was, in many ways, ideal for bringing up children. We were living in a quiet rural environment, in daily contact with a culture which had been purged from harsh pagan fears and superstitions. The people were eagerly receiving the teaching of Jesus Christ from the Bible and merging it with the best elements of Kayan culture.

Mina and Lukut were in early childhood now, and they were a delight to us. It was interesting to observe how these two children, one Kenyah and the other Kayan, responded as they grew up in this environment. Their biological heredity was identical with the people all around them, but they had been under our influence from infancy, and we had tried to show them the eternal values that God, their Creator, had revealed in the person of Jesus Christ. They were, therefore, good material for a case study.

From the time he had begun to talk, Lukut spoke both Kayan and English.

"Mina does not talk very much, being a silent and thoughtful type," Winsome noted at one point. "But when she does talk, she is trilingual."

Winsome was a good mother, and she lovingly observed and guided their behaviour. Her diary for 1954 records some of their sayings. In four-year-old Mina's vocabulary, mosquitos were called "sneakoes." She was also philosophical about life's harsh realities. One day Mina and Lukut were playing quietly together when Lukut remarked, "Where is your 'husbin'?"

Mina replied in a sad voice, "Oh he die! That's why I got you!"

Lukut, being a year younger, saw life in less complex terms. On one occasion he had been looking at the sky before going to bed. When he shut his eyes to pray he intoned solemnly, "O Lord bless the moon!"

Mina, by nature sensitive and conscientious, took quite a responsibility to care for her younger brother. Lukut, however, was an independent little fellow with quiet self-confidence. Winsome once asked Mina to peep into the room and see what Lukut was doing. "He is talking to Lukut," said Mina, meaning he was talking to himself. And early in life he developed his own ideas about how things should be organized. When a visitor asked him what he wanted to do when he grew up, Lukut replied, without hesitation, "I would like to tell other boys what to do!"

One day, two of the Long Tebangan Kayans went hunting and shot a large sambhur deer. It had a young male calf which the men caught and brought to us alive. Our two children were fascinated by this attractive little animal. To feed it we mixed some powdered milk with warm water and put it in a feeding bottle, and the little deer sucked ravenously. It soon adopted us and followed us everywhere. We named him Bambi, and he would come bounding to us when we called him.

Sometimes the Kayans passed our house with their hunting dogs. Responding to his instincts, Bambi would run into the river to escape the dogs. His long legs would carry him into deep water, leaving the dogs barking at him from the bank. The first time I saw this, I went to the river's edge and called his name and he came to me for protection. Soon Bambi learned to ignore his natural instinct to rush into the river when the dogs barked at him and would come directly to me.

Lukut, Mina and Bambi

Even more remarkably, Bambi learned to swim across the river following my boat — right across the river to the other side where there were dozens of barking dogs. Then he would follow me closely, up the bank to the village, trusting my protection as he walked with me, all the time surrounded by barking dogs. I marvelled that a young deer born in the forest should show such implicit trust in me as its protector.

During this second period at Long Tebangan, we faced growing concerns about the young people, not only in our own village, but everywhere in Sarawak and Sabah. The Government had started primary schools in the coastal areas and later extended them into the larger rural centres. This new access to education and exposure to the outside world was rapidly changing the pattern of society among the tribal people. We knew that we must respond to this momentum of change, especially among the young people in the villages who had accepted the gospel message and were now looking to us for guidance. They faced enormous changes in their lives, and to cope effectively they needed not only spiritual teaching, but also vocational training to adapt to the industrial and technical advances that were penetrating the very fabric of life in Southeast Asia.

To promote spiritual maturity, we felt the best way forward would be to establish Sunday classes which would give the young people an avenue for teaching others what they themselves had learned. In addition, we felt it would help to meld the whole village into a spiritual unit. I put this proposal to the village leaders, and they agreed. This was the beginning of Sunday school work in the Mission, and it became a well-established sphere of service in the national church.

Regarding vocational instruction, my own training and experience in technical school teaching had heightened my awareness of the emerging need for this type of program, adapted to the needs of a rural environment. I therefore advocated these ideas to the various government administrators with whom we were in close contact, hoping that the colonial Government of Sarawak would initiate a scheme of training in technical skills so that the people could themselves build better houses and furniture and advance their living standards. I realized that our Mission did not have the resources to undertake such a program, however, so I could do little more than discuss the vision I had. I did not, at that stage, anticipate that I would have any direct involvement myself.

During 1954, with our pilot on furlough, the mission plane was grounded. As the time approached for the biannual field conference in July of that year, I informed the Mission in Lawas that owing to the suspension of aerial transport, Winsome and I felt we should remain at Long Tebangan.

The long distance and the time consumed in travelling to Lawas were not the only factors, however, that made us reluctant to go to the field conference. I had come to realize that both Winsome and I had deep-rooted differences in viewpoint, attitude and policies from those who were in control of the administration of the Mission. The previous year, I had written a personal newsletter which touched on some of my perceptions and sense of frustration. I felt that if such differences came to the surface, they could undermine the harmony of the conference. However, in the end, we yielded to the wishes of others and set out for Lawas, travelling by river and sea.

Coming down the Baram we stayed overnight at the Chinese shop at Long Lama. While there, our children had a good time playing with a young Chinese girl whose father was a brother of the shopkeeper. The girl's father had been married to a Kayan woman from Long Laput who had since died, and he was planning soon to return to mainland China permanently, leaving his youngest daughter, Lee Kah Kim, at Long Lama. Seeing her playing with our two children, he asked if we would adopt her. We said that we would pray about it, and we continued on to Lawas.

Early on the first day of the conference, July 26, 1954, Winsome and I were sitting together, waiting for the proceedings to begin, and we were reading from *Daily Light*. The top text in the selection of verses for the day read, "By faith Abraham, when called to go to a place he would later receive as his inheritance, obeyed."[3]

I was immediately impressed with this verse, indeed with the whole selection of verses, and it seemed to come as a definite and direct message to me. I turned to Winsome and said, "Do you think this indicates that we should leave the Mission?"

"It could mean that," she replied.

During the next few days the conviction increased that this was God's direction for us.

I remembered the challenge that Hudson Taylor had given to prospective candidates for service with the China Inland Mission. "The Mission may cease to exist," he said, "but if God has called you, he will not fail you."

---

3. Hebrews 11:8

It was not a step that we could ever have taken lightly. God's call to me — and to Winsome — to serve him in Borneo had been clear and definite.

Nor were we self-supporting. Winsome had a small inheritance from her grandfather, but I had no other income, and we had recently taken on the added responsibility of Mina and Lukut as our children. To leave the Mission would be a major risk, but we felt that this was indeed the step we should take in faith and obedience to God, just as Abraham did.

So I wrote a letter of resignation, giving a six-month notice period from July 31, 1954 to January 31, 1955. Never for a moment did we consider leaving Borneo and going elsewhere, far less going back to Australia or trying to form a splinter group. I must admit that I secretly hoped that the situation would change and we would be able to withdraw our resignation during that six-month period. Also, we gave no indication of our resignation to any of the local churches or national Christians. What the future held we simply did not know. Although our hearts were heavy, our spirits felt free.

We did not discuss this decision with anyone outside the Mission except the Education Officer, Robert Nicholl. We had been operating a primary school at Long Tebangan, and although the school was not financed by the Government, it was under the supervision of the Education Department, and we were in duty bound to inform him.

Mr. Nicholl was a man of great scholarship. He had told me previously of his unusual career. He was born into a Methodist family but became a Roman Catholic priest, and then for ten years he had been a monk in Buckfast Abbey. During the Second World War he had been a chaplain in the Army, but he came to the point where, as he told me, "I had nothing to offer the troops." He became an atheist and resigned his chaplaincy. After the war he entered the Sarawak civil service and became the first principal of the Teacher's Training College at Batu Lintang in Kuching.

When passing through Marudi on our way back to Long Tebangan, we met with Mr. Nicholl. When I told him that we had given six months' notice of resignation from the Mission, he asked us about our future plans. I told him simply that we were looking to God for his guidance, but that we had no intention of leaving Borneo. We were prepared to stay on in some form of service in this land, even under the simplest of conditions.

The decision to stay on was soon put to the test. On our way up the Baram we stayed again with the Chinese shopkeeper. The seven-year-old girl, Lee Kah Kim, was still there, and once again they asked if we would adopt her. Winsome saw the child happily playing with Mina and Lukut, and she remembered the word spoken by the Egyptian princess, "Take this baby and nurse him for me, and I will pay you."[4] So we took Kah Kim with us up the Baram to Long Tebangan.

During the remaining months of 1954, the children were a delight to us, and we found that sometimes God spoke to us through them. One evening, in the short twilight of the tropics, Winsome found Mina sitting on the front porch all alone. From the back of the house towards the forest came the sound of the "six o'clock" cicada droning out its repetitive, harsh buzz, punctually at sunset. This large winged insect always made its rasping sound strictly on time, even when a storm or thick dark clouds made it difficult for human beings to guess the hour.

Mina was just sitting there quietly, looking out at the river and the village beyond where the people were returning from their farms and the birds were settling on the trees.

"What are you doing there, Mina?" Winsome asked.

"I'm listening to the peace, Mummy," said Mina quietly, in her charming, original expression. She herself was just that — peaceful and radiating peace.

For Winsome and me, inward peace was often tested during those months. Yet God did give us peace immediately when we took the step that Abraham had taken, and the Lord gave us the word that he had given to his disciples, "Peace I leave with you; my peace I give you. I do not give to you as the world gives. Do not let your hearts be troubled and do not be afraid."[5]

---

4. Exodus 2:9
5. John 14:27

To leave the membership of the Mission which God had guided me to initiate was the most difficult decision I had ever faced. But I believed then, and I still believe, that it was God who led me to that decision. He had a new sphere of service for me, for which he had been preparing me ever since I had enrolled as a teenager at the West Melbourne Technical School.

God gave me the persistent vision that his people in Borneo, having been delivered from the bondage of pagan worship, should now adopt a standard of living consistent with the new life and liberty that Christ had given them. How this goal could be achieved I did not know. But I did know that God oftentimes answers prayer in unconventional ways.

In the meantime, we continued on with the primary school, the Sunday school, and with Bible teaching for the Kayan adults and young people at Long Tebangan. But most importantly we prayed and waited for the next step to be shown.

Then, in early October, while listening to the morning radio call-up from Lawas, we received the text of a telegram from the Department of Community Development in Kuching. It was sent through Robert Nicholl, the divisional Education Officer, inviting me to draw up a proposal, including curriculum and financial estimates, for the commencement of a Community Development Project. This project was to be situated in the Baram River area, but was to encompass also the Murut and Kelabit peoples of the interior.

I sent a telegram in reply asking for more details, and Mr. Nicholl responded in specific terms stating that I would be free to submit my own proposal and that I would have a free hand in making estimates of expenditures. He also stated that in my own quarters and in my private life I could continue my missionary status. For instance, provided I conducted the project on a secular basis, I could hold services in the school room for Christian students during the weekend.

This offer took me completely by surprise, but I recognized it as the answer to our prayers, and it proved to be God's plan for our future service for him.

After receiving the second message from Mr. Nicholl I went downstream to Miri and met with him. He was an enormous help in drawing up the proposal and in devising a tentative curriculum. We both agreed that it should embrace technical training in manual crafts such as carpentry and the maintenance of tools, tinsmithing and soldering, plane geometry and geometrical development, and also building design and construction. All these I had learned and then taught at the West Melbourne Technical School. The project also was to include improved methods in agriculture and vegetable growing. We planned on selecting two boys from each village in the Baram and its tributaries so that they could go back and demonstrate to their own people what they had learned.

This new direction in our lives was wonderfully timed to coincide with Robert Nicholl's term as Education Officer in Sarawak's Fourth Division. He recognized the significance of the changes that were taking place among the young people of the Baram District, and he had the initiative and courage to turn that perception into action.

By early 1955, Mr. Nicholl wished to determine whether the proposed Community Development Project would be acceptable, at least in principle, to the Sarawak Government and the people most directly concerned. He arranged with the District Officer for a special meeting of the Baram District Council so that I could explain the purpose of the project and discuss the curriculum.

I presented our project proposal to the Council at Marudi in mid-March and felt that I had received a favorable hearing. The new District Officer, Ian Urquhart, who had replaced Alastair Morrison, appeared to have a good appreciation for the requirements of the people and seemed supportive. I was also encouraged by the response of the Government representative from Kuching. But apart from that, I was very glad just to see him again, for the representative was Roland Bewsher!

Following our release from the internment camp at Batu Lintang, Roland and Mary and their adopted twins had repatriated to Australia. From there, Roland applied for a position with the new Government of Sarawak administered by the British colonial office, and he and his family eventually returned to a posting with the civil service in Kuching.

Almost ten years had passed since the end of the war, and almost twelve years since Roland had jettisoned his Christian faith while in confinement at Batu Lintang.

However, Roland's story has an amazing sequel. Sometime after returning to Sarawak, he had visited England in connection with his sons' schooling. While there, he came in contact with some Christians, and the influence of their lives caused him to painfully re-evaluate his own life.

"In a miraculous way," he told me later, "God repossessed me." We had numerous contacts with Roland and Mary in subsequent years, and we soon saw that God certainly had graciously "repossessed" him. What a source of joy this was to us. As in Jesus' classic parable, the lost son had returned: "For this son of mine was dead and is alive again; he was lost and is found. So they began to celebrate."[6]

Undoubtedly, there was also great rejoicing in heaven. The lost sheep had been found.

"I tell you that in the same way there is more rejoicing in heaven over one sinner who repents than over ninety-nine righteous persons who do not need to repent."[7]

---

6. Luke 15:24
7. Luke 15:7

Part VI
Finishing Well

Life is love, enjoy it.
Life is a mystery, know it.
Life is a promise, fulfill it.
Life is sorrow, overcome it.
Life is a song, sing it.
Life is a struggle, accept it.
Life is a tragedy, confront it.
Life is an adventure, dare it . . .

– Mother Teresa

Chapter 26

While it was difficult to think of leaving the people we loved at Long Tebangan, the scene was now being set for us to enter an entirely new phase of service in Borneo. It was one we could render alongside and complementary to — and yet independently from — the organization of the Mission. As the months passed, it became clear that God was behind the scenes, guiding us step-by-step, and our main prayer was that we would recognize his leading. In fact, this entire experience was a poignant illustration of the need to seek to understand God's purposes, to watch for his controlling hand upon our lives, and to respond with our obedience.

Now that the Community Development Project had been openly discussed with the Sarawak Government, I felt free to mention this new opportunity to friends in Australia. I did so in a personal newsletter dated April 15, 1955, in which I also wrote:

> The indigenous church in Borneo now consists of many thousands of believers among the various tribes, but apart from those few being trained as pastors, almost none of these Christians are being trained for civil responsibilities. In many parts of inland Borneo the picture is not that of a few called-out believers in a vast pagan community, but rather of many believers in communities which have become largely Christian — though still awaiting the education and training which should accompany such a change. I have a strong feeling that we have a responsibility to meet the need for such training . . .

While we continued our more conventional missionary projects at Long Tebangan — teaching weekday Bible classes, supervising the large Sunday school, revising and enlarging the Kayan-English dictionary, and translating the initial chapters of Matthew's gospel into Kayan — we also corresponded actively with both the Education Department and the Department for Community Development. A program of technical education specifically designed to raise the standard of living of the rural people had not been attempted before in Sarawak, and I was invited to Kuching to discuss the project with the relevant Government departments. At subsequent meetings with the District Councils comprising representatives from the Kayans, Kenyahs, Ibans, Muruts, Kelabits and other minor ethnic groups, people enthusiastically gave their support. Yet our proposal was not without opposition. At all of these meetings I tried to emphasize that the project would be conducted on a strictly secular basis, with the understanding that in my private life I would be free to minister to and counsel any young Christians who may be involved in the program.

I felt that the ideal location for the project would be Long Lama where the land was typical of much of the Baram terrain and was suitable for agricultural training. This was also the natural trading centre for a large section of the tribal people as it was situated at the limit of navigation for coastal trading vessels. Thus, we were greatly encouraged when the big Kayan village at Long Laput, just a short distance upriver, spontaneously promised to make land available for this purpose.

In mid-July, with dramatic suddenness, on three successive days we received a cable from England, a letter from a Government official in Kuching and a letter from Australia. Although the one from Kuching was unofficial, it was from a friend in government service telling us that the Community Development Project had been approved, but there would be some delay in the allocation of government funds for buildings and other necessities. The letter also agreed with our suggestion that we should take a furlough in Australia, so that we could begin the four-year contract refreshed and in good health.

We were not left in doubt about our decision, for both the cable from England and the letter from Australia independently indicated that we should take our extended leave immediately. Again we had found God's timing perfect. And, in parallel with this, we were delighted to learn that our colleague Win Burrow had been appointed to take over from us at Long Tebangan.

We spent the first week of September in the Long Lama area looking at possible sites for the Community Development Project. I found an excellent block of land situated about 500 yards behind the Chinese bazaar and the historic old fort, a relic of the Rajah Brooke regime. The entire site was rising land which ensured that all buildings would be above flood level. An area of nearly twelve acres was made available, providing ample space to develop irrigated rice fields and vegetable gardens as well. This accomplished, all was now clear for our departure to Australia.

Upon our arrival at Sydney, Lukut, Mina and Kah Kim, dressed in Borneo style with their conical sun hats, caused quite a sensation among the press photographers. The children, now five, six and eight, respectively, were excited by the sights, and their excitement was contagious. Next morning the newspapers featured photographs of these so-called "wild children of the jungle." But fame is fleeting and things soon settled down.

Another event, however, was much more sobering. When we reached the home where we were to stay that night, my cousin Cyril Edwards drew me aside and said, "Hudson, your dear mother passed into the Lord's presence this morning."

Her death had occurred only five hours before our arrival that same day, October 6, 1955. She was ninety-three.

My mother had prayed that her two sons, my younger brother Howard and myself, would be there to bury her when the time came to leave this world, and even though we were not beside her at the time of her departure, we were both there to commit her body to the earth with the assurance that she would live on eternally in God's presence.

She was a wonderful mother. Looking back, I cannot remember any fault in her. She truly loved God and exalted him. For the last few months of her life Mother had been cared for in a nursing home in Sydney, and the nurses there told me of the gracious atmosphere of the Lord's presence in which she had lived. They said she had been a blessing to them all.

Our stay in Sydney was short, for Winsome's brother, Francis Howell, owned a sheep property named Rotherlea near Benalla, about 100 miles north of Melbourne, and he and his wife Jane invited us with open arms to stay and rest in the peace of the Australian countryside. For nearly a year Winsome had been in rather poor health, and this was an excellent opportunity for her to relax and quietly build up her strength again.

The weeks passed quickly and soon it was Christmas, much to the delight of the three children from Borneo. Dressed in red robes and a white beard, Winsome's brother provided them with their first unforgettable exposure to Santa Claus.

Meanwhile, I was able to catch up on my correspondence and make preparations for the upcoming Community Development Project in Sarawak. In February, I had a letter from the Government of Sarawak advising that the fully elaborated scheme, together with the estimates covering the period July 1956 to December 1960, had been approved by the Community Development Committee. They also informed the Australian Government concerning this scheme. As a result, I was invited to Canberra to meet with the administrators of the Colombo Plan, a program established within the British Commonwealth to provide technical and financial aid to developing countries in Asia. The Colombo Plan authorities showed every desire to assist and suggested that a list of the equipment required be prepared and submitted to them by the Government of Sarawak.

The delivery of this equipment would take some time, however, so I obtained some other equipment, with private funds, for immediate use upon my arrival at Long Lama. I was able to purchase secondhand a fully mounted circular saw, a simple planing machine, a moulding machine, some hand tools, a generator, some small electric motors, a battery charger, a twelve volt electric drill and a small wood turning lathe. I had all this equipment crated so that it could accompany me on my return to Borneo.

My target date for arrival in Sarawak was the beginning of July 1956, and I was able to book passage for myself and all my equipment on a cargo vessel which left Sydney on June 3rd, bound for Singapore.

We decided that Winsome and the children would follow in about five months time, leaving me free to get on with the hard pioneering phase of the project. This would involve building dormitories and cooking facilities so that the students selected could come into residence and commence the first two-year course in January 1957.

Once I arrived back at Long Lama, I could not wait to start construction. The first step was to cut a survey line from the river bank to the nearest area of rising ground. I knew exactly where it should go, so I cut that line myself using a *parang*. Next I marked out the sites for the various buildings — dormitory and kitchen, carpentry workshop, tinsmithing workshop, machine tool workshop, the power house for the electric generator, the site for my own house and quarters for the junior staff.

From the very beginning I endeavoured to enlist the interest and co-operation of the local people. As soon as the positions of the access road and the building sites were clearly laid out, I asked the District Officer to convene a meeting of the two local Chiefs and all the Headmen of the nearby villages, at the Long Lama fort, to explain the scheme and test the extent of their willingness to help. *Datuk* Mohammed Zin Galau from Marudi, the Liaison Officer for the whole Baram District, attended and gave great support.

During the balance of the year the people responded by supplying large quantities of construction timber at about half the market price, and each village gave two days of voluntary labour in felling trees and clearing and levelling the building sites. In addition I was able to hire contract workers whenever needed.

From July 1956 to February 1957, we saw a period of activity similar to the reopening of the Mission when I first returned to Borneo in August 1946, exactly ten years earlier. We finished the access road, complete with two bridges, and then laid a wooden railway track on which a hand-pushed trolley conveyed the heavy materials to the main site. At the end of the first term in 1957 we had twenty-seven students.

I taught all the technical classes, while J. Sing Anyi, himself a Kayan, taught the academic subjects. He also took a great interest in assisting with the wood-working classes.

Before the commencement of that first term, Robert Nicholl visited the central highlands and brought back with him five Kelabit girls to join the academic classes. These girls lived in a room at our quarters under Winsome's supervision. They did not take part in any of the technical classes, but helped with the vegetable gardens and the access road. Later these young women went on to train for teaching and nursing.

In spite of strenuous efforts from everyone, I had underestimated the time needed for completion of all the buildings required for the opening of the first two-year course. Nonetheless the students responded splendidly, and the later success of the scheme owed much to their dedicated work during that first year. They cleared the jungle, dug drainage ditches, and soon had gardens planted and producing vegetables for food.

During the first term most of the technical instruction was a by-product of the building program. It was "learning by doing," confined mostly to building and concrete work. Despite the fact that the students contributed so much to the work of building, however, we were able to maintain a half-day schedule for academic classes.

During the second term of that first year, we were able to start practical training with the power tools, and I was thankful to have the secondhand equipment I had purchased in Australia. The supply of equipment through the Colombo Plan was greatly appreciated when it came, but since it had to go through the normal process of contract, supply, acceptance, shipment and delivery to Kuching, and transporting to Long Lama, most of it did not arrive until mid-1958.

In the meantime, I was able to teach the students how to forge plane irons and chisels from spring steel, just as I had in the Japanese internment camp. By the second term we had made simple wooden planes and wood-working chisels, and the boys were busy making tables and doing other basic joinery in the buildings.

The tinsmithing classes also proved popular as I taught the boys how to use T-squares and drawing boards to produce a plan and elevation, and then develop a geometrical model from tinplate and solder the joints.

I was amazed at the aptitude of the students; by comparison with students I had taught at technical schools in Australia, the quickness with which these boys responded to teaching was much better. However, it must be remembered that I had hand-picked the brightest of the boys from the villages in the interior.

By the end of 1957, all the students had achieved some basic skills in carpentry, tinsmithing, concrete mixing and in the use of fertilizers for growing vegetables. During the 1958 term they applied this knowledge in erecting the workshop block which had a floor laid with properly mixed concrete.

Although one of my motivations for the project was expressed in the injunction: "As we have opportunity, let us do good to all people,"[1] I was especially anxious to help the Christians develop a lifestyle that reflected their liberation from the forces that had previously kept them in bondage. More than half of our students had come from Christian villages, so I arranged a morning prayer meeting, daily, at six-thirty. I was careful not to offer any inducement or bring pressure to bear on anyone to attend these early-morning meetings, but it was most rewarding to see that the Christian boys did attend. Also, on Sundays we had a normal church service.

In 1958, Shell generously donated a quantity of hand tools and other equipment, including a Petter diesel engine, overhead shafting, a lathe and a drill, and sent one of their engineering fitters to install all this equipment at no cost to us.

It was in 1958 that the achievements of our students gained greater recognition among the people of the Baram district resulting in an increase in volunteer labour. Even from Kayan and Kenyah villages two days' journey by boat, contingents came to help in clearing the jungle and digging fishponds.

1. Galatians 6:10

The second of the two-year courses ran from 1959 through 1960, and for that course we had ample equipment and hand tools. By that time Robert Nicholl had the assistance of Manson Toynbee, who had been sent by the Canadian Government to help upgrade the national headmasters of the local primary schools throughout the interior. As a result, when I enrolled students for the second course, I was able to select thirty-one boys who, with a stronger primary education, were better prepared to benefit from the agricultural and technical skills they acquired.

It was our policy to incorporate into the program those who had proven their ability and, by the beginning of 1959, I was able to appoint two of the graduates from the first course to our staff as assistant technical instructors.

In 1960, the Community Development Committee asked me to recruit a water buffalo trainer and ploughman in order to introduce the use of water buffalos in preparing irrigated rice paddies. For this purpose I went to Ranau in Sabah, where the local people recommended that I engage Sinit Gambiran. He came by ship with his wife and family and two buffalos, already trained for ploughing. For the next four years Sinit was attached to our project and instructed the students in the use of buffalos for wet rice cultivation, a process new to the Baram and of great interest.

The 1960 classes had a strong emphasis on agriculture. We taught the boys how to make light wheelbarrows with a frame of one-inch galvanized waterpipe bent to shape and a tray made from sheet iron. That year also we obtained an iron bending machine from Australia, and with this we made several large circular corrugated-iron water tanks, of 300 to 1,000 gallon capacity. The joints were riveted and soldered, and I also taught the boys to make some spouting and downpipe from galvanized sheet iron.

In carpentry, we taught them to make a wooden chair and a small kitchen cupboard, both with mortise and tenon joints. At the end of the year twenty-seven boys graduated, and each was given a set of tools to be used in his own village.

During 1960, the final year of the original pilot program, I corresponded frequently with the Community Development Committee in Kuching regarding the future of the scheme. The Director of Agriculture had always considered that the Long Lama project would eventually focus on farming. However, it was decided that the second phase would continue with the same content as before, but for three years only, 1961–63. As the enrollment in 1961 would be derived from boys who had passed primary six level, the course could now be accomplished in one year.

The Agriculture Department was not able to provide an instructor, so one of our own graduates, Sili Wan, was designated to fill the gap. He and Sinit Gambiran gave valuable training in the use of buffalos for wet rice cultivation. In addition, three of the most promising trainees from the 1960 graduates were chosen as student teachers and were given six months in-service training at the recently opened Tanjong Lobang Secondary School, under a Colombo Plan trade instructor. These student teachers proved excellent.

After only four years, the Long Lama project had demonstrated its worth. Fifty boys, drawn from the Fourth and Fifth Divisions of northern Sarawak, had graduated. From that time onwards I began to notice an improvement in both design and workmanship in the construction of villages in the interior. And the value of the program was not only in the technical skills that had been acquired. This I heard expressed again and again in feedback from the parents and elders of the various communities, as the students developed new social skills and a positive psychological outlook toward their rapidly changing environment.

The second phase of the Community Development Project should be viewed against the background of education in Sarawak as a whole. Government schools for primary education were non-existent in Sarawak before the Second World War. Even during the postwar colonial period, primary school education only became widespread in rural areas in the mid-1950s.

By 1960, the majority of children in Sarawak rural areas were educated to primary six, but the Common Entrance examination limited the number who could go on to secondary education. Hence for a number of bright students, especially those who were over the normal age group, the second phase of the Long Lama project was ideally suited and enabled them to receive further education, and learn leadership and other skills that were very useful in their rural situation.

In 1961, thirty-three boys were accepted for training, and during the second and third terms they applied their new skills by building a dormitory to replace the temporary structure. Also that year the access road was reconstructed and widened, and then some 200 tons of crushed stone were laid and the surface was sealed with "Colpave" bitumen.

The employment of three graduates as assistant staff enabled me to visit our students who had gone home after the pilot scheme and also to select suitable students for the 1962 course. In most cases the students had used their training well, and some clever students advanced into government secondary schools and teachers' training colleges.

During the remaining years of phase two, students were drawn from a wider area and included Ibans, Malays, Kelabits, Muruts and Penans, as well as the Kayans and Kenyahs of the Baram area. In our technical classes the same general pattern was repeated. The boys quickly learned the basic skills and then perfected them by producing useful products such as chairs, tables, wheelbarrows, kitchen cupboards, and in 1963 they built a maternity clinic at Long Lama. The building had a maternity ward with seven beds and separate living accommodation for a midwife and a medical dresser. A total of thirty students were admitted in 1962 and thirty-nine in 1963; all except five graduated.

Through the years, I have been rewarded many times over as I have seen the tangible results of the Long Lama project. In 1957, when we started, the Kayans of the Apoh district had not followed their animistic religion for some eight years; although their villages were much cleaner than before, they still retained the same general building patterns. Over the next dozen years, although the quality of building was not greatly different, changes in design began to occur and the animals and chickens no longer lived under the houses.

Then, in August 1989, almost thirty years later, I had the opportunity to visit Long Bedian, the furthest Kayan village up the Apoh River. I was amazed at the sight. The village had been transformed. The population had increased from 300 in 1949 to 2,000 in 1989, and the houses were solidly built using a modern style and an orderly plan.

Modern Longhouse Village

"Who did all this building?" I asked them.

"We did," was the reply.

"Did you hire qualified tradesmen to do the work?"

"No, we did it all by ourselves," they said. "We learned it from those who attended the Community Development Project at Long Lama."

Chapter 27

The year 1963 was one of momentous international transition. Sir Winston Churchill announced his retirement from public life. Dr. Martin Luther King made his famous civil rights speech from the steps of the Lincoln Memorial in Washington. President John Kennedy was assassinated in Dallas. Pope John XXIII died of cancer. And a new nation was born in Southeast Asia as Sarawak and Sabah officially became part of the Federation of Malaysia under the leadership of *Tunku* Abdul Rahman.

That year also, in his old, dilapidated house on Albion Street, London, Rajah Vyner Brooke passed away peacefully in his sleep.

At the memorial service in St. Paul's Cathedral, the Rev. Philip Jones paid tribute to the man in a sincere and moving address, reflecting on the Rajah's personal qualities and fairly recognizing his family's remarkable achievements in the country they had ruled for more than a hundred years:

> He was one of three great men: James Brooke, his great uncle; Charles Brooke, his father; and he himself, Charles Vyner Brooke. They were great in different ways. They were men of different character and they were molded differently by the demands of their times and purposes. But in one thing they were alike. One thread — and it was a thread of gold — ran through all their policies. They were concerned, all three of them, always, to serve not themselves, but their fellow men and their subjects. I am in no doubt at all that we can see something of both the gentleness and the strength of God in their dealings . . .[1]

For us, personally, 1963 was a year of transition too. As this final year of the Community Development Project at Long Lama was drawing to a close, I had hoped that the Community Development Committee would realize the value of the short-term technical and

1. Sylvia, Lady Brooke, *Queen of the Head-hunters* (London: Oxford University Press, 1990), 191.

agricultural training adapted to rural conditions. I felt that if such training were available at perhaps six centres throughout a sparsely populated state such as Sarawak, it would greatly advance social development and economic growth, thereby enhancing the standard of living of the people. To achieve this goal I offered to help train instructors to the limited extent needed for such a program of rural development. But no one at the required level of political power and policymaking caught this vision. Public attention was focused on the political relationship of Sarawak within Malaysia, rather than of development within the State of Sarawak itself.

Meanwhile, however, the Government authorities in Sarawak had recommended to Her Majesty the Queen that I be awarded the Decoration of Officer of the British Empire (OBE) for my services at the Community Development Project at Long Lama. The award ceremony was hosted by the British High Commissioner at Kuching in 1963.

Hudson Southwell – Community Development Project, 1963

In 1964, the Community Development Project became the Long Lama Farmers' Training Centre, and in order to ensure a smooth transition, I was retained for that year as a senior Assistant Agricultural Officer. My role was to assist in certain technical aspects of the Centre and to continue follow-up visits to Development Project graduates. Also, I was asked to prepare an evaluation study on the impact of the project on the communities from which students had been drawn.

With this most interesting phase of community development service drawing to a close, Winsome and I bought a block of land at Long Lama on which to build a house, and from there to continue our outreach and church planting among the peoples of the Baram.

Around that same time, a new government secondary school opened at Marudi, the administrative centre for the Baram District. Hundreds of young people were being drawn from their home longhouse villages and rural primary schools to this secondary boarding school. A large proportion of these teenagers came from Christian homes, and we saw this as a tremendous opportunity for nurturing the gospel which had already been sown in their hearts, and also as a responsibility to assist them as they were exposed to the pressures of an urban situation for the first time, without the influence and support of their parents.

We soon realized that if we built a home at Long Lama, we would not be able to work effectively among the students at Marudi. So I applied to the Department of Lands and Surveys to buy a block of land from the Government reserve land in Marudi between the new airstrip and the river, and this was granted.

When we left Long Lama in 1965, we gave the block of land we owned there to the Mission to be used as a site for a new church. At Marudi we were allowed to occupy a medium-sized house in a group of government quarters while we were building a cottage on our newly acquired land near the river, and I was able immediately to commence Inter-School Christian Fellowship (ISCF) work at the secondary school.

By early 1966, our little cottage was ready for occupation and we were able to move in. Although it had only one bedroom, it was adequate for the short term and even had a bathroom serviced with a septic tank. It was the first home Winsome and I ever owned!

After settling in at the cottage, the next job was to draw plans for a bigger two-storey house to be built along with a large workshop and storeroom on the same block of land. Having trained so many young people at Long Lama, it was not difficult to find some of them who were willing to work for wages on building the main house. It took longer than using a contractor, but it was more satisfying and we ended up with a good quality product. In mid-1967 we moved in and were finally able to have meetings for the young people in the spacious room we had designed on the ground floor.

All this time I was fully occupied with work among the students at the secondary school. We had a weekday meeting at the school with a regular attendance of over 100 young people and we held Sunday services in our house, not only for students but also for upriver people who were visiting Marudi.

Thus our home became the nucleus of the national evangelical church, the *Sidang Injil Borneo* (SIB), at Marudi. As the numbers grew, I applied to the Baram District Council for land for a church building, and two town blocks were provided free of charge.

Winsome and I had been in our new home for only about six months when on New Year's Day, 1968, a stranger appeared at our front door.

"Good afternoon, Mr. Southwell. I have a problem."

"Come in," I said, expecting that he had some spiritual concern. He was Chinese, had a beaming smile and spoke excellent English. He introduced himself as Michael Cheong.

He told me that several directors of St. Columba's Anglican Secondary School had decided to commence a private secondary school at Miri named St. Aidan's. They had already engaged some teachers, but the man they had hoped would serve as Principal could not come owing to ill health.

"Would you come as Acting Principal?" he asked.

We had never met before, and I knew nothing of Michael Cheong's background, but when he told me he was an industrial chemist, he immediately captured my attention! And, as he outlined the vision of St. Aidan's directors, I warmed to the invitation to take the job. I told him I would consider the offer if I could get replacements to take over the ISCF work.

I wrote immediately to the Mission at Lawas and asked if there were two missionaries who would be available to take over from us at Marudi. I offered our new house as accommodation and told of the great opportunities for ISCF work among the young people at the secondary school, as well as the growing ministry in the SIB church.

Once again, God's timing was perfect. He had his chosen servants all ready for the task. Irene Neville and Ursula Kohler had been seconded from the Overseas Missionary Fellowship and were immediately available for this new assignment.

With this settled, I confirmed my acceptance of the offer to serve as Acting Principal of St. Aidan's School. I went to Miri alone and stayed with Michael Cheong for a few weeks until Irene and Ursula arrived at Marudi and Winsome had introduced them to our house and to the work among the students. Winsome then joined me in Miri, where we were to share one of the staff quarters with Leonie Armour, an Australian lady who was on staff at St. Columba's. It was an excellent arrangement.

St. Aidan's School was governed by a Board of Management with John Leong as Chairman. John was a prominent oil executive who was involved with a great many public activities. After his retirement from business, he was ordained as an Anglican priest and later became Bishop of Kuching. Michael Cheong was the Supervisor of St. Aidan's and was concerned with the day-to-day running of the school.

The school had received many applications from prospective students, and the Board had engaged a staff of five teachers. As soon as I arrived in Miri I had to organize this teaching staff and then test the prospective students to determine which should be in the transition class and which should be in the first form.

Another responsibility which I particularly enjoyed was conducting the opening assembly each morning. I selected about sixty suitable hymns for young people and had them typed on stencils and duplicated to make simple hymn books. After we sang the opening hymn each day, I chose an appropriate parable or story from the Bible and explained its meaning, and then closed with a prayer. Although it was not compulsory, everyone attended and seemed to enjoy it.

It was not difficult to love the young people at St. Aidan's. Most of them had failed the Common Entrance examination to the government-aided schools, and they realized that they were getting a second chance to to advance within the education system. Also, the school had good support from all sections of the community, and the attendance increased each year.

Opening up this new school, however, heightened my concern about the education standards being offered to the students at the Mission bible schools at Lawas and elsewhere. My experience at the Community Development Project, followed by the three years of ISCF work among the students at the Marudi Secondary School, and now our educational work at St. Aidan's, all drew my attention to the fact that the standard of education in Sarawak was rising year by year, but the pastors graduating from the Mission bible schools were not keeping pace with these rising standards. Winsome and I both felt strongly that this increasing gap in the educational standards would severely limit the effective ministry of the pastors in the national SIB church. In fact, our view on educational policies had been one of the major issues involved in our disagreement with the Mission administration. As the years passed, we saw this problem becoming more acute. Although the membership of the SIB had grown dramatically, it was a startling fact that none of the church officers or pastors had even a junior secondary school education.

My burden was such that I prepared a paper which I hoped would form a basis for renewed discussion within the Mission. Knowing that the biannual field conference would be held in July 1968, the fortieth anniversary of the founding of the Mission, I decided to write to the field Chairman, Alan Belcher, requesting permission to present my paper.

After the conference, Dr. Bill Hawes, who had been elected the new Chairman of the Mission, wrote to me as follows:

> Dear Mr. Southwell,
>
> We really were delighted that you were able to attend a few sessions of our Conference and to present your Paper to us.
>
> Judging from discussions and comment since then, the burden that you have for outreach and ministry among the secondary school students is shared by a great majority, if not all, of the fellowship. We shall be having executive meetings during the next week or so and we shall certainly be discussing in full your detailed recommendations . . .

The need for secondary school education in a Christian environment had gripped many of the leaders of the SIB and some within the Mission. As a result, the Mission executive appointed a sub-committee headed by Dr. Bill Hawes, along with two leaders of the SIB, to make an extensive inquiry into all aspects of this issue. The sub-committee published a report of its findings and made firm recommendations to the Mission conference in July 1972. These recommendations led to the establishment of a Christian secondary school and a general upgrading of educational standards within the SIB.

Meanwhile, our family was growing up. Mina completed her studies at Tanjong Lobang College for both lower and upper sixth forms in 1969. During the four months' wait for the examination results from the Cambridge Examination Syndicate, she accepted a teaching position at St. Mark's Junior Secondary School at Marudi.

Lukut completed his form five School Certificate at St. Columba's where he had been a prefect and was admitted to the lower sixth form at Tanjong Lobang College.

Kah Kim had chosen not to go further with her schooling than primary six while we were still at Long Lama. However, being a practical-minded and naturally energetic girl, she was able to help for a few years at the home for missionary's children at Kota Kinabalu in Sabah. Kim then came back to live with us at Long Lama in 1964. She was seventeen that year, and she met and married Bilong, a fine

Christian Kenyah who came from across the Indonesian border. The next year they moved to the Limbang area where Bilong was employed by a Chinese company working a limestone quarry. Three years later they had two children, and Kim was expecting a third child when tragedy struck.

Bilong operated a crane lifting blocks of limestone. One day the cable jammed and he was reaching out from the control cabin, trying to set it free, when the boom suddenly jerked upwards. Bilong's head was crushed against the cabin, and he was killed instantly.

Winsome happened to be in Marudi for a short visit when Kim telephoned from Limbang. With providential timing, the mission plane had just arrived at Marudi airport on its way back to Lawas. The new pilot, Dennis Berry, had parked the plane on the airstrip near our house and was available to leave immediately. Winsome gathered a few things together and within an hour she was able to be with Kim in her time of deep distress.

Eventually, Kim and her two children went to Lawas to stay with some of Bilong's relatives who were living at the Mission bible school. While there, Kim found a clerical job with a timber company which enabled her to support herself and her children.

During our second year at St. Aidan's, we more than doubled the enrollment and many more young people wished to attend. By this time also the Principal, Father Eric Currie, had improved in health and was able to head up the school, and I became Deputy Principal. This considerably lightened my load to that of mainly a teaching role.

At the end of the first term that year, Winsome and I went to stay for a week during the term holidays in our house at Marudi. I was looking through some old papers and diaries I had stored there when I remembered that I had left two of my diaries and some other things, including my OBE medal, in my desk at Miri.

Suddenly the thought came, *What if those things left in Miri were destroyed by fire?*

It was a remarkable premonition, for within fifteen minutes the telephone rang and a friend in Miri told us that the staff quarters we shared with Leonie Armour had burned to the ground! A short time later Mina telephoned from her boarding school at Tanjong Lobang on the outskirts of Miri. Upon hearing the news of the fire, she had gone immediately to look in the ashes for any of Winsome's gold jewelry. It was clever of her, and she did find some.

"The fire started in the semi-detached kitchen, at eleven-fifty a.m.," I recorded in my diary, "and was all over in thirteen minutes! It started when some wax and kerosene being heated over a gas ring caught fire and then tipped over. There was an instant great blaze of fire which ignited the palm leaf thatch roof, and the fire quickly spread to the main house."

The fire brigade was slow to arrive, so all they could do was douse the ashes and prevent the fire from spreading to the house next door. Mina rang again in the evening and said many people had rushed to the scene and retrieved some of our belongings before the fire reached them. The entire typed manuscript for the Kayan dictionary and other papers had been tied together and stored in a cupboard. The fire had burned the cupboard and then the floor, but the bundle of tightly packed papers was so thick that only the outer sheets were destroyed.

It was an especially heavy blow to Leonie Armour. Many of our own personal possessions had been left in our house in Marudi, but she lost everything. One thing I greatly regretted losing was the OBE medal. It was either melted or taken by someone who found it in the ashes. But the inscription written on parchment paper and signed by Queen Elizabeth II had been left in Marudi, and so survived.

I tried to regard the fire as only an interlude. We found another house to rent, and carried on and had a successful school year. Many were gracious in helping us. The first to do so was Bishop Galvin, the Roman Catholic Bishop of Miri, who sent me a generous cheque for 500 dollars while we were still in Marudi! We had enjoyed a good relationship with Bishop Galvin over a number of years and always appreciated his insights. Later I heard that at a Congress in Rome, he had presented a paper calling for a wider adoption of New Testament teachings within the Catholic church.

That year proved to be a progressive one at St. Aidan's, but I remember it particularly by a great milestone in human history — the first landing of human beings on the moon. I was absolutely enthralled with the realization that men with God-given ingenuity could visit another celestial body that is part of his great creation. The whole school was listening to my radio receiver and I shall never forget the sense of awe I felt when we heard those memorable words spoken as Neil Armstrong took the first sure steps on the surface of the moon.

I have always liked looking at nighttime skies, and even now when I see a full moon I think of that historical moment in July 1969. I also think often about the Creator who not only set the moon in place, but who himself transcends human history:

> When I consider your heavens,
> the work of your fingers,
> the moon and the stars,
> which you have set in place,
> what is man that you are mindful of him,
> the son of man that you care for him?
> You made him a little lower than the heavenly beings
> and crowned him with glory and honour.
> O Lord, our Lord,
> how majestic is your name in all the earth![2]

2. Psalm 8:3-5,9

Chapter 28

As Winsome and I entered the year 1970, I noted somewhat ruefully that this was the year I would fulfill the normal human life-span of three-score years and ten! Still, I was convinced I should not think in terms of retirement, but rather try to keep myself young in mind and spirit, and remember that God is timeless; he speaks alike to young and old. Whether young or old, all face temptations and grapple with similar problems, and all are influenced by the pressures generated by an increasingly fast-changing world.

Although Miri was still a rather sleepy little town in those days, Winsome and I were finding urban life something quite new after living so many years in the interior. And we knew that if we felt this way, how much stranger it would be to the young people coming to the towns and cities for their education — those who had lived their entire lives in isolated longhouse communities in the Bornean rain forests.

The years we had spent in the interior learning the languages and absorbing the cultures of those with whom we had lived helped us identify with the various tribal peoples who were passing through times of dramatic transition. So it seemed a natural progression in our own experience when God afforded us opportunities to help young people from these ethnic groups meet the challenges of change, now in an urban environment.

At St. Aidan's, I was again filling in as Principal, since Father Currie, owing to ill health, had to return to Australia before the end of 1969. I continued on in this position in 1970, as the school enrollment increased to over 365.

During the Easter holidays, Winsome and I made arrangements to attend the SIB Easter Convention which that year was scheduled for Long Atip. The trip that had once taken us more than a day's journey by longboat with outboard engine now took only twenty minutes on the Mission plane.

About 3,000 Kayans and Kenyahs from the Apoh and Tutoh villages attended the Convention. Among those present was the Honourable J. Balan Seling, who was a Member of the State Legislative Assembly and a Cabinet Minister. He and his wife Meriam were longstanding friends of our family since the early 1950s when Balan had attended the Mission school at Lawas and later studied at the Melbourne Bible Institute (now the Bible College of Victoria) in Australia.

Balan and I both spoke to the gathering at Long Atip concerning the need for a Christian secondary school under the control of the SIB, and I told of our experience at St. Aidan's. We also discussed the building of a church at Marudi for which the Baram District Council had given two blocks of land. In several ways this convention was seen as a milestone in the life of the SIB in the Baram District.

That was just one of the significant events of 1970, a year for which my diary is full of yellow hi-light markings drawing attention to memorable occasions. Another such event occurred during the third week of May when officials of the British High Commission were visiting Miri and all citizens of the British Empire were invited to a reception for them. Winsome and I attended, and it was there we met Captain Alastair Young for the first time. We invited him to visit us, and he came the following week.

Early in his life, Captain Young had chosen a career with the Merchant Marine. During World War II he had piloted oil tankers all over the world for the giant Shell organization, and after the war he was stationed at Miri. When he retired at the end of a distinguished career, he continued to live in his own house in Miri. He was a benevolent man and was well-known for his educational work. He had even fitted up one of his rooms as a school where he taught young Malay and Chinese men the elements of seamanship to prepare them for marine examinations.

As we had all lived so long in Sarawak and because I had been in the Royal Australian Naval Reserve as a young man, we found we had much in common, and we enjoyed Captain Young's visits. He had a big garden and he often brought flowers for Winsome.

Captain Young had been educated at one of England's large public schools where he had had some exposure to religious teachings, but he had never developed a personal relationship with God.

One day he showed me an article he had cut from a newspaper criticizing the Bible and Christianity. It appeared to be written sincerely, but by someone who was not aware of the true teaching of the Bible, and therefore it was quite easy to show that the criticisms contained errors of fact. I outlined some of the reasons why I believed the Bible to be God's reliable and infallible truth.

Captain Young's response was, "This is just what I want."

Some weeks later he indicated his definite commitment to follow Jesus Christ.

He was then well past the age of retirement, but he found a new joy in life and liberty in spirit. He not only continued teaching seamanship, but also commenced regular hospital visitation as a friend to all who needed help.

By the end of the year I had completed three years at St. Aidan's, and the Board of Directors gave me five months' leave, so Winsome and I returned to Melbourne early in 1971. We had a wonderful few weeks of rest at Wollert, on a grazing property owned by Winsome's youngest brother, Geoffrey Howell. At the end of June, we celebrated my seventy-first birthday at Townsville with Prof. Jim and Dr. Laura Ward who had served with us in Sarawak in the early 1950s.

Two months later we were heading back to Borneo where I was to resume work as Principal of St. Aidan's Secondary School. However, the news had filtered through to the Education Department in Kuching that I was into my seventies, and some considered that I was too old to continue efficiently running a school.

I heard later that the Divisional Education Officer at Miri came to my defense by countering, "You don't know Mr. Southwell!"

In any event, I approached the St. Aidan's governing board and suggested that my senior assistant should take over as Principal while I would continue conducting the morning assemblies as Honourary Chaplain. For me this was a happy arrangement. The students seemed to enjoy having the morning assemblies continued as before, while the change allowed me to devote most of my time to making a thorough, final revision of my Kayan-English dictionary. This project had been laid aside for several years, but I now was able to give it my focused attention.

Hudson and Winsome – 1971

There were also other activities in which I was able to be involved, one of which was giving part-time assistance at the Miri Evangelical College, which was just then being started by Rev. Ken Coleman to meet the need for theological education at the senior secondary school level.

But the chief joy to me was my involvement in the Sunday morning services at the Government Senior Secondary College at Tanjong Lobang, since renamed Kolej Tun Datuk Tunku Haji Bujang. This college was the top secondary school in Sarawak and attracted the brightest students from all over the country.

Meeting with these young people was of special interest to me, as I had been involved with many of their parents and grandparents in very different circumstances. There had been no government schools in the interior in the prewar years. In fact I think the first school in this entire area was the one Winsome and I started while we were hiding from the Japanese among the Muruts of the upper Trusan in 1942. So apart from very minor exceptions, there was no one in the vast interior of Sarawak who could read or write in any language until after the war.

Following the Second World War, a way of life that had remained largely unchanged for centuries collided with the twentieth century. A government-funded educational system was instituted and exposure to the outside world increased dramatically. Concurrently, large numbers of the people of Borneo adopted a new spirituality. As a result, the generation that emerged was radically different from preceding generations.

Some of the more graphic examples of change occurred among the Kelabits as they were living in one of the most isolated parts of the island. Before the war, very few Europeans had ever travelled as far inland as the Kelabit highlands.

When I first visited the Kelabit highlands in 1939, I met a muscular young man at Bario who was keen-eyed and spoke very rapidly. He was dressed only in a loin cloth, but to indicate his upper class status he wore a necklace of rare and valuable beads along with two eyeteeth of the clouded leopard in holes which had been punched in the shells of his ears. Being a teenager, he would have been born around the time that headhunting was effectively banned in Sarawak. His father almost certainly would have taken a head.

I did not see this young man again until 1947 when I was visiting the Kelabit highlands after the war. By that time he was married and had a son of his own. He told me that his son was born within a few weeks of the arrival of the first "Z" Special group of commandos, led by Major Tom Harrisson. The new baby boy was given the name Tom, after the leader of the commandos, but this soon became the unaspirated name Dom, following the local Kelabit pronunciation.

After the war, to reward the Kelabit co-operation with the commandos, a primary school was opened at Mein, the largest and most central of the Kelabit villages. As soon as Dom was able to attend school, he was enrolled as a student. The Kelabit children were intelligent and made good progress climbing the ladder of the education system. From the lower primary school in the highlands, Dom went to the upper primary school at Long Lama, and then on to Tanjong Lobang.

After gaining his Upper Cambridge School Certificate, which was the tertiary entrance examination, he was awarded a scholarship to the University of Western Australia to study medicine. Upon graduating in the early 1970s, he married a girl from Australia and returned to Sarawak. After ten years of practicing medicine he went to England for further studies and passed the examinations for admission as a Fellow of the Royal College of Surgeons.

This is a remarkable example of advancement for someone born to illiterate parents, living in one of the most remote and isolated areas of central Borneo. And it was students of this calibre who were attending the Tanjong Lobang College when we lived in Miri.

On one occasion, these students asked me to give a special address on the subject "The Bible and Science," with particular reference to the issue of creation as opposed to evolution. The topic was a popular one, and a large number of students gathered in the assembly hall, not only Christians, but many from various other backgrounds as well.

My thesis was that the biblical account of the progressive steps in the creation narratives, when rightly understood, fitted in perfectly with the known facts of science, including biology, geology and the laws of physics. Following my address, some of the students asked questions which I endeavored to answer. Then one of the teachers I had not met before suddenly spoke up.

"I wish to say that I disagree with ninety percent of what the speaker has said!"

To support his case, he quoted from the writings of liberal and atheist philosophers. By then we were almost out of time, so I realized that I had to make my point quickly and unequivocally.

Afterwards, I had a chance to speak with this young teacher. His name was Ron Nugent. He was a graduate of the University of Western Australia and had come to Sarawak on a volunteer basis. His desire was to help students of developing countries improve their education and thus be better equipped to find their place in the modern world. He had high ideals, but despite a Christian upbringing, his views were decidedly atheistic. He told me, however, that he was seeking truth.

I was impressed by this young man's sincerity and commitment, and I invited him to come for dinner sometime. A fortnight after our first meeting, Ron visited us in the home we were renting. We had a good long chat, and I showed him some books by Christian thinkers and offered to lend him any of these books he might care to read.

Over the next year, Ron travelled among the people of the interior, including those in the upper Limbang and the upper Trusan. He met people in the longhouses, both those who were Christian and those who were still pagan, and he was impressed with the fact that Christian beliefs could be integrated positively into their native cultures. He also observed the lives of the Christian students at the College. This, along with his extensive reading, influenced his thinking, and the following year Ron began to slip into the Christian services which were held at the College on Sunday mornings. Towards the end of that year he made a life-changing decision to become a Christian, and at his baptism he gave a splendid address entitled "My Pilgrimage from Atheism to Christ."

Not long afterwards, his two-year contract came to an end and he returned to Australia. He applied for another posting in Borneo and, based on his excellent teaching record, was offered an assignment at a secondary school at Kota Belud in Sabah.

From Kota Belud, there was one road leading straight inland to a Dusun village named Taginambor. I had first visited this village in 1937 when I was making a survey of Sabah's spiritual needs. Ten years later, after the war, Trevor White worked among these people and they responded to the gospel. A church was built at Taginambor in full view of the beautiful and fascinatingly rugged Mt. Kinabalu, and many of the Dusun farmers moved down from the surrounding hills and built their houses in the valley to be near the church.

Now, years later, this young Australian teacher was glad to make the church at Taginambor his spiritual home. But sometimes during the school holidays Ron would still come to see us in Miri.

As the number of students qualifying for secondary education in Sarawak and Sabah increased, the demand for new schools grew throughout the more remote areas of both states. As a result of this demand, a junior secondary school was opened at Bario in the Kelabit highlands, and under God's sovereign planning he used this school as the venue for a dramatic outpouring of his Spirit in the 1970s.

It was a period when an increasing number of young people began coming to the towns from the interior; there they gained higher levels of education and sophistication. At the same time a reverse flow also began taking place, as students were trained as teachers and went back to staff the schools in the interior.

The parents of these young people had lived their early lives in an environment dominated by omens, dreams and taboos. Most of the older people had experienced the liberating power of the gospel, but to these young people the fear of evil spirits was a relic of the past. For this new generation, however, the old satanic powers were exchanged for more subtle temptations in modern civilization.

During this time a gifted Indonesian evangelist, Dr. Peterus Octavianus, came to Sarawak and Sabah, and on several occasions his preaching caused people to re-examine their lives. It was some time after Octavianus had gone back to Indonesia, however, that the true spiritual awakening took place.

Winsome and I were living in Miri at that time, but friends gave us firsthand accounts of the heart-searching confession, repentance and blessing of revival which started among the students of the secondary school at Bario. It was the work of the Holy Spirit entirely, for there was a real turning to God with deep humility and conviction of sin among both the Christians and non-Christians of the locality.

Another consequence of the revival was the desire of the people to share with others the blessing they had received, and so two groups prepared themselves to travel. One group went down the main course of the Baram, through the Saban area, to Lio Matu, and then visited the Kenyah villages. The other group travelled down the Akah River and visited all the Kayan villages. Both groups planned to meet up at the secondary school at Long Lama.

As it happened, at just that time Mina had started teaching at Long Lama Secondary School on the Baram. After completing form six at Tanjong Lobang, she had taught for a year at St. Mark's, then gained her teaching diploma after two years at Batu Lintang Teacher Training College in Kuching. Her letters to us from Long Lama were full of the good news of the revival: as the groups from Bario made their way downriver, sharing from their own experience, hundreds of people in the villages along the way, and particularly the young people, responded.

Hearing this news from Bario and now from Long Lama, Winsome and I decided to travel to Long Lama, both to visit Mina and to see what was happening. We arrived in early February 1974. As we knew many of the young people attending the secondary school, and could see the reality of changes in their lives, we again were in awe of what God had done.

During the more than sixty years we lived in Borneo, we were privileged to see tens of thousands of people become Christians. But there were three distinct periods during which God in his grace poured out his Spirit in a special way.

The first was in the middle years of the 1930s when among the Murut people on both sides of the international border there was a great turning to God resulting in completely changed lives. The second was among the Kayans and Kenyahs of the Baram at the end of the 1940s. And the third was in 1973 and 1974 beginning among the people of the Kelabit highlands.

From our involvement in all three periods, God taught us one important principle: a true work of the Spirit of God is given in his sovereign grace. We can no more generate nor manipulate a true spiritual awakening by our own efforts than we can cause the wind to change from east to west. Jesus himself said: "The wind blows wherever it pleases. You hear its sound but you cannot tell where it comes from or where it is going. So it is with everyone born of the Spirit."[1] Our part is to reverently watch God working and be obedient to his leading.

During those middle years of the 1970s we witnessed another remarkable evidence of God's working — and this time it was even closer to home.

Ron Nugent, the young secondary school teacher who had come to Borneo in 1971 as an avowed atheist, returned to Australia four years later to study theology. He came back to Sarawak again in 1976, but this time he had come to be married. The wedding ceremony was held in January of that year in the SIB church on the hill overlooking the town of Miri. And Winsome and I could not have been happier. His bride was our daughter Mina.

1. John 3:8

CHAPTER 29

Although Winsome was able to remain active, her health was deteriorating. She suffered from arthritis and was finding life in the tropics increasingly more wearing. So in 1979 we decided to return to Australia; we settled in Perth, partly because of the mild, dry climate but more particularly because Ron and Mina were living there. Winsome arrived in time for the birth of Mina's second baby, and I joined her several weeks later.

I remember the day I arrived back in Australia. It was in the early morning hours of December 13th, and Winsome and I went directly to occupy our new home. Perth is a lovely city and our little unit in a retirement complex was pleasant and convenient. Two things seemed very much out of place, however: retirement was the last thing on my mind, and my heart was still in Borneo.

After getting Winsome settled into our apartment, I returned to Sarawak to make arrangements for publishing the Kayan-English dictionary which I had recently finished compiling. It had been a laborious process, done on a manual typewriter with endless retyping to make corrections and additions. When I see the computerized systems available today, I cannot help but think how much easier things would have been if I had started later! The first copies of the dictionary were produced by a printing house in Miri later that year.

I was still active and healthy, but the aging process was making itself evident. A few days before my birthday in 1981, I had surgery on my right eye to remove a cataract and implant a tiny perspex lens. The operation was a great success and I was amazed at the precision of it all. Later that year, I returned again to Sarawak and travelled extensively, visiting churches and secondary schools in the major centres. I felt a particular responsibility to keep in touch with students who had been the focus of our service during the last twenty years of our time in Borneo.

While on this trip, I was privileged to meet Roy Gustafson, Guy Davidson and Franklin Graham, all of whom had been invited to participate in the annual Mission conference as representatives of the Billy Graham Evangelistic Association. They took a special interest in hearing about the early years of the Mission and suggested that I write a book telling of my life and times in Borneo. In fact a number of other people, both in Sarawak and abroad, had been encouraging me to write my memoirs. This only added to the increasing responsibility I felt to provide a more complete record of the things we had seen and experienced.

Winsome and I celebrated our golden wedding anniversary in Perth on April 29, 1982. It was a quiet but happy time with family and friends as we looked back and remembered all of God's goodness to us over the years and acknowledged with gratitude his gracious dealings with us.

Late in the year I visited Sarawak once again and travelled the length of the state. I was glad to be able to attend the SIB conference at Lawas, not far from Limbang where we had first brought the gospel to inland Sarawak more than a half-century earlier. It was stirring to see scores of delegates from hundreds of churches representing thousands of Christians throughout Sarawak; I was impressed with the harmony in their discussions and the spiritual maturity they demonstrated in working through their problems. In Sabah, a parallel conference was being attended by similar numbers of people.

I spent a very happy Christmas in Marudi with Luke, his wife Jane and their little son named John Hudson, and I was invited to speak on Christmas Day to an crowded congregation at the Marudi church.

Upon my return to Perth in mid-January 1983, I worked through a greater than usual amount of correspondence. Then, as was my practice following a major trip, I wrote a long letter relating the recent experiences — copies of which I sent to friends in various countries.

Two months later I had a cataract removed and a lens implanted in my other eye. While waiting for my eye to heal, I had more time to think about the prospect of writing my memoirs. Shortly thereafter, I wrote a letter to Hugh Steven, an author friend in the United States, outlining my thoughts on this potential undertaking:

> Whatever form the proposed book takes in the future, I feel that my first duty is to set down on paper my recollections of the historic events as they took place. The first twenty years, from 1928 to 1948, were the most decisive and dramatic; and since then the last thirty-five years have seen the building up of the church. During the last decade, and specially during the last few years, the national church has increasingly accepted responsibilities for its own ministry, as well as for evangelistic outreach.
>
> Ironically, it is because of this resurgence of activity in the national church that I am increasingly involved with my friends in Borneo. And it is this correspondence which hinders me from getting down to writing my own memoirs. Having pioneered the work, and knowing the parents and grandparents of the present generation, both they and I feel a mutual interest to keep in touch. They realize that I know their cultures, their languages and their background. However, I feel it my duty to both the church in Borneo and, in some measure, to the church in the world at large, to leave a record of some of the personal experiences in which my wife and I have had a share . . .

Despite my interest and enthusiasm, I was daunted by the enormity of this task. I had box upon box of material — diaries, personal letters, newsletters, tape recordings, photographs and copies of articles I had written for various publications. Around that same time, I read a book by Catherine Marshall, *Adventures in Prayer*.[1] One memorable chapter was entitled "The Prayer of Helplessness." While I reorganized some of my file boxes and as I thought about the task ahead, I, too, often prayed the prayer of helplessness. Then I began.

Since moving to Perth, Winsome had continually hoped to make a trip back to Sarawak but her frail health had prevented this. Now,

1. Catherine Marshall, *Adventures in Prayer* (Old Tappan: Chosen Books, 1975).

however, she seemed well enough to accompany me, and we both felt that it might be her last opportunity.

We arrived in Kuching in early December 1983 and spent several days with friends who arranged a surprise party for Winsome on the eve of her eightieth birthday. A number of old friends and many young people attended, and they presented Winsome with a beautiful beadwork wall hanging of a Sarawak hornbill.

On her birthday, December 19th, we took a small plane from Kuching to Miri which allowed us a magnificent view of the coastline of the land we both loved so much. What a vivid contrast to the same day forty-one years earlier when we had steamed into Kuching to enter the Japanese internment camp!

As was the case in Kuching, the church in Miri was strong and growing, and we spent an enjoyable week there. Then we continued on to Marudi where we stayed in our former home as guests of the Lee family and celebrated both Christmas and New Year's Day with Luke and his family.

We had hoped to go on to Lawas and Limbang and visit the site of our first home at Sungei Pranga but flights were fully booked over the holiday season, so we returned to Kuching earlier than expected. There, we walked along the wharf on the Sarawak River near the point where I first came ashore with Hendy in 1928. We strolled past the site of the Rajah's *astana*. And we visited the grave of Frank Davidson who had been with me throughout those prewar years and had died in the internment camp.

Our minds went back to those early years when the people of this land were walled in by fear of spirits and a pervasive darkness. In acknowledging how God had allowed us to share in the tremendous changes that had taken place, we experienced a special sense of joy and worship.

My next visit to Sarawak was an extended one; in addition to my usual travelling, I spent almost two months at Bintulu revising and expanding the Kayan-English dictionary. On previous visits the Sarawak Literary Society had asked me to undertake this project, as they wanted to publish a new series of dictionaries of the major languages of Sarawak. My expanded version was to include a number of new words from the Belaga dialect of Kayan, new words that had emerged during the translation of the Kayan Bible, and several appendices.

Christina Uyang Jau gave me a great deal of competent help as a Kayan language informant and typist. Although we had completed about 200 pages of revised typed work, there were still many months of work ahead for us, so Christina agreed to travel to Perth with me to continue this project. While there, she lived with Ron, Mina and their three children (we had gained another grandchild!) and came each day to work with me on the dictionary.

Australia was a new experience for Christina but she adapted well. Her English took on a decided Australian drawl, and Mina brushed up on her Kayan which she had not used in many years. On Sundays we all attended the Presbyterian church where Ron was senior pastor.

Christina was a diligent worker and, in order to keep up with her, I worked steadily, editing and proofreading the text. By the time she returned to Sarawak in mid-April we had completed the manuscript — all 650 pages — and sent it to the Sarawak Literary Society for printing.

Christina was not the only valued helper I had that year. Within a few days of my eighty-fifth birthday, Stephen and Helen Parson arrived from Canberra to assist me with my memoirs project. We made good progress during the next few months as the three of us spent hundreds of hours sorting my resource material and selecting the most relevant pieces.

In the meantime, I received a letter from Robert Nicholl who had been so much help to us more than thirty years earlier when he was the Education Officer in Miri. He was now an honourary Curator of the Brunei Museum, and he asked me to supply the Museum with photographs of Kayan beads along with notes and information on folklore associated with these ancient beads.

When I visited Sarawak again at the end of the year, I made a side trip to Brunei in order to deliver a number of beads from my own collection to be photographed along with some ancient beads belonging to Kayan friends from Long Pilah. The Museum authorities were keenly interested in all this bead lore, and I showed them ways to distinguish genuinely old beads from more recent ones.

Meanwhile, my dictionary project was progressing, and when I returned to Australia the proof sheets of typeset copy began arriving in sections from the printer in Malaysia's capital city, Kuala Lumpur. Unfortunately they were riddled with errors and, with each set of proofs, the situation worsened.

I continued making corrections to the printer's proofs, but they obviously were not comprehending some of the principles of the Kayan language so I made arrangements to meet with them in early October. While in Kuala Lumpur I stayed with the Honourable Luhat Wan MP, a Kayan we had known since he was a boy living on the Baram River, and who now was an assistant minister in the Malaysian Government.

Following my discussions with the printing firm I continued on to Sarawak, arriving at Miri in time for a series of special seminars sponsored by the Samaritan's Purse organization under the direction of Franklin Graham, Roy Gustafson and Guy Davidson. Nearly 500 pastors and full-time SIB workers attended these seminars. At one of the sessions I was asked to recount our early experiences in Borneo leading up to the dramatic conversion of the Muruts of the Trusan River. The seminar team also invited me to accompany them to Sabah the following week for another series in the newly opened SIB church in Kota Kinabalu.

After the Sabah seminar I stopped in Marudi for an especially enjoyable visit with Luke and Jane who now had two children and were expecting a third.

This trip also provided an unexpected opportunity for reconciling past differences. Among those who had attended the seminars were Alan and Madge Belcher whom I had not seen for some time. As we reminisced about past days, Alan said something that struck a particularly responsive chord in my heart.

"Hudson," he said, "when I think about all the amazing things we've seen in this country, I sometimes feel as though God made it all happen in spite of us."

In Perth, I renewed my efforts to make corrections to the printer's proofs of my Kayan dictionary. This had become tremendously frustrating because I was finding hundreds of mistakes. I felt I had no choice but to press on as so much time and effort had already been invested, but I was acutely aware that this was preventing me from making much progress on my memoirs. And I knew some of my friends were thinking, "What if he dies before he gets at least the first draft done!"

I made another trip to Kuala Lumpur in late October 1987 to follow up on the progress of the printing. Much to my dismay, I found that the printing firm had just gone out of business and all the proofs I had already carefully checked were lost! The loss of a year's work is difficult to accept under any circumstances, but at age eighty-seven and with so much work left to finish, I felt a heightened sense of devastation.

The Literary Society felt very badly about this fiasco and quickly made arrangements with another printing house. I advised them, however, that I simply could not devote the time to another complete checking of the proof sheets; they would have to ensure that the printing firm they selected was competent and capable of checking their own work. I offered to do a random check for accuracy of typesetting and to ensure that correct linguistic principles were being followed, but I made it clear that I was now committed to another project.

From Kuala Lumpur I continued on to Sarawak and had another memorable visit, making twelve separate trips throughout the state, mostly by plane, and returned home in time to celebrate Christmas with Winsome.

During the next year, apart from two trips to Borneo, I made good progress on writing my memoirs. "What a year this has been," I wrote in my September 1988 newsletter, "a wonderful year of God's guidance and his providence in ways I little dreamed possible."

In June, at the SIB's invitation, I attended the opening of their new administrative headquarters in Miri. As I stood beside this new building, I vividly recalled how fifty-nine years earlier to the exact day, June 4, 1929, Carey Tolley, Frank Davidson and I were levelling the hilltop at Sungei Pranga for our first headquarters. My reading for that day from *Daily Light* included a message which seemed particularly fitting: "The glory of this present house will be greater than the glory of the former house," was God's promise. "And in this place I will grant peace . . ."[2]

My second visit to Borneo that year was in direct connection with my memoirs project for I wanted to visit old friends as well as a number of the familiar places. Don Richardson was my travelling companion and we covered much territory. We visited the larger centres of Kuching, Sibu, Miri, Marudi and Limbang, and some of the surrounding longhouse villages. We called in at Long Lama, the location of my former Community Development Project. We spent a night at the Kenyah longhouse at Long Ikang where *Penghulu* Aban Gau had lived, and another night at the Kayan village at Long Pilah with its cluster of seven longhouses overlooking the river and mountains.

The highlight for me, however, was our visit to the Murut (Lun Bawang) village at Ba Kelalan. We travelled by plane, and I thought back to the many times I had trekked into this isolated, fertile valley filled with irrigated rice fields right next to the international border. More than twenty years had passed since my last visit to Ba Kelalan, and I was amazed at the changes. The population of the valley had quadrupled since I had first been there in 1933. There were now five churches in the area, beautifully constructed with varnished timber. Just the year prior, a government panel of multiracial judges had voted Ba Kelalan the best village in Sarawak. The people exuded

2. Haggai 2:9

health and harmony. As Don Richardson commented, "Even the hunting dogs didn't fight each other!"

On my trip home, I stopped to visit some friends in Jakarta in connection with my memoirs project and then continued on to Perth to resume work on the stacks of resource material that awaited me. I worked throughout the remainder of the year and, apart from a three-week visit to Sarawak in August, I continued through 1989.

That year, Winsome's health became increasingly frail and we noticed that her short-term memory was slipping markedly. She required more nursing care but she retained her sense of humour. She had undergone surgery the year before to remove an intestinal tumor and we were thankful indeed when x-rays taken at the end of 1989 showed no further malignancy.

Eventually the doctors diagnosed Winsome as having Alzheimer's disease, and in 1991 she entered a nursing home which provided twenty-four hour care. For several weeks after she left, my days became very long and I struggled with a feeling of helplessness — there seemed to be so little I could do for her. I read whatever I could find on Alzheimer's syndrome and visited her whenever possible.

After a few months, she moved into a room which became available in the nursing home next door to our retirement unit. This was a much better arrangement as I could now spend time with her each day. Winsome could still remember events that had happened a long time ago, so to assist in keeping her mind active, I reminisced with her about our early days in Borneo.

Friends wrote to us often, and this stimulated me to resume work on my manuscript. I had completed a draft the previous year, and I now began reworking the entire text. Life took on its old flavour again.

Several other events also made 1991 a memorable year. The first was the publication of the Kayan-English dictionary by the Sarawak Literary Society. Anyone who has ever had a book published will know what a special feeling it was the day I went to the mailbox and opened the package containing the first hardcover copy of the book. And despite all the previous problems with printing, the quality was even better than I had dared hope for.

Then at Christmastime, Roland Bewsher flew in from Brisbane to visit us. Apart from Enid Davidson, Winsome and myself, he was the only other living Mission member from the earliest years in Borneo. At eleven years younger than I, Roland looked very fit. We had a great visit together and I was thrilled to be able to share with him another amazing thing that had happened that year.

I had received a letter from a woman in Thailand, Khattiya Jalayanateja, who was engaged in researching the life of Colonel Suga, the commandant of the internment camp at Batu Lintang. She knew that immediately following the war, the Colonel had taken his own life — believing his wife and children had all perished in the atomic bomb explosion at Hiroshima. To further her research, she was asking for any information I could give her on my perception of Colonel Suga and the events of that time. From her letter I learned that the Colonel's wife and four of his six children had actually survived the atomic bomb at Hiroshima — and each of the surviving children are grandparents today!

In response to this delightful news, I sent a package of material to Mrs. Jalayanateja telling of the war years and my remembrances of Colonel Suga. I suggested that she forward this material to his surviving children. I believe that we would not have survived the war without Colonel Suga's influence. Under God's grace, we owed our lives to him.

More than that, I acknowledge God's grace throughout my entire life, and it is on this note that I come to the end of the very memoirs I have been referring to in the previous pages.

Though at ninety-one I am becoming increasingly forgetful of day-to-day occurrences, I often waken very early in the morning to find my mind focused on Borneo, and the images are as clear as my first breathtaking view of Mt. Batu Lawi in 1928.

My life's work was exactly what I was best suited to do. I loved what I did. It fascinated me. And above all, through what I was enabled to accomplish, I saw God at work in countless marvelous ways, large and small. For all of this, I cannot thank him enough.

EPILOGUE

Measure not the work
Until the day's out and the labour done;
Then bring your gauges.
– Elizabeth Barrett Browning

Hudson Southwell will not celebrate his hundredth birthday with us in the millennium year as he had hoped. His time on earth ended peacefully during the morning of December 6, 1996. Winsome, who had lovingly complemented his life, followed him eight months later.

Those who knew Hudson best will retain indelible memories of him. He was unique, and he was exceptional. I was fortunate to come to know him over the last twenty years of his life. One of the last times I visited him was during the Christmas season of 1991.

In earlier years, Hudson was well-proportioned, tall and athletic-looking; at ninety-one, he now stood considerably shorter, his once powerful back stooped from a lifetime of packing loads along jungle trails. The jet black hair had receded into a fringe of white.

Still, he had retained his charm. His blue eyes sparkled with vitality and genuine interest. His handshake was firm. His speech was distinguished, with a mild Australian drawl softening a proper British accent acquired from his father and some of his early teachers.

When someone asked him a question about the war years, he paused, but only momentarily. "Well, before I can properly answer that," he responded, "I should begin with something that happened in 1928 . . ."

He was still physically active. "I've always been quite fit," he reminded us. "Perhaps it's because I try to do things quickly."

"I walk fast," he added. "When I'm on a busy sidewalk, my natural gait has always been such that I pass everyone. Up until quite recently that is. Nowadays I stay more or less even with the faster ones."

In Hudson's apartment, shelves were lined with books, diaries and file boxes filled with notes and letters which he had used to prepare his memoirs. His desktop was arranged with a collection of letters to answer and another stack of material to read — *Time, Decision Magazine* and *Science News*.

On a night table lay his well-worn Bible, a small flashlight, and his *Daily Light* book stuffed with notes and held together by an elastic band.

The measure of a man is often best gauged by the assessment of informed observers who are not necessarily in sympathy with his views. Malcolm MacDonald, who was the Governor-General after the Rajah ceded power in 1946, chronicled his time in Sarawak in a highly-regarded book entitled *Borneo People.*[1] In one revealing chapter he discusses Hudson Southwell and his work among the people of that land:

> I was skeptical about the efforts of certain Evangelicals whose headquarters were on the neighboring Lawas River. During an earlier trip to Sarawak I had visited the place briefly, and gained a superficial knowledge of their activities. I met their principal, an elderly Australian named Southwell, whose lanky, angular figure and gaunt, bearded face made him look like an Old Testament prophet. His faith burned in his deep-set eyes and earnest conversation, and it was shared eagerly by his wife and small band of helpers.
>
> They worked then mostly among the Muruts of the Lawas and Limbang districts, and had achieved gratifying results in curing those wild tribesmen of dipsomaniac tendencies. Consequently the Murut's health, as well as their conduct, had distinctly improved. Their maternal and infant mortality started to decline, and their society in general began to stand, like countless individual Muruts themselves, more steadily on its feet.
>
> No one could fail to be impressed at this miracle performed by Southwell's dynamic religious zeal. But it was not the whole story. I was told that in some directions his enthusiasm carried him too far, making him insist on outlawing from native society much more than jars of rice-wine. At his order, I was informed, traditional dress suited to the tropical climate was abolished, and old pagan songs, games and dances which had their origin in savagery were swept away in a flood-tide of reform. When I heard this from his critics, I felt sad, for I admired the indigenous arts and crafts of the Borneans, and felt that they were a harmless as well as vital expression of the people's racial character. Why should their preservation be any more incompatible with Christianity — if the Muruts must become Christians — than our maintenance of the folklore connected with Santa Claus and his reindeers? I jumped to the conclusion that the worthy members of the Evangelical mission were zealots

1. Malcolm MacDonald, *Borneo People* (London: Jonathan Cape, 1956).

whose goodness ran to fanaticism, and whose labors might perhaps be more destructive than creative.

This impression seemed to be confirmed when I learned some time later that the Southwells had extended their activities from the Lawas to the Baram, and that they were making multitudes of hasty converts among the Kenyahs and Kayans. Tales reached me of their preaching the gospel to entranced crowds in long-houses, and of wholesale baptisms of entire communities within a few days. The Evangelicals seemed to be embarked on a militant crusade against heathenism which exploited an emotional mood among the natives to register them as Christians, without giving them careful grounding in Christianity. I did not feel much sympathy with that type of proselytism, especially as I suspected that with it went a forbidding intolerance of many innocent native customs.

When [Rodney] Needham lunched with me in Johore I had recently heard of this development on the Baram, and I remarked upon it to him, adding that I was not sure of the report's accuracy, but that it seemed to be supported by evidence. If it were true, then I thought the activities of the missionaries unfortunate. In my opinion our policy should be to persuade the pagans to abandon only such of their ancient habits and beliefs as were harmful, and to introduce them only to those modern ideas which would help them. We must encourage them to preserve all that was good in their indigenous culture.

Needham [a young Oxford-educated anthropologist working in Borneo as a field ethnologist] agreed with this view, and expressed concern at the rumors of the Evangelicals' excess of zeal. Now, several months later, he had made a considerable journey from the deep jungle especially to tell me that the rumors had been false.

"Southwell and his mission are doing wonderful work," he said enthusiastically.

I asked him to tell me more about it.

"You know that I hold no particular brief for missionaries," he answered. "Sometimes they do great harm among native peoples, because they don't really understand them and their needs. But Southwell doesn't belong to that type of preacher. He feels true sympathy with the pagans, and deals wisely with them. He's doing remarkably constructive work."

"That's very different," I observed, "from what I've heard. Tell me what constructive things he's doing."

"He and his wife and their Evangelical colleagues are turning the natives . . . into people with a sense of cleanliness, from heavy drinkers into abstemious beings, and from an unhealthy race into a race with a good prospect of life. It's on the health side that they've achieved so far their greatest successes. Everywhere they go they teach people the simple facts about proper medical treatment for ailments, the importance of proper sanitation and hygiene in a house, and the prudent care of children. They make them take pride in the spotless neatness of their homes. It's all very elementary; but done in a systematic way it's something new in these communities, and it's producing good results. The people see those results and are very grateful."

"That's admirable," I agreed. "But . . . I was under the impression that in his hurry to smash the natives' pagan beliefs and convert them to Christianity he destroys more quickly than he creates, and so tends to leave the natives without any deeply felt faith at all."

"That's not true," Needham answered emphatically. "Southwell doesn't force Christianity on the natives. He doesn't preach it in a house unless the leaders there invite him. In any case he couldn't compel changes in the people's faith unless they wished them, for the pagans are strong-minded, self-respecting characters who don't abandon old beliefs against their will. Change has its origin in their attitude of mind, not in Southwell's. If they want a change, the Evangelicals offer them an alternative to their old religion, and the measure of the missionaries' success is generally a measure of the people's spontaneous desire for change."

"But isn't Southwell too intolerant of harmless old pagan customs which make some of the brightness in the pattern of native society — of their hallowed songs and dances, for instance? Doesn't he, in his puritanical fervor, forbid them to enjoy these pleasant pastimes? Doesn't he, in fact, sweep away a lot of the good with the bad in local life?"

Needham shook his head and answered. "The stories about that are exaggerated. He doesn't stop the natives singing their old tunes. What he does is write new Christian words to the old tunes, and the natives sing these latest hymns with their accustomed pagan enthusiasm."

> "As an anthropologist," continued Needham, " . . . My approval of the Evangelical mission is chiefly for their medical, material and educational care of the people. Their first-aid for wounds, ointments for sores and medicines for ailments show healing powers which win the native's gratitude; and many of the missionaries' lessons in better household management, food storage, child care and the like bring practical benefits to these simple folk which they badly need and deeply appreciate. Moreover, the friendly, inspiring power of the Evangelicals' personalities works its own magic. They're good, admirable men and women. Southwell's astonishing influence over the natives springs from the strength of his own character, from his spiritual force. He's a fine man, an inspiring man."
>
> There was a ring of deep sincerity in Needham's voice. I felt that only a man of God of rare quality could capture so completely his enthusiasm.

One minor — and amusing — inconsistency stems from Malcolm MacDonald's remembrance of Hudson's physical appearance. His description of the "lanky, angular figure and gaunt face" would have been accurate during those tough, strenuous years just after the war. And perhaps MacDonald's perception of what "an Old Testament prophet" looked like is not far wrong. But the "gaunt face" was certainly not "bearded" when they met. Hudson was always particular about shaving, even during his three years in the internment camp.

Hudson would have agreed with the statement that "he couldn't compel changes in the people's faith unless they wished them, for the [Borneans] are strong-minded, self-respecting characters who don't abandon old beliefs against their will."

He would not have agreed, however, that the changes were effected by the "inspiring power" of his own personality. Hudson was convinced that the transformation of people comes about "Not by might nor by power, but by my Spirit, says the Lord Almighty."[2]

---

2. Zechariah 4:6

In the interior of Borneo, Mt. Batu Lawi towers above its surrounding hills, a magnificent pinnacle, seemingly timeless and permanent. But God's word tells us that even Batu Lawi will not always be there.

Human experience tells us also that one day each of us will no longer be subject to the confinements of time and space as we now know them.

"I sometimes ponder the thought," Hudson once told me, "what will I be like?"

"I try to visualize eternity in scientific terms," he added. "But my mind can't comprehend it."

On this point he knew he was in good company, and he quoted from memory:

> No eye has seen,
> no ear has heard,
> no mind has conceived
> what God has prepared for those who love him.[3]

Although Hudson Southwell had many admirable qualities, perhaps his greatest strength was his ability to trust. His faith had been forged through adversity — when he would say calmly, "We can trust God in this," it was with conviction shaped by a lifetime of extraordinary experiences.

By venturing into uncharted waters, Hudson came into contact with countless numbers of people who recognized his faith to be genuine and integrated that spiritual faith into their own lives.

Sarawak has long been a land of romance and mystery, of legends and heroes. For much of the twentieth century, a number of outstanding figures shaped the direction of that country, among them an English rajah, a Kenyah *penghulu,* a Japanese colonel and a British commando. It may prove, however, that none had a greater impact than a scientist from Australia who genuinely trusted God.

---

3. Corinthians 2:9

ACKNOWLEDGEMENTS

It has been well said that a book sometimes takes on a life of its own. Certainly, that was the case with this book as the efforts of a diverse group of people were integrated over a period of more than twenty years into a finished product.

The major contribution was clearly that of Hudson Southwell. It was not until he was in his mid-80s that Hudson felt sufficiently free from other obligations to begin writing his memoirs. Based on his exceptional recall, and supported by stacks of diaries, letters, published articles and photos, he produced a manuscript — 316 pages in all — painstakingly drafted on a manual typewriter.

Rod Blair undertook to assist Hudson with the entire project from conception through publishing. In addition to providing the required funding, he researched descriptive material and quotations from other published sources and worked with Hudson to rewrite various sections of the original manuscript; he also compiled the prologue and drafted the epilogue.

Lydda Vetrov and Terry Mack reviewed the manuscript in detail and suggested numerous revisions to improve the narrative and eliminate repetition. Terry also transferred the manuscript onto a desktop publishing program. Mo Keshavjee was instrumental in designing the cover.

Judith Markham, who Charles Colson accurately referred to as "the master craftsman of her trade," edited the text. Her assistance in restructuring Hudson's material into a more readable format was invaluable. By her own admission, Judith loves "messing with other people's words." She possesses a superlative ability to do just that without altering the precise thoughts an author wishes to convey.

Others contributed to the process by way of recommendations, advice and encouragement. Roland Bewsher provided all three through discussions and letters about his early days in Borneo with Hudson and Winsome. Ron and Mina Nugent supported the project from the outset with their time and background information.

Stephen and Helen Parsons assisted Hudson in organizing his research material. Philip Sinden was gracious in giving advice during difficult times. Bob Reekie, Don Richardson and Dan Runyon provided input on the business of publishing a book.

Khattiya Jalayanateja generously supplied background information on Colonel Tatsuji Suga along with photographs obtained from the Suga family. Judith Heimann provided a photograph and information regarding Major Tom Harrisson.

Most importantly, the process of producing this book has been underpinned by a spiritual component. On one level, the book is a human-interest story; on another level, it is the account of one man's faith in extraordinary circumstances. Although everyone's situation is different, the call to true spiritual faith is universal; consequently, those most closely involved with the book came to recognize something of their own spiritual journey in Hudson's story.

This book will honour Hudson Southwell's faith, the practice of which has infinite value: "Without faith, it is impossible to please God, because anyone who comes to him must believe that he exists, and that he rewards those who earnestly seek him."

That, in fact, is the main reason for publishing the book. Hudson's fondest desire would be that each reader is able to identify in some way with the spiritual struggle the story embraces, and that he or she earnestly seeks God, and is rewarded accordingly.

Bibliography

Bonhoeffer, Dietrich. *The Martyred Christian.* London: Collier Macmillan Publishers, 1983.

Brand, Dr. Paul, & Yancey, Philip. *Fearfully & Wonderfully Made.* Grand Rapids: Zondervan Publishing House, 1987.

Brooke, Sylvia, Lady. *Queen of the Head-hunters.* Singapore: Oxford University Press, 1990.

Broomhall, A.J. *Hudson Taylor & China's Open Century: Assault on the Nine.* London: Hodder & Stoughton, 1988.

Collis, Maurice. *Raffles.* Singapore: Faber and Faber Ltd., 1966.

Colson, Charles. *Kingdoms in Conflict.* Grand Rapids: Zondervan Publishing House, 1987.

Elliot, Elizabeth. *Amy Carmichael.* E. Sussex: MARC, 1988.

Harrisson, Tom, ed. *The Peoples of Sarawak.* Kuching, Sarawak: Government Printing Office, 1959.

Harrisson, Tom. *World Within.* Singapore: Oxford University Press, 1990.

Houston, James. *The Transforming Friendship.* Oxford: Lion Publishing plc, 1989.

Howell, David L. B. *Through the Long Grass.* West Sussex: Gooday Publishers, 1991.

Keith, Agnes. *Land Below the Wind.* London: Michael Joseph Ltd., 1949.

Keith, Agnes Newton. *Three Came Home.* U.S.A.: Little, Brown and Company, 1947.

Lapierre, Dominique. *The City of Joy*. London: Arrow Books Limited, 1986.

MacDonald, Malcolm. *Borneo People*. London: Jonathan Cape, 1956.

Marshall, Catherine. *Adventures in Prayer*. Old Tappan: Chosen Books, 1975.

Morrison, Hedda. *Life in a Longhouse*. Kuching, Sarawak: Borneo Literature Bureau, 1962.

Payne, Robert. *The White Rajahs of Sarawak*. Singapore: Oxford University Press, 1991.

Pearce, E. K. Victor. *Who Was Adam?* Exeter: The Paternoster Press, 1969.

Piper, John. *Desiring God*. Portland: Multnomah Press, 1986.

Pollock, John. *Wilberforce*. Herts: Lion Publishing plc, 1977.

Richardson, Don. *Eternity in Their Hearts*. California: Regal Books, 1981.

Runciman, Steven. *The White Rajahs, A History of Sarawak*. Kuala Lumpur: S. Abdul Majeed & Co., 1992.

Rutter, Owen. *The Pirate Wind*. London: Hutchinson & Co., 1930.

St. John, Spenser, Sir. *Life in the Forests of the Far East*. Kuala Lumpur: Oxford University Press, 1974 [1862].

St. John, Spenser, Sir. *Rajah Brooke*. London: T. F. Unwin, 1899.

Solzhenitsyn, Alexander. *One Day in the Life of Ivan Denisovich*. London: Penguin Books, 1963.

Yancey, Philip. *Disappointment with God*. Grand Rapids: Zondervan Publishing House, 1992.